Mark Twain in Virginia City

Mark Twain

in Virginia City

by PAUL FATOUT

INDIANA UNIVERSITY PRESS

Bloomington .

ACKNOWLEDGMENT

The author is indebted to the Bancroft Library, University of California, Berkeley, for use of the following illustrations: map on pages xiv-1; both pictures on page 13; Second and Carson Streets on page 14; all pictures on page 91; B Street on page 92; both pictures on page 161; R. C. Gridley on page 193.

Also to the History Room, Wells Fargo Bank, San Francisco, for Virginia City on page 14; firemen on page 92; Mark Twain, 1864-65, on page 112; Mark Twain, 1870, on page 176.

Also to The Mark Twain Papers, University of California, Berkeley, for Mark Twain, 1862, on page 98, and Mark Twain, 1865, on page 168.

FOR MY BROTHERS AND SISTER:

Ray, Ruth, and Hugh

CONTENTS

ILLUSTRATIONS

PREFACE

OF LIFE in Virginia City, Nevada Territory, when he was a reporter on the *Territorial Enterprise* from September, 1862, to May, 1864, Mark Twain gives illuminating glimpses in thirteen chapters of *Roughing it*: of mining hysteria, staggering bullion statistics, nabobs rolling in money, free spending by everybody, seething humanity, high-spirited pranks, reckless gun play. This narrative, distorted by his erratic memory and habitual exaggeration, may be faulty in precise detail, but it is graphic in its impressions of a hardy locality riding a great surge of wealth and energy.

Of the many thousands of words he wrote for the paper, not many have survived because no file of the *Enterprise* is known to exist for those years. Mark Twain apparently kept his own file, but in 1866 he said that he had burned "a small cartload" of *Enterprise* and other clippings. In a letter from Buffalo in 1870 he spoke of having received a "coffin of 'Enterprise' files," but they seem to have disappeared. Hence the day-by-day account of Virginia City's most famous writer is a fragmentary one. His news stories, off-duty gambols, congenial sessions with friends, and conflicts with enemies: such things are only partially revealed.

Some of the gaps may be filled by *Enterprise* items reprinted in other papers of Nevada and California, by letters from their Washoe correspondents, and by editorial comments on doings in silverland, penned sometimes with admiration, often with almost audible gasps of horror. If such remarks throw no light directly on Mark Twain, they are valuable in establishing the physical and emotional climate of the time and place.

Because the *Enterprise* was a provocative journal, editors throughout the West raided its pages to fill their own, and thus preserved a good many column inches of Virginia City reportage. The purpose here is to recreate, in part, Mark Twain's life in Washoe by the aid of reprinted material gathered from extensive files of Nevada and California papers in the Bancroft Library at Berkeley. Contributions to the lost *Weekly Occidental,* a literary paper published in Virginia City in 1864, have been recovered by this method: specifically, from *The Golden Era,* San Francisco *Evening Bulletin,* Downieville *Mountain Messenger,* and Unionville *Humboldt Register.*

Although the authors of lifted *Enterprise* stories are only rarely identified, some items, by reason of style and mannerisms, are clearly by Mark Twain; others, only probably or inferentially so. I have avoided heavy reliance on examples of his Western writing available elsewhere: as in *Mark Twain of the Enterprise*—thirty of his newspaper letters that came to light in 1952—*Mark Twain in Nevada, Mark Twain's Western Years,* his contributions to *The Golden Era,* and so forth. Occasionally I have used these sources but not, I hope, excessively.

Contemporary evidence indicates that his stay in Virginia City did not make him the foremost writer of the West, as some critics have claimed. His fame came later. Yet his experience there was useful to him and certainly exciting. In old age he fondly remarked that those days were "full to the brim with the wine of life." The vintage was heady, but at the time it did not always have for him the sparkling vitality or the enticing bouquet his reminiscent affection suggests. Hence, another purpose is to see Washoe through his eyes and those of others while they lived there, and thus avoid the legendary and the sentimental that seem inevitably to affect the backward view.

His news writing may have no great literary value, but it aids in defining the character of the man, and points toward his literary destination. From the start of his reporter's career it shows flashes of the manner that would become characteristic of the Mark Twain we know today. Those interested in stylistic growth may find seed ground and sprouts there.

The word "Washoe," which frequently appears here, was a familiar or pet name for Nevada Territory. Many inhabitants hoped that it would be adopted as an official name when statehood arrived.

I am indebted to Harper & Row for permission to quote from *Mark Twain's Autobiography*, *Mark Twain's Letters*, *Mark Twain: A Biography*, *The Innocents Abroad*, and *Roughing It*; to the University of California Press for excerpts from *Mark Twain of the Enterprise*; and to Mrs. Doris Webster for quotations from *Mark Twain, Business Man*.

My best thanks to Emerson G. Sutcliffe, an informed Twainian and excellent critic, for his careful reading of the manuscript and always sensible suggestions—particularly on the influential relationship of Twain and Artemus Ward. I am grateful to the efficient and friendly staff of the Bancroft Library: John Barr Tompkins, Helen Bretnor, Vivian Fisher, Cecil Chase, Jim Kantor, Julia Macleod, Estelle Rebec, and the many pages and others who assisted. The Bancroft is a splendid place manned by admirable people. I thank the Purdue Research Foundation for a grant in aid. Miriam S. Farley, of the Indiana University Press, is a sagacious editor whom it is a pleasure to work with. Finally, a citation to my wife, Roberta, for enduring once again the trials of book-making with fortitude and encouragement, for poring over microfilms and coping with proofing and indexing.

PAUL FATOUT

Lafayette, Indiana
August, 1963

This topographical map of the Comstock Lode, drawn by
Hugo Hochholzer in 1865, has only recently been discovered and is now in the possession of the Bancroft Library.

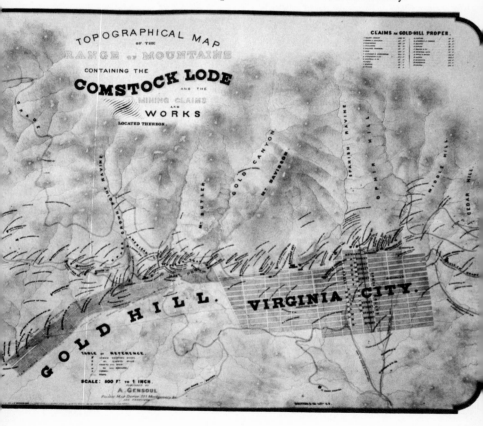

Chapter One

MINER BECOMES REPORTER

❦❦

WHEN Sam Clemens, aged twenty-five, gave up piloting on the Mississippi River at the outbreak of the Civil War, he shortly thereafter took off for the Far West with his brother, Orion, newly appointed secretary to the governor of the Nevada Territory. After an overland stage journey of some three weeks, they arrived in Carson City about the middle of August, 1861. Before the end of the year Sam, like many another demented citizen unhinged by this region of gold and silver, had been touched with mining mania. He invested in Esmeralda mines, and with three companions made a laborious midwinter trip two hundred miles northeast to Unionville, Humboldt County, a locality hailed as extraordinarily rich. Here he hoped to make a fortune—in *Roughing It* he confesses that he expected to pick up bushels of silver nuggets covering the ground like fallen snow—but all he got out of the foray was hard experience.

Back in Carson City after a month or two, he remained there some weeks, then set out for the Esmeralda district, about a hundred miles south by east of the territorial capital. There his frantic mining adventures ended at Aurora, a small town close to the California line, known as the roughest camp in the Territory.

With a partner, Horatio "Raish" Phillips, he lived in this

town a dismal five months during the spring and summer of 1862, their residence described in his *Autobiography* as "a cotton-domestic lean-to at the base of a mountain." The life was grubby, the quarters cramped and cold, the food supply uncertain. In May a correspondent of the Sacramento *Bee* reported that Aurora "is bare of everything but whisky, cigars, tobacco and some clothing. We, as well as our neighbors, are living on beef and coffee straight: no flour or corn meal, no beans. . . . The men are too weak to work."[1] Nevertheless, during this year the camp enjoyed a short-lived boom that intensified the fever of treasure-seekers. Sam ran as high a temperature as any of them. In his letters from there he glibly rattled off data on claims and ledges—Antelope, Yankee, Flyaway, Fresno—often asked his brother for money, expressed a determination to "make or break," and reiterated an abounding assurance of riches soon to come. In May he said confidently to Orion:

> To use a French expression I have "got my d——d satisfy" at last. Two years' time will make us capitalists, in spite of anything. Therefore, we need fret and fume, and worry and doubt no more, but just lie still and put up with privations for six months. Perhaps three months will "let us out." . . . I have got the thing sifted down to a dead moral certainty. I own one-eighth of the new "Monitor Ledge, Clemens Company," and money can't buy a foot of it; because I *know* it to contain our fortune. . . . I have struck my tent in Esmeralda, and I care for no mines but those which I can superintend myself.[2]

His optimism was so strong that he even, so he said, put in hours of hard pick and shovel work digging a shaft, an occupation that no hope of wealth could make congenial to Sam Clemens.

Fortunately for everybody, he was not solely a miner. Soon after his arrival, in early April, he began sending facetious letters to the Virginia City *Territorial Enterprise*, some of them narratives about a Professor Personal Pronoun, said to have been take-offs on Chief Justice Turner, who was over-fond of referring to himself in his speeches. To his surprise, the paper printed these burlesques. As the letters kept com-ing, editor Joe Goodman, always happy to discover talent, turned a favorable eye upon this breezy unknown corre-spondent who signed himself "Josh." By the middle of May Sam had written several, for he instructed Orion to put the *Enterprise* letters "in the scrap book—but send no extracts from them *East*."[3] He thought that his humor was too highly flavored for home folks, although the scrapbook has not sur-vived to give us a taste. As a Fourth of July offering he in-vented a flamboyant speech by a patriotic spouter who began with the stirring statement: "I was sired by the Great Amer-ican Eagle and foaled by a Continental Dam." This oration is lost, but it was probably similar to the following examples, labeled "Western Eloquence," that appeared in California papers in late July, 1862:

Americans! This is a great country—wide—vast—and in the southwest unlimited. Our Republic is yet destined to re-annex all South America—to occupy the Russian Possessions and again to recover, the possession of those British provinces which the prowess of the old thirteen colonies won from the French on the plains of Abraham! All rightfully ours to re-occupy. Ours is a great and growing country. Faneuil Hall was its cradle, but whar—whar will be found timber enough for its coffin? Scoop all the water out of the Atlantic Ocean, and its bed will not afford a grave sufficient for its corpse. And yet America has scarcely grown out of the gristle of boyhood. Europe! what is Europe? She is no whar, nothing, a circumstance, a cypher, a mere obsolete idea. We have faster steamboats, swifter locomotives, better fire engines, longer rivers, broader lakes, higher mountains, deeper cata-racts, louder thunder, forkeder lightning, braver men, hand-somer weemen, and more money than England dar have![4]
Who discovered the North Pole? Who, I say who? Our

own immortal Jefferson! Certainly—or any other man; and more too! Who discovered the route to Cape Cod through Cappadocia? That fearless Moorish navigator, James H. Polk. Who planted the stars and stripes on the heaven piercing summit of the Andes? Who, but the sainted Franklin! With these significant facts in view, let us, with the horoscope in one hand, and the Magna Charter in the other, plunge boldly into the foaming billows of the angry Mississippi, and pressing our way forever onward, never stop until Tivolio is joined to Tripoli—Kamchatka to Nicaragua—and yet onward, until we shall have triumphantly gained Tarantula—that long lost isle of bliss of which a Plutarch reasoned and a Galen sang.[5]

Since editors of small-town weeklies often lifted material from other papers without credit, the authorship of these parodies is unidentified, but touches in the second excerpt suggest the manner that would be characteristic of the future Mark Twain: garbled history, the angry Mississippi, Tarantula, and the absurd assortment of proper names. At any rate, the Fourth of July speech moved the editor of the *Enterprise* to offer Sam a job as local reporter at $25 a week. The offer came in late July, when neither the Monitor nor any other mine had yielded a fortune, or even enough to live on, when, broke, he could borrow money only at eight per cent a month, and had been reduced to the drudgery of sledging rock and screening tailings in a stamp mill at ten dollars a week. He had already considered applying for a place on the Sacramento *Union*. Orion wrote the editor of that paper a strong recommendation of his brother, and Sam said he was prepared to write as many letters a week as the *Union* wanted, all for the same modest ten dollars.

He accepted the offer of the *Enterprise* but only after a delay of about two weeks, which Albert Bigelow Paine, Mark Twain's biographer, turns into a mystical session of soul-searching over whether to take a steady job at a wage considerably below the expectations of a would-be tycoon, or to continue the struggle with resistant nature in Esmeralda, Humboldt, or some other mining region. When Sam told Orion on August 7 that he "guessed" he would go to Virginia City, he also said: "I shall leave at mid-night tonight, alone and on foot for a walk of 60 or 70 miles through a totally uninhabited country. . . ."[6] Out of that projected solo journey, Paine makes an ambulatory vigil: "So he had gone into the wilderness to fight out his battle alone."[7] Yet a week later Sam was writing to his sister, Pamela, from Aurora. For a physically lazy man like Sam Clemens, a walk of some 140 miles in seven days—loaded down with enough food and trappings to survive in uninhabited country—seems far out of character. Probably he wrestled with the problem of whether to be or not to be a reporter, and particularly on which of two possible papers. The hope of riches died painfully, no doubt, as it did many times during his life, but if he fought any battle with himself he surely did not tramp all that distance to start hostilities.

Finally committing himself to the *Enterprise,* he left Aurora about the middle of September, setting out by way of Carson City for Virginia City, 122 miles away. He always maintained that he was too hard up to afford stage fare, hence walked the whole way. But he was generally averse to walking when he could ride, and the road was well traveled by many ore wagons plying between Aurora and Carson City. It is hard to believe that sociable drivers did not offer him a lift.

When he landed in Virginia City, sometimes in the latter part of September, he was a rusty-looking specimen corroded by the wear and tear of rugged months in Esmeralda. Rollin M. Daggett, looking back a generation later, said that Sam "had been living on alkali water and whang leather, with only a sufficient supply of the former for drinking purposes, for several months, and you may imagine his appearance when I first saw him."[8] Coatless, wearing a slouch hat and a blue woolen shirt, and as he himself recalled with a likely dash of romancing, "whiskered half down to the waist," he seemed hardly a prepossessing addition to the staff of the *Territorial Enterprise.* Yet it is difficult to conceive of any other newspaper berth that would have suited him better, both professionally and socially. The move was a good one for both sides. Having had newspaper experience as a youth in Hannibal and Keokuk, Sam was no tyro, although he had never worked for a paper of so springy a pace as the *Enterprise.* Taken in hand by Dan De Quille (William Wright), city editor, called Local or Localitems, he caught on fast as he plunged into a swirling stream that became more turbulent as it rose to flood stage.

Three years before, Virginia City had been a camp of various names: Ophir, Ophir Diggings, Pleasant Hill, Mount Pleasant Point. The next year, christened by a miner from the Old Dominion, it was described as a sleepy "Pi-ute sort of town." At that time J. Ross Browne called it "a mud-hole; climate, hurricanes and snow; water, a distillation of arsenic, plumbago, and copperas; wood, none at all except sage brush; no title to property, and no property worth having."[9] But then, stimulated by the electrifying discovery of the Comstock silver lode in 1859, the town began sprawling over the slope of Mount Davidson so fast that when Sam arrived it was a place of about five to seven thousand, well on the way to becoming a sagebrush metropolis of four-story hotels, impressive stores, a brick courthouse, even large churches. The town had the makings of what one visitor later called "a whaler" that "smells all over of city airs! . . . huge saloons and restaurants . . . wonderfully large theatres, houses and grave yards."[10] C Street was the equivalent of San Francisco's Montgomery; on D was a busy red-light district, where a thrifty girl could amass a better stake than many a miner. Below D was Chinatown. Suburbia, discreetly removed from the vulgar herd, consisted of elaborate houses well up on the slope of Mount Davidson, and east of town in Six-Mile Cañon.

Erratic, unplanned growth made a crazy jumble of buildings and thoroughfares. A tourist from California remarked:

This burgh is not handsome, nor picturesque, nor even comely, for there are no two streets of the same width, nor two parallel streets, and the lots and blocks are of every conceivable size and shape. . . . the stranger is taken aback when he enters a hotel to find that the main entrance on one street is a flight of stairs above that on another street, and that the doorsteps on one side of the street are on a level with the ridges of the one story houses on the opposite side. Also there are no cross streets of any account, and one has to travel a long ways to get around to the next street above or below.[11]

To old-timers who had been there since 1860, such irregularities were trifling compared to signs of progress like hundreds of new buildings, the grading of B Street, and the importation of a glossy new fire engine in time to be in the Fourth of July parade. Aldermen recognized urban qualities when, in the revised charter of December, 1862, they removed the superfluous "City" from the name and made it officially "Virginia."

Up and down Six-Mile Cañon and extending beyond Gold Hill at the head of Devil's Cañon were ore dumps, tunnel tracks and smoking quartz mills of many mining and milling companies: Gould & Curry, Central, United States, Ophir, American, Madison, Sierra Nevada, La Crosse, Potosi, Chollar and others. The Burning Moscow smouldered, its vitals deliberately kept aflame, it was darkly hinted, to burn out rather than freeze out dispirited stockholders. A multitude of companies claimed not only ore veins, but also mill sites, streams, stone quarries, wood lots, springs—about every sort of natural commodity except sagebrush, which nobody had yet figured out how to convert into a profitable product.

Attracted by the supposedly endless wealth of the Comstock Lode, prospectors swarmed in, canny entrepreneurs, Chinese, storekeepers, laborers, trollops, and a horde of lawyers—called the "Devil's Own"—who struck it rich in continual litigation over mining claims. A modest quota of eminently respectable ladies were said to insure community stability and moral tone. Territorial editors pridefully stressed cultural aspirations and refinement. A Carson City correspondent pointed out that every Nevada town of any size had a public school besides an Odd Fellows' and Masonic Lodge, furthermore that there were "seven church edifices in the Territory, besides several rooms where preaching is had nearly every Sabbath."[12] In early 1862, the *Enterprise,* boasting of the uplifting assets of Virginia Sunday schools, a Temperance Society, and a Literary Association that had sent off $916 to buy a library, purred smugly:

Descriptions of Washoe society written a year or two ago, would not be applicable to our present status. True, we may still hear, occasionally, of an appeal to deadly weapons for the settlement of a difficulty, but the sale of revolvers and bowie knives is about over. Law and order has taken the place of anarchy and passion. Such men as boast of the number of men they have slain, as well as their toadies and admirers, have almost entirely disappeared. . . . Owners of mines and mills are bringing their wives and little ones, and settling down in our midst; beautiful private residences and cozy cottages are springing along the hillsides, beautifying with their terraced door-yards and tasteful inclosures the outskirts of our city. Yes, we are fast becoming a civilized people![13]

That idyllic view was premature. Among the incoming thousands were gamblers, roughs, thieves, thugs, sharpers, and assassins, many of whom, more savage than civilized, were to turn Virginia into a shooting gallery the like of which had not been seen since the stirring days of '49.

The Enterprise, oldest paper in the Territory, had started as a weekly in Genoa, at that time western Utah, in 1858, then had moved to Virginia in 1860. In 1862, under the able editorship of Joseph T. Goodman, it was a thriving daily employing half a dozen printers, several editorial writers, and a corps of reporters: Dan De Quille, Captain Joe Plunkett, Rollin M. Daggett, C. A. V. Putnam, Howard P. Taylor, and others. Goodman, a versatile writer with a reputation as a poet, handled his temperamental employees with a loose rein that was good for both staff and paper. The efficient business management of Jerry Driscoll made profits roll in. Organization was more big-city than that of any other Western paper outside of San Francisco, and pungent writers gave the Enterprise a virility and humor that made it popular, prosperous, and influential. The New York Herald, which seldom noticed such faraway sheets, regularly paid $16 a year for a subscription to this one. The office, a small rickety frame building at the corner of A Street and Sutton Avenue, was a crowded turmoil of work and high spirits. While the press clanked at their elbows, reporters wrote at a fifteen-foot table that was also useful for food continually dished up by a Chinese cook known as Old Joe. Sam Clemens slid into this milieu with no trouble at all.

In *Roughing It* he says that he began by manufacturing news out of one hay wagon, multiplying it by sixteen and bringing them into town "from sixteen different directions," thus stirring up a local "sweat" about hay. This item is lost, yet he evidently wrote it, to judge from the remark of Joe Goodman, who once tagged him "Recorder of . . . Hay Wagons." To sensationalize another piece of news, the cub reporter says that he increased to more dramatic proportions the casualties of an emigrant train that had weathered a brush with Indians. Stories of Indian encounters appeared so often in Western papers that identification is uncertain, but a good candidate for Sam Clemens' account is a half column entitled "The Indian Troubles on the Overland Route," published in the *Enterprise* of October 1.

It told of "twelve or fifteen wagons" that arrived in Virginia, all but five of which soon moved on to California. From an Iowa man the reporter learned of a fight near Fort Hall, where the train was attacked in daylight by Snake Indians, the emigrants losing six men and one woman. "The Indians also captured the teams belonging to thirteen wagons, together with a large number of loose cattle and horses." The survivors, overtaken by a much larger train, reached Humboldt safely after beating off another attack and passing on the way numerous corpses, "all minus their scalps," and the wrecks of many wagons.

To this account the reporter added that of another group of forty emigrants that, assailed near City Rocks, put up such feeble resistance that only one man escaped; fifteen women and children were carried off. "This train was called the 'Methodist Train,' which was not altogether appropriate, since the whole party knelt down and began to pray as soon as attack was commenced." That observation faintly suggests the Clemens touch. A third story told of emigrants surrounded by the Snakes and fighting for eight hours before cutting a way out at the cost of unstated numbers of killed and wounded. The several battles, kidnappings, thievery, scalped corpses, and wagon covers "transformed into magnified nutmeg graters by Indian bullets" adequately illustrate the remark in *Roughing It*: "I put this wagon through an Indian fight that to this day has no parallel in history."

The "Washoe Zephyr," a capricious gale from over the mountains that playfully strewed portable property around

Mark Twain and Clement
T. Rice, the Unreliable (*center*),
at Steamboat Springs, 1863

Dan De Quille, 1863

Above: Virginia City in the 1860's; *below*: Second and Carson
Streets, Carson City, Nevada, in the 1860's

the landscape, received attention in the report of "a sudden blast of wind" that

picked up a shooting-gallery, two lodging houses and a drug store from their tall wooden stilts and set them down again some ten or twelve feet back of their original location, with such a degree of roughness as to jostle their insides into a sort of chaos. . . . There were many guests in the lodging houses at the time of the accident, but it is pleasant to reflect that they seized their carpet sacks and vacated the premises with an alacrity suited to the occasion.[14]

The braying jackass, known as the "Washoe Canary," appeared in the story of a newly arrived young woman who, living near a private hospital, had been disturbed by the howls and moans of a patient in the throes of delirium tremens:

Shortly after dark one evening, a jackass came to a halt near the young lady's residence, and having firmly braced his feet, threw his whole soul into a grand imitation of saw filing, reluctantly dying out, when completely exhausted, in a heart-rending moan. "There!" exclaimed the young lady, "dear me, there goes that terrible fellow again! Goodness sake, what a terrible thing the delirium tremens must be!"[15]

Whether or not Sam Clemens wrote those items, they are his sort, for he was not a routine reporter amenable to the humdrum chore of factual newsgathering. He could not pump up enthusiasm over the bare bones of mining statistics that filled columns in Western papers. He was not excited by measurements and capacities of stamp mills, by new buildings, new businesses, and the like. Preferring the out-of-the-way, he liked to adorn a tale by embellishments upon the truth or by editorializing, as in this kind of squib: "A very neat hearse arrived here yesterday, for Wilson & Keys. This is something that has long been much needed."[16]

Best of all, he enjoyed spinning a yarn entirely out of his

imagination. After about two weeks on the job he turned his fancy loose on a hoax aimed at what he called "the growing evil" of the mania for digging up petrifactions. Undertaking this joke in a spirit afterward described as one of public service performed in a mood benign and fatherly, he published in the *Enterprise* of October 4 a straight-faced report of a petrified man discovered near Gravelly Ford:

Every limb and feature of the stone mummy was perfect, not even excepting the left leg, which had evidently been a wooden one during the lifetime of the owner—which lifetime, by the way, came to a close about a century ago, in the opinion of a *savant* who has examined the defunct. The body was in a sitting posture, and leaning against a huge mass of croppings; the attitude was pensive, the right thumb rested against the side of the nose; the left thumb partially supported the chin, the forefinger pressing the inner corner of the left eye, and drawing it partly open; the right eye was closed, and the fingers of the right hand spread out. This strange freak of nature created a profound sensation in the vicinity.

An inquest conducted by "Justice Sewell or Sowell of Humboldt City" concluded with the verdict that "deceased came to his death from protracted exposure." When charitable citizens proposed to give him decent burial by blasting him from his limestone seat, the judge vetoed this move as a desecration "little less than sacrilege."

Newspapers near and far reprinted this story; according to Mark Twain, it crossed the Atlantic to appear in the London *Lancet*, a journal of medicine, chemistry, criticism, literature, and news. The ingeniously distributed nose-thumbing, wink, and wooden leg, the solemn absurdity of an inquest, the absence of a justice named Sewell in Humboldt City, the 125 miles between that place and Gravelly Ford: these pointers enabled sharp San Francisco newsmen to see the joke at

once. Those in less sophisticated places were more than half
prepared to believe, like the Downieville, California, editor
who would have accepted all details except for that wooden
leg, which, said he, was "rather too stiff for our digestion."
Some, cautiously running the story without comment, implied half-way conviction. One man, pondering the marvel
of the stony figure, reflected solemnly upon

the strange power and the singular motive of nature in thus
arresting the process of decay and transforming into shapes,
indestructible by the elements, things which chance merely
has thrown in the way. It would seem as though the Genius
of the enchanted realm were a sworn foe to the decree of
"dust to dust."[17]

To set everybody straight, the author wrote a follow-up:

Mr. Herr Weisnicht has just arrived in Virginia City from
the Humboldt mines and regions beyond. He brings with him
the head and one foot of the petrified man, lately found in
the mountains near Gravelly Ford. A skillful assayer has
analyzed a small portion of dirt found under the nail of the
great toe and pronounces the man to have been a native of
the Kingdom of New Jersey. As a trace of "speculation" is
still discernible in the left eye, it is thought the man was on
his way to what is now the Washoe mining region for the
purpose of locating the Comstock. The remains brought in
are to be seen in a neat glass case in the third story of the
Library Building, where they have been temporarily placed
by Mr. Weisnicht for the inspection of the curious, and where
they may be examined by any one who will take the trouble
to visit them.[18]

Possibly even those hints did not undeceive all trusting readers taken in by the matter-of-fact manner. It would be interesting to know how many gullible people accepted the invitation to view the remains. Several years later Mark Twain
concluded: "To write a burlesque so wild that its pretended

facts will not be accepted in perfect good faith by somebody, is very nearly an impossible thing to do."[19]

Besides being a reporter he was also drawn into the frenetic business of buying and selling feet in mines that were represented as promising, but were more likely to be worthless or wildcat. This gamble was as chancy as roulette or a lottery offering ten blanks to one prize. If a claim were rich, the owner of feet in it might be too poor to buy bread because he had no capital to develop the mine. If he enlisted the aid of capital, he could almost count on being frozen out. One observer called Nevada Territory "the rich man's paradise and the poor man's purgatory."[20] A monied man could do well, it was said, if he had been schooled in rascality by a penitentiary apprenticeship or by experience as a New York City councilman. Otherwise, a player could win only if he gave his whole time to the game, particularly if assisted by a San Francisco confederate, "who requires a conscience like india-rubber, willing to cheat his own brother if he can get a chance."[21]

Hysteria over feet was indecent and continual, aggravated by smooth salesmen and fraudulent assays. The *Enterprise,* in a travel guide entitled "How to See Washoe—Advice Gratis to Visitors," instructed the tourist to divert himself by inspecting the Ophir several times a day, and in his inquiries about sound investments never to take the word of an actual miner, but to "Listen and give heed only to the words of the kid-gloved, gentlemanly dealers in mines. They, of course, are incapable of uttering a single word not strictly true in regard to the mines. Their only object is to see you get a 'good thing.' "[22] A newcomer in 1862 described the methods of the kid-gloved gentlemen. "On your arrival here," he said,

you will be told of speculations just offering for a small sum, out of which you can realize in a short time any amount, varying from seven hundred and fifty thousand to a million of dollars! The investment, your informant will tell you, is perfectly safe, as the tunnel is commenced, and the rock, rich in auriferous substances, is to be struck in a few weeks. . . . They will further show you it is a continuation of Gold Hill, Comstock, Ophir or Gould & Curry, and the parties holding are only induced to sell as their business in other places imperatively calls them away, or they have something bigger in view, or their health is seriously impaired by a too free use of the water which flows from the barren hills of this desolate clime.[23]

That confidence-man technique was familiar and foolproof. In *Roughing It* Mark Twain tells how reporters, puffing an undeveloped mine, "driveled and driveled about the tunnel" and waxed ecstatic over "a shaft, or a new wire rope, or a dressed pine windlass, or a fascinating force pump," but said of the rock only that it "resembled the Comstock (and so it did—but as a general thing the resemblance was not striking enough to knock you down)." Mining region papers were full of such data: "The El Dorado Company are said to have struck a very fine ore . . . . which it would be impossible to distinguish from Ophir or Gould & Curry ore;" "The Old Michigan Mine . . . a well defined ledge of quartz has been struck, resembling, and believed to be a continuation of the main Gold Hill ledge;" the Charles Caney Company's "fine Cornish pump . . . . is the first pump of its kind ever imported into the Territory, we believe." Small wonder that Sam Clemens found no pleasure in that sort of composition. Every mining outfit that professed to be a company got itself written up, all the accounts drearily similar, all effusively noncommittal. No matter about that. Anything was salable that pretended to be a claim. Wild-eyed speculators, excited by a boulder smelling of sulphur or looking as if it came from a spur of the main lode, recklessly threw their money into useless holes in the ground.

Charles R. Luddington, a Virginia merchant, once arranged a window display of over one hundred varieties of wildcat stocks, handsomely decorated in shades of red, green, blue, yellow, purple, and variegated: all gaudy and elaborate but of no more value than waste paper. The *Enterprise,* observing that the monthly food of these wildcats was assessments, said that some of them

are of a nature so ferocious that few brokers—brokers are his principal visitors—care to touch them, knowing by sad experience how liable they are to be bitten; others, by a proper course of treatment, have become quite tame, and may be safely handled, even though these have been known to relapse into wildness, when there is always sure to be some one bitten.[24]

Such an object lesson deterred nobody, least of all Sam Clemens. According to his own story, he was bitten by wildcat as often as the most rabid speculator. Some years later, writing to the California Pioneers of New York City, he claimed kinship with forty-niners on the score of all the "dips, spurs and angles, variations and sinuosities" of foolish experience. After mentioning his mining failures in the Humboldt and Esmeralda districts, he told the Pioneers:

I entered upon an affluent career in Virginia City, and by a judicious investment of labor and the capital of friends, became the owner of about all the worthless wildcat mines there were in that part of the country. Assessments did the business for me there. There were a hundred and seventeen assessments to one dividend, and the proportion of income to the outlay was a little against me. My financial barometer went down to 32 Fahrenheit, and the subscriber was frozen out. I took up extensions on the main lead—extensions that reached to British America in one direction, and to the Isthmus of Panama in the other—and I verily believe I would have been a rich man if I had ever found those infernal extensions. But I didn't. I ran tunnels until I tapped the Arctic ocean, and I sunk shafts till I broke through the roof of perdition; but those extensions turned up missing every time.

I am willing to sell all that property and throw in the improvements. Perhaps you remember that celebrated "North Ophir"? I bought that mine. It was very rich in pure silver. You could take it out in lumps as large as a filbert. But when it was discovered that those lumps were melted half dollars, and hardly melted at that, a painful case of "salting" was apparent, and the undersigned adjourned to the poor-house again. I paid assessments on Hale & Norcross until they sold me out, and I had to take in washing for a living—and the next month that infamous stock went up to $7,000 a foot. I own millions and millions of feet of affluent silver leads in Nevada—in fact, I own the entire undercrust of that country nearly, and if Congress would move that state off my property so I could get at it, I would be wealthy yet. But no, there she squats—and here am I. Failing health persuades me to sell. If you know of any one desiring a permanent investment, I can furnish him one that will have the virtue of being eternal.[25]

Allowing for exaggeration, that recital has some truth in it. He owned feet that he either bought or received gratis from generous owners. *Roughing It* remarks upon the openhanded custom of making such gifts to reporters, who could cash them in for board money if caught short. In a letter to his mother he said: "I pick up a foot or two occasionally by lying about somebody's mine."[26] George E. Barnes, of the San Francisco *Call*, remembered that Sam availed himself "of legitimate opportunities to acquire 'feet' in the Comstock and shares in different outlying mines. He was accounted quite rich in this kind of property at one time;" furthermore, he accumulated "a good deal of money, every stiver of which he sunk in Hale & Norcross."[27] Like others who speculated in those no-account "outlying mines," he caught the "feet" disease and paid for it. The North Ophir stirred up great excitement in 1863, when the company struck rock alleged to assay an incredible $6,000 to the ton. North Ophir stock shot up spectacularly until the discovery of the melted half

dollars caused instant deflation. Mark Twain put that story
into *Roughing It,* but says nothing there of having invested
in this fraudulent claim.

By the middle of November or early December, Sam was
in Carson City to report the second Territorial Legislature,
which convened on November 11 and remained in session
sixty days. Surely he also became a hanger-on of the Third
House, described as "a peculiar institution" composed of
jokers who made fun of legislative procedings. Newspapermen belonged to this informal body, lawyers, businessmen,
even legislators like Councilmen Roop and Hannah and Representative William H. "Billy" Claggett. In gatherings ribald
and inebrious they met every evening, said one observer, "in
a rear building, as Mrs. Malaprop would say 'contagious' to
a drinking saloon," where proceedings were sometimes "quite
witty, but occasionally the wit is 'as broad as it is long.' "[28]
Minutes of these meetings would be illuminating, but none
have survived.

Territorial Solons, like any others—lobbying, caucusing,
buttonholing, politicking—were vulnerable to satire. The ex-
periment of an evening session, with guests, stirred mild derision. "It is true that but very little was accomplished," said
a reporter,

but there was a full and fashionable audience, including Mr.
and Mrs. Buncombe, who are proverbially fond of speeches.
The Representatives' Hall, with a lady sitting at every other
pine desk, and every desk illuminated by two tallow candles
(total, fifty-six candles), presented, if not a majestic, at least
a lively spectacle.[29]

Led by Hal Clayton, a Carson City attorney, the wags of
the Third House published a broadside entitled *Annual Message of Captain Jim, Chief of the Washoes, and Governor
(de facto) of Nevada, Delivered Before the Third House of
the Territorial Legislature, Friday, November Fourteenth,*

One Thousand Eight Hundred and Sixty-Two. Captain Jim, a bona fide Indian known as Chief of all the Washoes, was a familiar territorial character described as a man of splendid physique and possessed of "a degree of intelligence rarely found among the Diggers." He was also called "a keen old rascal" who had such a high regard for truth that he never meddled with it. Armed with a letter of introduction from Nevada's Governor James W. Nye, who admired the Indian's political skill, Captain Jim once triumphantly descended upon San Francisco, where he was royally entertained by General Wright, commandant at Alcatraz, and other important citizens. In Virginia, the captain put up at the International Hotel.

The Third House "message," attributed with as much sense as irony to this capable chief, appeared three days after the official message of Governor Nye. The burlesque parodied political bombast in florid rhetoric, and set forth ridiculous legislative proposals by the *de facto* executive. He rhapsodized about "the prosperity and glory of our rich, fertile and beautiful young Territory . . . onward progress in morality, enlightenment and civilization. . . . this powerful, gigantic and stupendous Government," and so forth. Sam Clemens probably had no part in the writing of this effusion, and he may not have arrived in time to hear its delivery, but at some point he must have edged into deliberations of the Third House to add his voice to its rowdy debates.

On an evening in mid-December, while legitimate legislators met in candle-lit rooms, the Third House, in the satanic glow of bonfires on the street outside, raised an uproar of shouts, drunken speeches impassioned and profane, and a brass band blaring away directly under legislative windows. The noisy demonstration was a protest against absentee ownership of Washoe mines by monied men living in San Francisco, and there was much raucous yelling about "California capitalists," "Montgomery street speculators," and "hired newspapers of San Francisco." This issue was the crux of a corporation bill that, having failed to pass the previous session of the legislature, was now being hotly debated by this one. When it squeaked through the Council by one vote, despite the determined opposition of Councilman D. G. Hall, who was bitterly denounced by the Third House—"Where is the ⸻ of a ⸻?"—the act contained the desired provisions: that a majority of stock in all Nevada mining companies be owned by residents of the Territory, that company offices be established there, and that corporations formed under the laws of other states and territories be prohibited from doing business in Nevada.

Whereupon another street meeting, addressed by exultant speakers frequently refreshed at a nearby bar, evolved into a celebration that attracted most of the permanent and floating population of Carson City. Tremendous bonfires flared, firecrackers popped, guns roared, dogs barked, and the band blatted away manfully as everybody immersed himself in a flood of champagne, whiskey, and brandy. A hurried dispatch to the *Enterprise,* presumably written by Sam Clemens, said:

Great excitement exists. Half the population is drunk—the balance will be before midnight. The flags are flying, and a general looseness prevails. Four hundred guns are now being fired on the Plaza.[30]

The crowd paraded around town, stopping for restoratives at the homes of Governor Nye and other prominent citizens, and making a night of it in a general carouse. What part Sam Clemens played in this spree he did not reveal. The next day a colossal community headache did not halt transaction of legislative business, although a reporter noticed that "the worthy legislators were not all in their places . . . and those that were mostly wore a dolefully solemn expression of countenance."[31]

The solemnity may have been partly the result of morning-after second thought upon the wisdom of the corporation bill. Governor Nye was so dubious of its merits that he signed it only with some reluctance. California editors had naturally been against it as an unfair discrimination against their state. The territorial press hailed the result as a victory for the sovereign people. The *Enterprise* celebrated in verse:

> Rejoice, ye mountains!
> Send word to the sea,
> The people have spoken—
> Nevada is free![32]

On the other hand, the moblike eruptions in Carson City troubled a correspondent of the San Francisco *Evening Bulletin*. Disapproving of government by such coercive tactics as riotous street meetings, he said that they reminded him of ancient Rome. "But one feature of despotism was missing. There was no legion of Pretorian Guards to force the Senate."[33] In the overheated oratory he found too much of the hated doctrine of states' rights, and he was horrified to hear the band playing "Dixie," even maudlin fools loudly singing it.

The immediate effects of the corporation bill were to make hesitant San Francisco capital more cautious than usual, and to depress the value of Washoe mining stocks. In February, 1863, Congressman A. A. Sargent, of California, acting with the approval of Governor Nye, introduced in the House a bill to disallow the Foreign Corporation Act of Nevada Territory. When the bill passed both House and Senate, its effect was to annul the action of the Nevada legislature. The cancellation occurred quietly, without protest other than some grumbling in the papers. The Washoe

Times snorted: "In gaining the hollow admiration of the speculators and sharpers of Montgomery street, a Congressman may run the risk of losing the esteem of a vast army of hard-working men."[34] Montgomery Street was the Western counterpart of Wall Street; in the popular mind both were inhabited only by thieves and scoundrels.

In Carson City, Sam Clemens, *Enterprise* correspondent, did his duty so well that at the end of the session the Council passed a resolution of thanks to him and Clement T. Rice, of the Virginia *Union,* for "full and accurate reports of proceedings." In addition, Sam sent letters about people and things in general: playful remarks about the Nevada Supreme Court and toll roads, illustrated by a satirical map; a ludicrous view of Representative Williams, feet on desk, nonchalantly munching a turnip during the chaplain's prayer; the tryout of the new engine of the Empire City Eagle Fire Company; a description of a quadrille at the White House, written with an engaging humor that forecast the style of the future Mark Twain.[35] He had a fling at the Hon. Thomas Hannah, the Hon. John K. Lovejoy, Mr. Speaker Mills, and other politicos in the story of a "Grand Bull Drivers' Convention" that purportedly assembled at Washoe City on December 22: speeches, a ball—"one lady to several gentlemen"—much liquid jollification, and disapproving remarks about the unseemly behavior of his friend Rice, the *Union's* reporter, dubbed "the Unreliable."[36] In a similar key was a racy greeting to a newly-formed pioneer organization, called "Pah-Utes":

Ah, well—it is touching to see these knotty and rugged old pioneers—who have beheld Nevada in her infancy, and toiled through her virgin sands unmolested by toll-keepers; and prospected her unsmiling hills, and knocked at the doors of her sealed treasure vaults; and camped with her horned toads, and tarantulas and lizards, under her inhospitable

sage brush; and smoked the same pipe; and imbibed lightning out of the same bottle; and eaten their regular bacon
and beans from the same pot; and lain down to their rest
under the same blanket—happy, and lousy and contented—
yea, happier and lousier and more contented than they are
this day, or may be in the days that are to come; it is touching, I say, to see these weather-beaten and blasted old patri-
archs banding together like a decaying tribe, for the sake
of the privations they have undergone, and the dangers they
have met—to rehearse the deeds of the hoary past, and rescue
its traditions from oblivion! The Pah-Ute Association will
become a high and honorable order in the land—its certifi-
cate of membership a patent of nobility. I extend unto the
fraternity the right hand of a poor but honest half-breed and
say God speed your sacred enterprise.[37]

While Clemens was in Carson City, Dan De Quille left
for the "states" sometime in November on an extended leave
of about eight months. The *Enterprise*, in a notice undoubtedly written by Sam, said that Dan had gone East to recu-
perate because he had broken down under the strain of

creating big strikes in the mines and keeping all the mills in
this district going, whether their owners were willing or not.
These herculean labors greatly undermined his health, but
he went bravely on, and we are proud to say that as far as
these things were concerned, he never gave up—the miners
never did, and never could have conquered him. He fell,
under the scarcity of pack-trains and hay-wagons. These had
been the bulwark of the local column; his confidence in them
was like unto that men have in four aces; murders, robberies,
fires, distinguished arrivals, were creatures of chance, which
might or might not occur at any moment; but the pack-trains
and hay-wagons were certain, predestined, immutable!
When these failed last week, he said "*Et tu* Brute," and gave
us his pen. His constitution suddenly warped, split and went
under, and Daniel succumbed. We have a saving hope,
though, that his trip across the Plains, through 1,800 miles
of cheerful hay-stacks, will so restore our loved and lost to
his ancient health and energy, that when he returns next fall

he will be able to run our five hundred mills as easily as he used to keep five-score running.[38]

The departure of this popular reporter made Sam Clemens sole arbiter of city news in the *Enterprise*. He became the Local when he returned to Virginia upon adjournment of the legislature in early January, 1863. Town items that got into other papers are not always identifiable, but such a squib as the following sounds like him:

A beautiful and ably conducted free fight came off in C street yesterday afternoon, but as nobody was killed or mortally wounded in a manner sufficiently fatal to cause death, no particular interest attaches to the matter, and we shall not publish the details. We pine for a murder—these fist-fights are of no consequence to anybody.[39]

At an Odd Fellows ball in Gold Hill on January 7, some rascal stole his hat. In a pretended display of sympathy for the thief, he predicted that the headpiece would give the fellow an irritating malady:

We have been suffering from the seven years' itch for many months. It is probably the most aggravating disease in the world. It is contagious. That man has commenced a career of suffering which is frightful to contemplate; there is no cure for the distemper—it must run its course; there is no respite for its victim, and but little alleviation of its torments to be hoped for; the unfortunate's only resource is to bathe in sulphur and molasses and let his finger nails grow. Further advice is unnecessary—instinct will prompt him to scratch.[40]

That was an early example of the inelegant humor that later literary and social mentors, like Mrs. Fairbanks and his wife, Livy, would strive to suppress on behalf of refinement.

On the street he found, or said he found, a carelessly dropped billet-doux signed "Your Madeline." "Darling," she said, "I have not had time to write you to-day—I have worked hard entertaining company. *Do* come and see your little pet.

I yearn for the silvery cadence of your voice—I thirst for the bubbling stream of your affection." The Local printed this tender missive, and added:

> We feel for that girl. The water privilege which she pines for so lovingly has probably dried up and departed, else her sweet note would not have been floating around the streets without a claimant. We feel for her deeply—and if it will afford her any relief, if it will conduce to her comfort, if it will satisfy her yearning even in the smallest degree, we will cheerfully call around and "bubble" awhile for her ourself, if she will send us her address.[41]

There is no further word on that helpful offer. Another item without a by-line bears the unmistakable Clemens stamp. He wrote up "The China Trial":

> We were there, yesterday, not because we were obliged to go, but just because we wanted to. The more we see of this aggravated trial, the more profound does our admiration for it become. It has more phases than the moon has in a chapter of the almanac. It commenced as an assassination; the assassinated man neglected to die, and they turned it into assault and battery; after this the victim *did* die, whereupon his murderers were arrested and tried yesterday for perjury; they convicted one Chinaman, but when they found out it was the wrong one, they let him go—and why they should have been so almighty particular is beyond our comprehension; then, in the afternoon, the officers went down and arrested China-town again for the same old offense, and put it in jail—but what shape the charge will take this time no man can foresee: the chances are that it will be about a standoff between arson and robbing the mail. Capt. White hopes to get the murderers of the Chinaman hung one of these days, and so do we, for that matter, but we do not expect anything of the kind. You see, these Chinamen are all alike, and they cannot identify each other. They mean well enough, and they really show a disinterested anxiety to get some of their friends and relatives hung, but the same misfortune overtakes them every time: they make mistakes and get the wrong man, with unvarying

accuracy. With a zeal in behalf of justice which cannot be too highly praised, the whole Chinese population have accused each other of this murder, each in his regular turn, but fate is against them. They cannot tell each other apart. There is only one way to manage this thing with strict equity: hang the gentle Chinese promiscuously until justice is satisfied.[42]

Such original reporting of news is a good reason why the *Enterprise* was one of the best known papers in the West, and one of the best known Western papers in the East.

To write a full column on "Silver Bars—How Assayed" he visited the office of Theall and Co., assayers, where he marveled at five bricks of silver worth $10,000: "We are very well pleased with the Hoosier State mill and the Potosi mine—we think of buying them." The label on each, stating ounces of gold and silver and the value in dollars, he called "Poetry stripped of flowers and flummery, and reduced to plain common sense." Then, said he, "We absorbed much obtuse learning, and we propose to give to the ignorant the benefit of it." So he discussed amalgam in a crucible "of the capacity of an ordinary plug hat . . . composed of some kind of pottery which stands heat like a salamander," and heated "in the midst of a charcoal fire as hot as the one which the three Scriptural Hebrew children were assayed in," thus showing a fondness for Biblical allusion that would be typical of Mark Twain.

He told of silver chips, cut from a bar, "placed in a little shallow cup made of bone ashes, called a cupel, and put into a small stone-ware oven, enclosed in a sort of parlor stone furnace, where it is cooked like a lost sinner;" spoke of scales so delicate that "You might weigh a mosquito here, and then pull one of his legs off, and weigh him again, and the scales would detect the difference," its smallest aluminum weight, one-thousandth of a grain, looking like "an imperceptible atom clipped from the invisible corner of a piece of paper whittled down to an impossible degree of sharpness—as it were—and they handle it with pincers like a hair pin;" described the method of separating base metals from precious and of gold from silver, the latter in solution being "precipitated with muriatic acid (or something of that kind—we are not able to swear that this was the drug mentioned to us, although we feel very certain that it was,) and restored to metal again." He apologized for only hazily remembering some steps in the process, "owing to lager beer," and concluded:

This is all the science we know. What we do not know is reserved for private conversation, and will be liberally inflicted upon any body who will call here at the office and submit to it. After the bar has been assayed, it is stamped as described in the beginning of this dissertation, and then it is ready for the mint. Science is a very pleasant subject to dilate upon, and we consider that we are as able to dilate upon it as any man that walks—but if we have been guilty of carelessness in any part of this article, so that our method of assaying as set forth herein may chance to differ from Mr. Theall's, we would advise that gentleman to stick to his own plan nevertheless, and not go to following ours—his is as good as any known to science. If we have struck anything new in our method, however, we shall be happy to hear of it, so that we can take steps to secure to ourself the benefits accruing therefrom.[43]

Taking the time to assemble the technical details for this article of about 1,500 words, and putting the whole into coherent form, called for remarkable self-discipline from a man usually uninterested in that sort of data. Dan De Quille, reminiscing about Virginia days, said that Sam was "earnest and enthusiastic in such work as suited him," but that he gave "only a lick and a promise" to "cast-iron items" involving "figures, measurements and solid facts, such as were called for in matters pertaining to mines and machinery."[44]

This time he took pains to dilate upon scientific facts, yet in a typically easy manner that makes livelier reading than the more precise, but generally duller, style of the better informed technologist. In the same vein was the notice of a mining device invented by William L. Card, of Silver City:

a sort of infernal machine, which is to turn quartz mills by electricity. It consists of wheels and things, and—however, we could not describe it without getting tangled. Mr. Card assures us that he can apply his invention to all the mills in Silver City, and work the whole lot with one powerful Grove battery. We believe—and if we had galvanic sense enough to explain the arrangement properly, others would also.[45]

Such slapdash reporting as that would be unappreciated in the modern city room, but the method suited the Local and the *Enterprise*. Fortunately for Sam Clemens' development as a writer, the paper allowed its staff more freedom than any journalist except the most pampered columnist could expect today. Sam throve under this casual regime; he could not have put up with the regimented life of a reporter assigned to the City Hall or the police court. Anything that looked like hack work bored him. Covering dull meetings, drowsy with droning talk, he amused himself by decorating the margins of his copy paper with weird drawings of the talkers, and far-fetched representations of the subjects they talked about. When the Virginia Board of Aldermen dealt with a traveling menagerie that had failed to pay the city tax, Sam sketched the City Marshal leading an elephant by the trunk, the mayor mounted on a giraffe, a policeman holding a lion by the tail, another with a captured rhinoceros. These drawings were no doubt in the same free style of those he later put into *A Tramp Abroad*, "How to Make History Dates Stick," and other works.

None of his illustrations got into the paper, but they entertained the boys at the office, especially Dan De Quille, with whom, when he was on duty, Sam shared the city beat. They often cruised in company, and always wrote at the same baize-covered table, Sam's end much slashed by his habit of "clipping" news items with a pocket knife. They were a good team, very friendly, both humorists, but not at all alike. Dan, who had joined the staff only a few months before Sam, was six years older than his partner. As Joe Goodman's first lieutenant, he was a man of mild disposition and placid temper that made him a stabilizer, a sort of presiding genius or mentor of the whole unruly crew. A model craftsman, he practiced methodical work habits and exercised a meticulous care for accuracy. Because he was shy, gentle, loath to offend, his humorous pieces, which he called "quaints," were droll, whimsical, puckish, sometimes mildly sentimental. At the time, he was the best known, best liked, and most promising writer on the paper, having published many sketches in *The Golden Era* and attracted the attention of the New York *Knickerbocker Magazine*. Nevertheless, he made no effort to seek a national audience; contented with his berth in Virginia, he remained there until the *Enterprise* died in 1893.

Sam Clemens, on the other hand, was audacious, impulsive, erratic, and haphazard. Given to outrageous eruptions of temper and flagrant personalities, he was neither gentle nor inoffensive. His humor was more slashing than whimsical, and it was never merely quaint. He made readers take heed, by either amusing them or irritating them, but he was an uncertain quantity, sometimes approaching brilliance, sometimes falling into the commonplace and gauche; thus far his reputation, such as it was, did not extend beyond local limits. Joe Goodman believed, and many others shared his opinion, that of the two men Dan was the one destined for fame. But Sam had powerful ambition that would not permit him to be satisfied indefinitely with a reporter's job, and that would aid materially in confounding those critics.

Chapter Two

ENTER MARK TWAIN

❧❧

IN LATE January, 1863, Sam Clemens, sent on a one-day mission to Carson City, stayed there a week, unable to resist the attraction of balls, weddings, and bonhomie. These he described for the *Enterprise* in several dispatches animated by his usual exaggeration and by horrified remarks about the outlandish behavior of the Unreliable.[1] The trip was significant because one Carson letter, dated January 31 and signed "Mark Twain," publicized for the first time a *nom de plume* that was to become world-famous. About ten years later he explained, as a sort of afterthought, how he came by this pseudonym:

"Mark Twain" was the *nom de plume* of one Captain Isaiah Sellers, who used to write river news over it for the New Orleans *Picayune*: he died in 1863, and as he could no longer need that signature, I laid violent hands upon it without asking permission of the proprietor's remains. That is the history of the *nom de plume* I bear.[2]

Convinced of the truth of these facts, as he called them, he said that they were among the few things he was sure of. He repeated that explanation so often to correspondents—to anybody who inquired—that by the eighteen-eighties he said he had given it three thousand times. He put it into Chapter L of *Life on the Mississippi,* and for over twenty years after that

periodically produced the same information when asked. As
part of his autobiographical dictations of 1906, dutifully recorded in Paine's biography (1912), the Sellers story bore
the stamp of authority that made it generally accepted.

Nevertheless, those "facts" become improbable when examined. For one thing, Sellers died in 1864, over a year after
Clemens "laid violent hands" upon the name. For another,
the captain's humdrum river news—which Sam burlesqued
for the New Orleans *Crescent* over the name of "Sergeant
Fathom" in 1859—was so uninspired that the invention of an
imaginative pen name seems unlikely. The usual signature
attached to those prosaic *Picayune* items was a plain "I.
Sellers." Furthermore, diligent research has failed to discover that the captain or anybody else used the name "Mark
Twain" while Sam Clemens was a pilot on the Mississippi
River.[3] The Sellers origin of the pseudonym appears, then,
to have been either a deliberate invention or one of those
curious aberrations of Twain's inaccurate memory.

A more plausible explanation came from George W. Cassidy, of the Eureka, Nevada, *Sentinel,* in the eighteen-seven-
ties. Claiming acquaintance with Clemens "in the early
days," he said that the pen name originated in John Piper's
bar, known as "Old Corner saloon," a favorite Virginia City
haunt of reporters and Bohemians. The proprietor, said Cassidy,

conducted a cash business, and refused to keep any books.
As a special favor . . . he would occasionally chalk down
drinks to the boys on the wall back of the bar. Sam Clemens,
when localizing for the *Enterprise,* always had an account
with the balance against him. Clemens was by no means a
Coal Oil Tommy, he drank for the pure and unadulterated
love of the ardent. Most of his drinking was conducted in
single-handed contests, but occasionally he would invite Dan
De Quille, Charley Parker, Bob Lowery or Alf. Doten, never
more than one of them . . . at a time, and whenever he did his

invariable parting injunction was to "mark twain," meaning
two chalk marks. . . . in this way . . . he acquired the title
which has since become famous wherever . . . English . . . is
read or spoken.[4]

A variant of that story, told in the vernacular by a narrator
described as "a Washoe genius," got into the Nevada City,
California, *Transcript*:

> "Wall now, d'ye see," says he, " 'Mark'—that is Sam, d'ye
> see—used to take his regular drinks at Johnny Doyle's. Well,
> 'Mark' that is Sam, d'ye see, used to run his face, bein' short
> of legal tenders. Well, 'Mark,' that is Sam, d'ye understand,
> always used to take two horns consecutive, one right after
> the other, and when he come in there and took them on tick,
> Johnny used to sing out to the barkeep, who carried a lump
> of chalk in his pocket and kept the score, 'mark twain,' where-
> upon the barkeep would score two drinks to Sam's account—
> and so it was, d'ye see, that he come to be called 'Mark
> Twain.' "[5]

These stories are more convincing than the Sellers version
because they are consistent with Washoe ways and with the
Western life of Mark Twain. Out there he was no stranger
to barrooms and barkeeps. In a hearty society where drinks
were the order of the day and night, where the saloon was
an accepted institution, where the over-persistent toper
might be laughed at but not ostracized, and where refusing
a proffered glass violated the code of the gentleman, he con-
formed with every evidence of enjoyment. Nobody had to
force him up to the bar. An habitué of Piper's saloon and of
many another in the Territory, he probably knew Cassidy,
likewise the Johnny Doyle who was a barkeeper in the Bank
Exchange, Gold Hill, and another Johnny Doyle who was
proprietor of a saloon in Dayton, a small town near Virginia.

A reminiscence in the San Francisco *Chronicle* in 1872 tells
of an informal club of ten or a dozen men, including Mark

Twain, Dan De Quille, and Joe Goodman, who first styled themselves "Companions of the Jug," then changed the name, at Goodman's suggestion, to "The Visigoths." They met every afternoon in a brewery on D Street, where beer was a dollar a gallon; plentiful Limburger, radishes, mustard, and caraway-seed bread came forth at twenty-five cents a platter. They entertained visiting actors, and enlivened their gatherings with impromptu wit and poetry that became more inspired as the lager flowed and flowed.[6] Paine tells a story of Mark Twain and Alf Doten on the trail of a news story at Como, but not going after the story because every morning for three days Mark Twain led his partner into a brewery, where they stayed all day.[7] Perhaps that occurrence was responsible for an item in the Como *Sentinel*, which boasted that hometown lager was "the best in the Territory, as we can prove by 'Mark Twain,' who has sat in the brewery and drank 'gallons and gallons' of it without arising from his seat."[8]

Plentiful testimony shows that in Washoe he was a sturdy bottle man who was far from being the Model Boy of Virginia. Hence, when he later met the respectable Langdons, of Elmira, during an impetuous courtship of their daughter, he had reason for apprehension over a harum-scarum past. His story of failing to win for the parents of his beloved Olivia an endorsement of character from Western friends may be exaggerated, but there was some truth in it, for they had good cause to doubt his qualifications as a potential husband of steady habits. According to his own testimony, the opinion of the Rev. Horatio Stebbins, San Francisco Unitarian, was that Sam Clemens would fill a drunkard's grave.

When he settled in the more austere moral climate of New England, he may have evolved the Sellers story, or somehow pulled it out of the haze of mistaken remembrance, as a means of suppressing knowledge of that free Nevada life, knowing full well that barroom escapades were scarcely correct in Connecticut. Such a conjecture rests upon the mixed impulses of his character, in which the outspoken rebel vied with the conventional citizen fearful of offending public opinion. This caution appears in several other incidents that look evasive: his attempt, late in life, to repudiate the early, crude Thomas Jefferson Snodgrass Letters, written for the Keokuk *Post* in 1856-57; his dubiety over the deterministic dialogue, "What is Man?;" and his unwillingness to publish during his lifetime the sardonic *Mysterious Stranger*. In the same category is the surprising remark he contributed in 1882 to a symposium entitled *Study and Stimulants*: "I have not had a large experience in the matter of alcoholic drinks."[9] A heavy weight of Western evidence, his own and others', flatly contradicts that statement, as he surely must have been aware. After he had moved to the East, he developed a sensitivity that often made him timid about risking social disapproval.

The leadsman's call "Mark twain!," said to have been sung out to and by bartenders, was part of the river language that crept into the writing of this former steamboatman, and no doubt into his speech also. In spirit Mark Twain was never far from the Mississippi River, and anybody who listened to him surely knew it. That barkeepers and cronies quickly took up the name is easy to believe. Possibly friends in Virginia knew him as Mark some little time before he signed the January 31 letter from Carson City. In that dispatch, which describes a gay party at Governor J. Neely Johnson's, Mark Twain says:

The Unreliable intruded himself upon me in his cordial way and said, "How are you, Mark, old boy? when d'you come down? It's brilliant, ain't it? Lend a fellow two bits, can't you?" He always winds up his remarks that way. He appears to have an insatiable craving for two bits.

The words of the Unreliable imply that the pseudonym was already familiar. That his casual use of "Mark" was probably interpolated fiction does not invalidate the inference. Surely the pen name did not suddenly spring into being overnight; it must have been bandied about in Virginia before public adoption, long enough to convince everybody that it was a brilliant invention.[10]

When Sam Clemens became Mark Twain, his news stories were more often than heretofore identified by other editors. They were alert to his sorties in the *Enterprise,* and diverted by the running battle of wits between him and his friend Rice, the Unreliable, of the Virginia *Union.* The pair continually joshed each other in their respective papers. "This poor miserable outcast," said Mark Twain,

crowded himself into the Firemen's Ball night before last, and glared upon the happy scene with his evil eye for a few minutes. He had his coat buttoned up to his chin, which is the way he always does when he has no shirt on. As soon as the management found out he was there, they put him out, of course. They had better have allowed him to stay, though, for he walked straight across the street, with all his vicious soul aroused, and climbed in at the back window of the supper room and gobbled up the last crumb of the repast provided for the guests, before he was discovered. This accounts for the scarcity of provisions at the Fireman's supper that night. Then he went home and wrote a particular description of our ball costume, with his usual meanness, as if such information could be of any consequence to the public. He never vouchsafed a single compliment to our dress, either, after all the care and taste we had bestowed upon it. We despise that man.[11]

In the *Enterprise* office the Local found a missive signed by one "Solon Lycurgus" who, while admiring the panorama from Sugar Loaf Peak, wrote his sweetheart in the language of love mixed with that of the law. Addressing "my Mary,

the peerless party of the first part," he spoke of the grand
view "of this portion of what is called and known as Creation, with all and singular the hereditaments and appurte-
nances thereto appertaining and belonging" and of the desert
glowing "with the warm light of the sun hereinbefore mentioned, or darkly shadowed by the messenger-clouds aforesaid." Said Mark Twain:

what a villain the man must be, to blend together the beautiful language of love and the infernal phraseology of the law
in one and the same sentence! I know of but one of God's
creatures who could be guilty of such depravity as this: I
refer to the Unreliable. I believe the Unreliable to be the
very lawyer's cub who sat upon that solitary peak, all soaked
with beer and sentiment, and concocted the insipid literary
hash which I am talking about. The handwriting closely
resembles his semi-Chinese tarantula tracks.[12]

Day after day they sniped at each other, often enough to
fill a small volume that might be known as the Unreliable
Papers. After a sally by Rice, Mark Twain came up with an
obituary of his fellow journalist:

He became a newspaper reporter, and crushed Truth to
earth and kept her there; he bought and sold his own notes,
and never paid his board; he pretended great friendship for
Gillespie [clerk of the first Territorial Legislature] in order
to get to sleep with him; then he took advantage of his bed
fellow and robbed him of his glass eye and false teeth; of
course he sold the articles, and Gillespie was obliged to issue
more county scrip than the law allowed, in order to get them
back again; the Unreliable broke into my trunk at Washoe
City, and took jewelry and fine clothes and things, worth
thousands and thousands of dollars; he was present, without
invitation, at every party and ball and wedding which tran-
spired in Carson during thirteen years. But the last act of his
life was the crowning meanness of it; I refer to the abuse of
me in the Virginia *Union* of last Saturday, and also to a list
of Langton's stage passengers sent to the same paper by him,

wherein my name appears between those of "Sam Chung" and "Sam Lee." This is his treatment of me, his benefactor. That malicious joke was his dying atrocity. During thirteen years he played himself for a white man; he fitly closed his vile career by trying to play me for a Chinaman.

He is dead and buried now, though; let him rest, let him rot. Let his vices be forgotten, but his virtues be remembered; it will not infringe much upon any man's time.

P. S. By private letters from Carson, since the above was in type, I am pained to learn that the Unreliable, true to his unnatural instincts, came to life again in the midst of his funeral sermon, and remains so to this moment. He was always unreliable in life—he could not even be depended upon in death. The shrouded corpse shoved the coffin lid to one side, rose to a sitting position, cocked his eye at the minister and smilingly said, "O let up, Dominie, this is played out, you know—loan me two bits!" The frightened congregation rushed from the house, and the Unreliable followed them, with his coffin on his shoulder. He sold it for two dollars and a half, and got drunk at a "bit house" on the proceeds. He is still drunk.[13]

Some days later, reporting the celebration at Almack's over the organization of the Washoe Stock Exchange, Mark Twain said that, happening to arrive "by a sort of instinct . . . just at the moment that the corks were about to pop," he drank toasts, listened to speeches, and shared the general conviviality until

that everlasting, omnipresent, irrespressible "Unreliable" crowded himself into the festive apartment, where he shed a gloom upon the Board of Brokers, and emptied their glasses while they made speeches. The imperturbable impudence of that iceberg surpasses anything we ever saw. By a concerted movement the young man was partially put down at length, however, and the Board launched out into speech-making again; but finally somebody put up five feet of "Texas," which changed hands at eight dollars a foot, and from that they branched off into a wholesale bartering of "wild cat"—for their natures were aroused by the first smell of blood of course—and we adjourned to make this report.[14]

The foolery of those exchanges between the pair made Comstock journalism unusual, if not unique. The banter also illustrated a principle Mark Twain adopted when he became a seasoned after-dinner speaker: that lies about friends may be outrageous but should never be malicious. There was certainly no malice in the assumed indignation over the disgraceful behavior of the Unreliable.

The *Enterprise* Local was a sort of roving columnist, most himself when he traveled at his own pace on whatever subject struck his fancy. Now and then he glanced at the news, as in one of those interminable mining items:

> After remaining for a long time in a partially developed state of agriculturality—so to speak—Honey Lake has shown the features of the Nevada family at last—the earmarks of the Washoe litter—and suddenly cropped out as a mining district. Several promising ledges have been discovered round about Susanville, and the people are already beginning to use the language of "feet." Specimens from two new locations—the Union and the Bridges leads—look exceedingly well. They seem to contain no silver, but are sprinkled with free gold, easily seen with the naked eye.[15]

Such a notice was of the "cast-iron" kind that by this time he could write automatically, yet with enough flair to lift it above the ordinary. The making of another piece of news showed his reporter's instinct for going after a story. While writing to his mother one night he interrupted his letter to say: "I have just heard five pistol shots down the street—as such things are in my line, I will go and see about it." Returning several hours later, he added: "The pistol did its work well—one man—a Jackson County Missourian, shot two of my friends, (police officers,) through the heart—both died within three minutes. Murderer's name is John Campbell."[16]

The policemen were Dennis McMahon and Thomas Reed. Campbell, having blown into town from Santa Rosa, had become involved with them in a beer cellar row in which all three were said to have been drunk. When the officers got his dander up by accusing him of singing "Dixie," he shot them. These details were sordidly routine, but the sequel aroused the interest of Mark Twain when a rumor gained currency that five Indians had been smothered to death in a tunnel back of Gold Hill. Since the story was generally regarded as a sensation hoax for the edification of strangers, the Local went after the facts. Gold Hill, he said,

was electrified on Sunday morning with the intelligence that a noted desperado had just murdered two Virginia policemen, and had fled in the general direction of Gold Hill. Shortly afterward, some one arrived with the exciting news that a man had been seen to run and hide in a tunnel a mile or a mile and a half west of Gold Hill. Of course it was Campbell—who else would do such a thing, on that particular morning, of all others? So a party of citizens repaired to this spot, but each felt a natural reluctance about approaching an armed and desperate man, and especially in such confined quarters; wherefore they stopped up the mouth of the tunnel, calculating to hold on to their prisoner until some one could be found whose duty would oblige him to undertake the disagreeable task of bringing forth the captive. The next day a strong posse went up, rolled away the stones from the mouth of the sepulchre, went in and found five dead Indians!—three men, one squaw and one child, who had gone in there to sleep, perhaps, and been smothered by the foul atmosphere after the tunnel had been closed up. We still hope the story may prove a fabrication, notwithstanding the positive assurances we have received that it is entirely true. The intention of the citizens was good, but the result was most unfortunate. To shut up a murderer in a tunnel was well enough, but to leave him there all night was calculated to impair his chances for a fair trial—the principle was good, but the application was unnecessarily "hefty." We have given the above story for truth—we shall continue to regard it as such until it is disproven.[17]

Twainian irony shows in that one, also humanitarian sympathy for the mistreated, even for a murderer. Later indignation over injustice led him to write sharp protests on behalf of the maltreated Chinese of San Francisco, and of beaten-down underdogs generally. The Indians smothered in the tunnel may have occurred to the author of *Tom Sawyer* when he contrived the death of Injun Joe in a cave, similarly sealed up, near St. Petersburg.

After about eight months in free-and-easy Washoe, Mark Twain was fairly well known to the press of the Western country. Though not a general favorite, like Dan De Quille, he had a reputation: as a perplexing mixture of the offhand, irreverent, profane, mad, laughable, and diabolic. Some serious-minded editors dismissed him as only a frivolous fool. Others might gasp at his effrontery, yet they were ready enough to spice their columns with his peppery words lifted from the *Enterprise*. In Virginia, a blend of fame and notoriety made him a man of some importance. Joe Goodman satirically emphasized local prestige by describing him as reigning "by the Grace of Cheek," as

Monarch of Mining Items, Detailer of Events, Prince of Platitudes, Chief of Biographers, Expounder of Unwritten Laws, Puffer of Wildcat, Profaner of Divinity, Detractor of Merit, Flatterer of Power, Recorder of Stage Arrivals, Pack Trains, Hay Wagons and Things in General.[18]

Around the office he was a positive character distinguished by a foul-smelling pipe, which his colleagues dubbed "The Remains," and by a sulphurous temper that made associates call him, in a mood compounded of camaraderie and exasperation, "the Incorrigible." To provoke an explosion the boys sometimes played tricks on him. When the printers now and then hid his lampshade, he came to a boil by slowly ambling around the room while he released his rich vocabulary of profanity and worked up to a fine pitch of malediction. A story says that the Episcopalian rector, happening along during one of these outbursts, paused to listen, enthralled and horrified by the magnificently impious flow. Mark Twain was said to have apologized thus:

"I know you're shocked to hear me, Mr. Brown. It stands to reason you are. I know this ain't language fit for a Christian man to utter nor for a Christian man to hear, but if I could only get my hands on the ___ ___ ___ ___ who stole my shade, I'd show you what I'd do to him, for the benefit of printers to all time. You don't know printers, Mr. Brown; you don't know them. A Christian man like you can't come in contact with them, but I give you my word they're the ___ ___ ___ ___ that a body ever had anything to do with."[19]

Since he freely published pointed personalities, ruffled readers applied to him the same kind of language he expended on the printers. An anecdote tells of an irate citizen who stormed into the office threatening to boot the Local all over the Territory. "Well," drawled Mark Twain, "if you think you've got money enough to put me over all these toll-roads, just start in!"[20]

Most of the cheeky *Enterprise* stories that gave him such a devilish reputation are lost to us, likewise the insulting gibes and pieces profane and irreverent. Undoubtedly they stirred strong feelings that made him a marked personage likely to be regarded with apprehension or aversion. On his relations with his fellow man the testimony is mixed. Russell K. Colcord, reminiscing at the age of ninety, remembered that back in Aurora days Sam Clemens had seemed "cold, selfish and unsocial," but added: "Unfortunately for me I did not know him at all except to nod in passing."[21] In 1887

George E. Barnes, of the San Francisco *Call*, said that Mark Twain did not have many friends in Nevada. "There were some who affected his company on account of his writings, but he had not the faculty of winning friendships."[22] In 1893 Arthur McEwen, a reporter for the San Francisco *Examiner*, seconded that opinion:

> Not many people liked Mark Twain, if one may judge by the tone of deprecation in which he is spoken of on the Comstock to this day. . . . It is the villager's way of impressing upon the stranger the villager's superior, intimate knowledge of the great man. They say that Mark was mean—that he would join in revels and not pay his share, and so on. Those who knew him well, who had the requisite intelligence to be more than surface companions, tell a different story.[23]

McEwen added the ironical note that "Mark, being a man of sense, never neglected his interests. The fact that to know a particular man might at some time be advantageous did not deter Mr. Clemens from making his acquaintance." There is something in that view; Mark Twain was not slow to cultivate people who could be of use to him financially or socially: tycoons, prominent clergymen, literary lights, generals, and politicians.

Nevertheless, in Washoe a strong attachment for Dan De Quille, Joe Goodman, and the Unreliable, not to speak of others like Steve Gillis, Denis McCarthy, and Alf Doten, did not depend merely on their practical usefulness. He liked them for their intrinsic qualities, as people who meant more to him than "surface companions." Dan De Quille testified to their warm friendship, and Joe Goodman recalled with great affection:

> Back in the old days Sam was the best company, the drollest entertainer and the most interesting fellow imaginable. His humor always cropped out.[24]

If he had few close friends in Nevada, that circumstance is in accord with the experience of a long life in which he became acquainted with a great many people all over the world, but reserved friendship for a few, possibly only for two: Joe Twichell and William Dean Howells. Mark Twain himself admitted in 1869 to Mrs. Jervis Langdon, his prospective mother-in-law, that whereas every man in California knew something about him, not more than five were close enough to speak authoritatively. He could be genial enough, good-humored and chatty, but he had too much reticence to be the kind of grinning gladhander who effusively exudes good fellowship that is often spurious. Among the many pictures of Mark Twain, not one is a smiling portrait. He did not—probably could not—give of himself easily. Howells touches upon that point astutely when he says in *My Mark Twain*: "He glimmered at you from the narrow slits of fine blue-greenish eyes, under branching brows, which with age grew more and more like a sort of plumage, and he was apt to smile into your face with a subtle but amiable perception, and yet with a sort of remote absence: you were all there for him, but he was not all there for you."

In Washoe, friends or no friends, he seemed reasonably contented insofar as such a disturbed man ever could be. In the *Enterprise* he mused upon the theme of happiness:

We take happiness to be the aim of life. The varied pursuits of mankind all tend, directly or indirectly, to this object. The strife for wealth, power and fame, is instigated by the faith that we shall be happier in their possession. Our idols of to-day will be broken by ourselves tomorrow. They are only images of the real objects we worship. They are means, not ends. We use them as ladders to climb to the point of our ambition, and kick them away when we have attained it. Remembering that happiness is always the aim, if it can be reached by little trouble, is it not clearly folly to spend time and labor in seeking it? Clearly. You would say a man who

could honestly stoop and pick up a treasure, would be a fool
to unnecessarily work a lifetime for it just because its real
value was worth a life's labor. This is our philosophy. Likewise Charley Funk's and Wilson's. Wilson, you know, is the
reporter of the Union. While the senior wranglers of the two
papers befoul each other in the editorial columns, we lay off
in a lager beer saloon, and feel as much pity for both as they
feign contempt for each other. And Charley Funk, too. We
have formed a select Lager Beer Club, for the purpose of
imbibing ourselves and making it fashionable to indulge in
the healthful Teutonic beverage. It is a pleasant pastime, and
the cheapest happiness we ever struck. Give us our jolly
companions and a pot of foaming beer, and the Rhine flows
through Washoe, the merry vintagers sing on our hillsides,
and we live in the golden reign of King Gambrinus.[25]

The emergent philosopher foreshadowed the speculative
Mark Twain of later life. The abrupt descent from solemn
reflection to the beer cellar illustrates the combination of
serious and flippant that he was often to use in after years,
particularly on the lyceum circuit. If happiness means seren-
ity, peace of mind, a balance free from mercurial ups and
downs, his spirit was too turbulent for that. He told his
mother that he was well satisfied in Virginia, but as for happiness, he seemed to be continually pursuing it without ever
catching up. His sister, Pamela, retorted that he would find
it if only he returned to the religion he had deserted.[26] But
neither that anodyne nor any other was of use to him, nor
ever would be. Still, Virginia offered substitutes of a sort
congenial to a man fond of the stir of life. The place was
something like the Mississippi River in its kaleidoscope of
shifting scenes and multitudinous characters. A reporter
there, said Mark Twain some years later, had a great opportunity to observe a wide variety of human beings and human
ways.

No other occupation brings a man into such familiar sociable relations with all grades and classes of people. The

last thing at night—midnight—he goes browsing around after items among police and jailbirds, in the lock-up, questioning the prisoners, and making pleasant and lasting friendships with some of the worst people in the world. And the very next evening he gets himself up regardless of expense, puts on all the good clothes his friends have got—goes and takes dinner with the Governor, or the Commander-in-Chief of the District, the United States Senator, and some more of the upper crust of society. He is on good terms with all of them, and is present at every public gathering, and has easy access to every variety of people. Why I breakfasted almost every morning with the Governor, dined with the principal clergymen, and slept in the station house.[27]

Yes, all that was agreeable, and there were besides affable beer cellar companions and plenty of lager.

Chapter Three

FLUSH TIMES

ᵾᵾ

RESTLESS as always, weary of months of sagebrush and desolate hills, Mark Twain took off for San Francisco about the first of May, 1863. The Unreliable went with him, and they were like recruits making the most of city lights after long restriction to the rigors of boot camp. For two months, spending money with carefree abandon, they reveled in the high life of balls, bars, and restaurants: out on the town all day and most of the night, roaming around the popular resort known as the Willows, jaunting to Hayes Park, excursioning to Oakland and San Leandro, yachting on the Bay, dining sumptuously at the Lick House with claret and champagne. In a spirited letter to the *Enterprise*, Mark Twain also mentioned a rowdy performance at the Bella Union Melodeon, and reproved the "reckless and unprincipled" Unreliable for appearing uninvited at the Davenport-Spangler wedding and stealing the spoons.

Joe Goodman gave the departing Local a *bon voyage* in the *Enterprise* manner:

As he assigned no adequate reason for this sudden step, we thought him the pitiable victim of self-conceit and the stock mania. He possessed some wildcat, and had lectured the Unreliable on manners till he fancied himself a Chesterfield. Yes, the poor fellow actually thought he possessed some breeding—that Virginia was too narrow a field for his graces and accomplishments; and in this delusion he has gone to display his ugly person and disgusting manners and wildcat on Montgomery street. In all of which he will be assisted by his protegee, the Unreliable. It is to be regretted that such scrubs are ever permitted to visit the Bay, as the inevitable effect will be to destroy that exalted opinion of the manners and morality of our people which was inspired by the conduct of our senior editor. We comfort ourselves, however, with the reflection that they will not be likely to shock the sensibilities of San Francisco long. The ordinances against nuisances are strictly enforced in that city.

He went on to say that Mark Twain left town because he was running away from a girl.

Who ever thought beneath that ingenuous face was concealed a heart that could wrong confiding innocence? Yet the angels fell, and why not Mark Twain? . . . The subjoined tender verses tell the story—the same sad story of maiden love betrayed. . . . Since Ariadne wept her Theseus, since Oenone mourned her Paris, nothing more passionate has gushed from a loving, lonely heart:

> ———— to Mark Twain
>
> At morn, at noon, in evening light,
> As in a dream I move around,
> For Heaven has lost its loveliest sight
> And earth its sweetest sound.
> Do fond emotions softly swell
> For her from whom your steps have strayed—
> Or has some flaunting city belle
> Eclipsed your plighted sage-brush maid?
> Mark Twain, Mark Twain,
> Ah, haste again
> To her whose true love you betrayed.[1]

It is too bad that this forlorn damsel created by Goodman, and her touching verses, are not genuine so that they might throw a glimmer of light upon the cloudy subject of Mark Twain and women in Washoe. Tantalizing questions keep popping up: Was he a diligent squire of dames there? Did he pay special attention to any woman or women? Did he ever fall in love? Did he think of marrying a sagebrush belle? No satisfactory answers clarify obscurity.

Women were not plentiful in Virginia. According to the United States Census of 1860, men there were in a majority of seventeen to one. The "fallen angels" of D Street and the taxi dancers of hurdy-gurdy cellars were in adequate supply, and female dealers at faro tables flashed gold-toothed smiles, but of proper girls there were not nearly enough to go around. When emigrant trains paused in town for a breather after a long trek across the plains, their sunbonneted misses swirling down Virginia streets brightened masculine faces with the hope that these attractions might be persuaded to remain. But then the trains pulled out for California, taking the girls along, and the faces fell. In *Roughing It,* Mark Twain dwells upon the womanlessness of the whole region, and the pleasure of seeing any female, regardless of age or pulchritude. Yet in his letters to the *Enterprise* from Carson City, remarks about balls and parties show that there was feminine companionship, and that he was a social being who was neither hermit nor misogynist.

He liked the girls, and he knew how to comport himself in mixed company. Fond of dancing, a regular attendant at Firemen's and Odd Fellows hops—where the papers once in a while reported as many as one hundred ladies—he cut a dashing figure in the plain quadrille, his agility complemented by ballroom manners more urbane than the roughhouse behavior of the Virginia newspaper and barroom crowd. As he said many years later when the papers accused him of familiarly patting the shoulder of King Edward VII: "an impertinence of which I was not guilty; I was reared in the most exclusive circles of Missouri and I know how to behave."[2] Having been brought up by a firm-minded mother like Jane Lampton Clemens, he knew more about correct behavior than many people suspected. If not a model of Chesterfieldian polish, the wild humorist of the Pacific slope, even in his wildest days, knew something of social graces. Shaggy and shocking as he still appeared to the decorous Olivia Langdon in 1868, he nevertheless fascinated her and eventually won her over.

Some of the Washoe girls surely liked him, too, notwithstanding his penchant for teasing mockery and the air of devilment that hung about him like a sultry aura. Even at his most disconcerting—as when, for instance, he ridiculed feminine dress, came out with a salty remark, or flouted convention—he was, to some at least, attractive. After his marriage in 1870 the *Enterprise* spoke of the "soft glances" that had been cast upon "his manly form as he strode forth, notebook in hand," and mentioned "his many narrow escapes [from matrimony] in this land of sage."[3] But no reliable evidence shows that in Nevada he courted any woman, plighted troth with a maid, or jilted one girl for another. Betrayal in the usual sense of adept seduction is too far out of character to merit consideration. The former Mississippi pilot, having observed on the river the loose living of gamblers and thieves, con men and professional seducers, fancy women and drabs less fancy, never fell into such ways himself. Always he maintained an admirable Victorian regard for womanly virtue.

On the obscure subject of the ladies and their appeal, the Local of the Gold Hill *Daily News* made a provocative contribution. Visiting Virginia in search of copy, he said that the sight of school children carried him back

to the time when we made dirt pies, spun tops, and played "keep house" with the little girls. But now we are a man; like Mark Twain, we can't find nary a one to keep house with. Mark says he "popped it" to one the other day, but she couldn't see it. Guess we won't try it.[4]

That rejection was perhaps one of those narrow escapes. It is reasonable to suppose that a well-favored young man like Mark Twain, slim, bushily red-haired, susceptible to feminine charm and himself capable of radiating charm, popped the question to somebody. If he did, her identity would be interesting to know, likewise what sort of person she was, but no word about that episode has come down to us, either from him or the fair unknown. If she was anything like the woman he did marry—as surely she was, to satisfy his highly selective taste—the wonder is that so carefully nurtured a flower should have bloomed on Mount Davidson.

While he and the Unreliable roistered in San Francisco, the fortunes of Virginia surged upward to the high water mark of prosperity. In June, 1863, the Gould & Curry hit the ledge with a half-mile tunnel 430 feet below A Street, one blast having turned up a ten-thousand-dollar lump loaded with silver. The *Enterprise* hailed the discovery of "extremely rich" ore as "another and incontrovertible evidence of the permanence and exhaustless wealth of that mysterious depository known as the Comstock range, compared with which the mines of other latitudes sink into insignificance."[5] The president of the company, in his annual report, stated that the ore down there was "in quantity and value fully equal to any found in the works above." Actually the rock was disappointingly low-grade, but that information was not passed on to the general public, which retained unimpaired confidence in the Gould & Curry. Its stock shot up to $6,000 a foot—the Virginia *Union*, in an hysterical moment, announcing a quotation of $12,000—but holders were not eager to sell; the dividend was $150 a foot.

Swollen with riches, the company put up a huge mill of wood and hammered granite two miles east of Virginia: in the form of a Greek cross 250 feet long, the arms 75 feet, the structure was said to be the greatest work of its kind in the world.

Even the leather belting, custom-made in Boston, was four inches wider than any other had ever been. The whole place was like an hacienda, with gardens and an oval basin, in the center of which three nymphs held a stone shell that supported a swan spouting a fountain from its beak. The outlay for this fancy establishment was about three quarters of a million, yet operation was not economical because the cost of extracting ore turned out to be too high. Economy, however, was unbecoming on the Comstock and particularly so in this company, which was the industrial giant of the region. It employed 500 men, furnished rock to sixteen mills, and disbursed enough money to keep half the town going. No Gould & Curry stockholder quibbled about expenditures. The company president, in a lush San Francisco office, high-ceilinged and walnut-paneled, lived up to his importance by handsomely entertaining callers with the aid of a gold-braided flunkey bearing cigars and whiskey decanter on a silver tray.

In July the Ophir, having its best year, struck a rich vein said to assay $2,500 or better to the ton. Its stock also went up, and it, too, had a huge but inefficient mill. As a gauge of Comstock well-being, the Ophir was as good as the Gould & Curry, though there was somewhat less fanfare about it.

The town hummed with frenzied human beings and a chronic congestion of traffic. Swearing drivers navigated six-mule teams through a haze of dust on narrow streets crowded with other teams, horsemen, and pedestrians pushed into the gutter by sidewalk auctions of all sorts of merchandise: horses, brass watches, haberdashery, and a great deal of mine stock being sold for nonpayment of assessments. Stages arrived piled high with boxes, awkward bales of hoopskirts, blanket rolls, and dressed pork carcasses, the passengers' heads sticking up grotesquely above the clutter. Omnibuses made sixteen round trips a day to Gold Hill and Silver City. Wells Fargo transported a million dollars' worth of bullion a month, expressmen carelessly tossing silver bricks around as if they were made of common clay.

Immigrants fresh from the plains mingled with pigtailed Chinese shuffling along under burdens attached to yokes over their shoulders, Mexican vaqueros with silvered saddles, Germans smoking long pipes, miners looking the worse for wear in tattered hats and ragged coats. Contrasting with them were suave fellows as nattily dressed as if straight from Brooks Brothers, and ever alert to sell the greenhorn anything from stock in the Ophir to Mount Davidson itself. True gentlemen and the socially prominent could be distinguished by dignified black broadcloth and Havana cigars. Cigarettes were for Mexicans and D Street girls. Dodging furtively among the throng were mysterious "process" men, laden with chemicals and crucibles guaranteed to reduce ores cheaply and fast—a needed improvement when rich rock could be shipped to England, processed there, and the precious metals returned, all at less expense than the cost of milling at home. Above the hubbub sounded the round-the-clock clatter and whomp of stamp mills, and from the mines beneath came the dull boom of charges that periodically jarred the whole place with window-rattling blasts.

Fifty wagon loads of lumber, averaging 4,000 feet to the load, rolled into this treeless region daily; other wagons hauled every day about one hundred tons of ore to mills in Washoe valley. The big companies, owning most of the pay rock on the main Comstock Lode, garnered the big money, yet everybody seemed to have money and to spend it freely: laborers at four to six dollars a day, saloon keepers, clerks, Chinese laundrymen, harlots. Mrs. Warren was an opulent madam, highly respected. Julie Bulette, another brothel-keeper regarded with equal esteem, rode in a lacquered brougham, its panel decorated by a painted heraldic device that one historian said looked like "four aces crowned by a lion couchant."[6] A hurdy-gurdy girl—who was not a prostitute, incidentally—got a quarter per dance, besides a treat. If a man became enamored, as often happened after a few drinks, he gave her a bonus of five dollars, or ten or twenty. A saving girl could build a substantial estate out of these takings.

Highly-paid mine superintendents and others who had struck it rich were nabobs of lordly luxury. Clusters of impressive suburban homes had pretentious names worthy of a twentieth-century realtor: Clifton, Silver Terrace, Golden Terrace. The flashier sort of monied men sported huge gold watches, heavy chains, and immense diamonds; kept stables of fast horses and harems of fast women; had an amazing capacity for hard liquor; and played cool hands of poker. There are stories of silver doorknobs, harness mountings of silver and horses shod with silver shoes, guests at a party refreshing themselves at a water tank filled with champagne, these showy displays marking the familiar behavior of ready spenders who do not know what to do with all their money. The streets of Virginia, paved with low-grade refuse rock, were literally metaled with gold and silver, and the inhabitants appeared to be similarly equipped.

Prospectors, sometimes carrying heavy mortars described as "not good for any use except to make hominy," pecked away at the barren earth everywhere, collected sackfuls of specimens, and so often rushed into town with news of allegedly sensational strikes that wildcatting reached the summit of lunacy. As one observer said: "The streets of Virginia City are literally crammed with crazy people who talk incoherently about 'feet' when most of them have no other feet than those they stand on."[7] Another remarked eloquently:

The people have all gone mad on "feet." It is "feet" in the morning, "feet" all the time. They have given up all amuse-

ments except music—retaining that only because it has "feet."
They may now and then let fall a word about the war, but
it ends in hoping that Hooker will soon perform some brilliant "feat."[8]

The mania spread to San Francisco, where big-time and
small-time speculators watched stock quotations as closely as
office boys buying on margin in the soaring bull market of
1929. Said the San Francisco *Journal*:

> The luck of a few of our citizens upon the Comstock has made
> all mad, from the merchant prince to the laborer, from the
> jeweled lady to the chambermaid and cook. It is all feet; feet
> on the sidewalk, feet in the cars, in bar-rooms and reading-
> rooms, in hotels and restaurant, and counting houses and in
> work shops. In the parlor, the mistress speaks of the Gould &
> Curry, Ophir, and in the kitchen the servant talks of the Nor-
> ton and Burnside. The wealthy trade their mansions for feet,
> and the poor their hard earned homesteads. . . . Other thou-
> sands who had been saving money to buy homes, have now
> neither homes nor money, but have stock that is not worth a
> dollar a cord.[9]

The wild dealing in feet concerned chiefly undeveloped
"outside" claims off the main lode, hence of uncertain value
and subject to rapid fluctuation. Anything might start a
flurry. The established companies themselves were not above
the trick of keeping a shift of miners working overtime to
create the impression that a big strike was imminent, and
thus induce a swift rise in stock prices. Another device
was to assay a rich piece of rock, give out the news that the
whole claim was equally rich—as of course it was not—and
when the stock soared, declare a substantial dividend, then
sell out fast before the inevitable decline. Yet another dodge
was to dump a load of Comstock ore into a worthless mine.
Even cruder frauds were no less effective. One clever fellow
was said to have rubbed a twenty-dollar gold piece over a
boulder until it showed color, staked a claim, pointed out the

obvious indications, and cashed in before anybody discovered the swindle.

Some of the most profitable mining ground was never on the market. It belonged to a closed corporation, usually one man, and it was not for sale—like the twenty feet of L. S. "Sandy" Bowers in Gold Hill. It yielded a total of about one million dollars and gave him a good income, though nothing like the fantastic $70,000 a month of popular report. Adjoining Bowers was the Plato claim of ten feet, also the property of one man. In September, 1863, Plato declared the record dividend of the Territory, $1,335 per foot, a tidy monthly total of $13,350, which the owner did not have to share with any stockholders.

Editors remonstrated against witless plunging, and humorists satirized it. One ironist invented imaginary claims called "The Rising Moon," "It's All in Your Eye," "The Captain Kidd," "The Freeze Out," "The Nip and Twitch." Dan De Quille had one of these that he named "The Pewterinctum." Another wit, in "Advice to a Verdant Stock Operator," said solemnly:

If I was in your place and thought the Baltic was going up, I would hold on; if I thought it was going down I would sell. As a general rule in stock operations, buy at the lowest price and sell at the highest; get all you can and keep the money.

I have sold my Baltic, and am sorry for it. I have plenty of other stocks on hand, for which I am also sorry. . . . I think the Baltic is a good mine if it only pays dividends. There are two kinds of mines—those that pay dividends and those that require assessments. The dividend-paying mines are generally considered the most desirable to hold.[10]

Neither raillery nor serious reproof slowed down maniacal feet-trading in Virginia. All booms induce aberration, but this Washoe performance proceeded with utter disregard for reality. At the time only three mines were paying dividends: Gould & Curry, Ophir, and Savage. Most of the others were levying assessments, and no outside claim had shown any sign of becoming a paying one. Yet the hope of buying into a bonanza obliterated these hard facts and produced behavior as zany as the most hysterical boom ever saw. The shrewd ones made money, as they usually do; the unskillful, who held on too long, lost their shirts. But that is an old story.

The rapid increase of population pouring over the mountains from California made new buildings so much in demand that as soon as a foundation went down, the owner put up a sign: "This building is rented." A shortage of living quarters jammed hotels and lodging houses, skyrocketed the price of real estate, and boosted rents. A good-sized house for a family, or a suite of elegant bachelor rooms, rented for as much as $250 a month; small wooden stores, $300-$500. The owner of a lot with a twenty-five-foot frontage refused $12,000 for it. High freight rates on furniture and provisions brought over the mountains made the cost of living about twice that of San Francisco: a home-town economist estimated a minimum of $100 a month for each adult, $30 for every child. Home life was rare, all bachelors and many families sleeping in rented rooms and eating in restaurants, where board at $12 a week was the rule in the few places fit for ladies. But nobody grumbled much about crowding or inflation. The prevailing maxim was: "Go it while you can."

Mortality was considerable, not only because of fatal illnesses that resulted, some thought, from the arsenical water of the region, but also because of frequent resort to the five-shooter, a lethal weapon likely to be unlimbered at the drop of a surly word. The revolver was a popular settler of arguments, whether about a dog, a mine, a woman, or a drink. A California undertaker, after a visit to Washoe, said of Virginia: "It's bully! the best business place I ever saw. If I had a shop there I could get 5 coffins a day to make."[11]

While the Civil War raged in Eastern states, the political temper of the town and of Nevada Territory generally was of continual concern to editors and politicos. Governor Nye was an ardent, even fanatical, Unionist. In a strong message to the first Territorial Legislature in 1861, he had cited the federal constitution as the source of national power, repudiated neutrality, and denounced secession as heresy. In subsequent speeches he bore down heavily upon the pernicious doctrine of states' rights as the prime reason for all the nation's ills, and berated sluggards whose failure zealously to support the government gave aid and comfort to the foe.

On June 18, 1863, at a dinner in the Astor House, New York, for Brigadier General Thomas F. Meagher, commander of the famous Iron Brigade, Nye said that in Nevada he would not permit anyone to speak against the Lincoln administration. "As Gen. Nye," quipped the New York *Leader*, "claims to own the people of that locality, would it not be proper to call it Nye-vada Territory?"[12] He also said that, although he believed in freedom of opinion, nobody had a right to disseminate lies to subvert a grand Republican government, and that if he had his way he would fill Fort Lafayette so full of disloyal traitors that their feet stuck out the windows. The implication was that among those suspected of treason were all Democrats, naturally, and anybody else who presumed to object, however mildly, to anything done in Washington. "At times," said a news report, "he seemed to be denying the right of criticism, and was slightly biased."[13] This uncompromising stand, at a time of much agitation over threats to free speech and press, drew some cheers, but provoked a much louder storm of hisses and heckling, howls of "Sit down!" and cries of "Police!" The uproar went on for several minutes, violently gesticulating gentlemen jumping up and yelling incoherently, the chairman adding to the din by banging his gavel and bellowing for order. Nye belligerently confronted the tumult with true Western readiness to fight everybody then and there.

When a later speaker, the Hon. Thomas C. Fields, took the opposite position by excoriating Nye and the federal government, he too ran into a noisy outburst of raucous boos and orders to sit down. His response was: "Let me alone, God d—n it."[14] The riotous occasion reflected the strained emotions of the period, loyalties divided, and the constant difficulty of drawing a sharp line between honest criticism and treason. Superficial harmony returned to the banquet only when a toast to the ladies "was drank," as the papers always put it, "with enthusiasm."

Like many another politician who fancied himself in uniform, Nye telegraphed the Secretary of War an offer to raise and lead a brigade of territorial infantry. The government considered the offer favorably, but nothing came of it. About 1,000 Nevada volunteers enlisted in the Union army, but none saw service at the front. The governor, though he donned a uniform as commander of territorial militia, and became an active promoter of recruiting, did not take the field.

Nye once called Mark Twain "nothing but a damned Secessionist," but that label was inaccurate. Whatever else he was, he was not that. At the outset of the war his home state, Missouri, nominally Southern with 114,000 Negro slaves, was a critical border region. The governor, Claiborne Jackson, of covert Southern sympathies, believed that slaveholding states should stand together; after the firing on Fort Sumter he rebuffed Lincoln's call for 75,000 volunteers as a move in "an unholy crusade." The lieutenant governor, Thomas A. Reynolds, an extreme Southern rights Democrat, was an outspoken secessionist. Both tried to maneuver the state into the Confederacy, but when the issue was put up to the voters they rejected secession by an overwhelming majority of 80 to 1. Yet for all that the state might have been lost to the Union had not Captain Nathaniel Lyon, on May 10, 1861, ·decisively asserted federal authority by moving in on Confederate troops at Fort Jackson, near St. Louis, and capturing the entire command. Six weeks later a convention ousted Jackson and Reynolds, and elected a provisional governor, Hamilton R. Gamble, who maintained a state government that was officially loyal to Lincoln. Nevertheless, Missouri, torn by conflicting allegiance throughout the war, sent volunteers into the armies of both sides.

In early '61, while his state wavered between staying in the Union and getting out of it, pilot Sam Clemens, steaming up and down the Mississippi, felt the winds of variable opinion. In a sketch entitled "The Private History of a Campaign That Failed," published twenty years after Appomattox, he remarks upon his shifting attitudes during those parlous times. This essay purports to be an account of his two weeks in a homespun Southern military unit—military only by a great stretch of the imagination—in the spring of 1861. It is chiefly humorous exaggeration of the futility of inexperienced young men blundering around the countryside, being alarmed by rumors of enemy approach, doing their best to avoid conflict, falling into ridiculous misadventures. Whether the narrative contains any reliable facts scholars have not yet discovered, but some points of view expressed in it seem genuine. The author says:

Out West there was a good deal of confusion in men's minds during the first months of the great trouble—a good deal of unsettledness, of leaning first this way, then that, then the other way.

Sam leaned various ways, he admits, starting out strong for the Union, then becoming a rebel when the political air got thicker and hotter on the lower Mississippi. It has been conjectured that, in New Orleans in January, he went so far as to drill with a Confederate company there. Nowhere, however, does he concede that he ever dallied with the thought of secession. According to his mother, he never swayed in that direction. In a letter to her sons out West in 1862, she spoke of the intransigence of a "Mr. B." (Horace Bixby), a strong Union man who did not want to pay Sam a debt of $200 plus interest:

He said no secesh should ever have $1.00 of his money—he would see him starve and go to h— before he should have a dollar, if he owde him a thousand he would not pay it. He kept on in that strain until I said, Mr. B., Sam is no secesh. O, no, he knew that. He heard Capt O say that when Sam and W[ill] B[owen] were on the Alonzo Child they quarreled and Sam let go the wheel to whip Will for talking secesh and made Will hush.[15]

Mark Twain himself has left us no evidence to suggest that he was ever an ardent secessionist; as a temporary rebel he seems to have been only lukewarm, nothing like a rabid fire-eating states-righter. In later days, when he became acquainted with prominent Union generals and was a favored speaker at reunions of northern armies, he made light of his transitory adherence to the Southern cause.

Because he casually detached himself from that so-called military company, called Marion Rangers or Ralls County Rangers, some critics have accused him of desertion from the Confederate Army. As recently as 1940 Congressman Shannon, of Blue Springs, Missouri, delivered in the House a scathing denunciation of Sam Clemens' treasonable act, which showed that he "was not of the same kidney as real Missourians," put on record a fanciful tale of Sam's running away from a fight all the way to Keokuk, and excoriated his "dismal failure as a belligerent."[16] Others, if less flamboyant than the politician, have taken a similar attitude.

The charge of desertion is difficult to substantiate. This company of Rangers, like many another that sprang up in Missouri, was composed of ten or fifteen young men in and around Hannibal, who surreptitiously banded together in a loosely cohesive way, collected a strange assortment of armament and mounts, then tramped through the neighboring country for a short while, making themselves more of a nuisance than otherwise to farmers roundabout. Mark Twain says in "The Private History" that at the end of their first march, ten miles to New London, they bivouacked, dead beat, in the barn of Colonel Ralls. The colonel, the narrator goes on, made a speech, then

swore us on the Bible to be faithful to the State of Missouri and drive all invaders from her soil, no matter whence they might come or under what flag they might march. This mixed us up considerably, and we could not make out just what service we were embarked in.

Despite that impromptu swearing-in, there were none of the accompaniments of induction into military service: no formal enlistment, no oath of allegiance, no proper uniforms, no organization to speak of.

The company was theoretically in the Missouri State Guard, Second Division, commanded by Brigadier General Thomas A. Harris, but he had about as little authority over it as its own elected officers, one of whom was 2d Lieutenant Sam Clemens. No discipline prevailed in this outfit, or in many another homebred organization like it; the sergeant flouted the lieutenant, the privates thumbed their noses at the sergeant. It is absurd to ascribe army status to a company that was extraordinarily ramshackle, even by the very casual standards of '61. As the New York *Times* remarked, in rebuking the outburst of Representative Shannon:

Will Mr. Shannon kindly take notice that the lieutenant walked, not ran, to Keokuk. Whether the desertion was anything more than technical, one doesn't know or care. On both sides that war was singularly rich in desertions. Lieutenant Clemens might have been killed, instead of completing his education. So we praise his absquatulation as we do Horace for abandoning his shield.[17]

In that "Private History" Mark Twain says he "resigned" because he concluded that he was not cut out for a soldier. He tells of an episode, no doubt imaginary, in which five Rangers fire at a man on horseback. When the man falls out of the saddle and dies, Sam, believing that his bullet was the fatal one, is much disturbed by somber reflections:

The thought shot through me that I was a murderer; that I had killed a man—a man who had never done me any harm. That was the coldest sensation that ever went through my marrow.

The thought of him got to preying upon me every night; I could not get rid of it. . . . and it seemed an epitome of war; that all war must be just like that—the killing of strangers against whom you feel no personal animosity. . . . My campaign was spoiled. It seemed to me that I was not rightly equipped for this awful business. . . . I resolved to retire from this avocation of sham soldiership while I could still save some remnant of my self-respect.

Whatever of mature afterthought influenced those supposedly youthful ruminations, they are germane: he was not good combat material. It is impossible to believe that he would have been of much use in an army; only an intractable precisionist would wish him to have served in one.

For Tom Fitch, a writer for the Virginia *Union*, he made of his unceremonious separation from military service a characteristic Mark Twain story:

I was troubled in my conscience a little, for I had enlisted, and was not clear as to my lawful right to disenlist. But I remembered that one of the conditions of joining was that the members of the Guard should not be required to leave their homes except in cases of invasion of the State by an enemy. The Confederate forces had invaded southwest Missouri. I saw at once that in accordance with the terms of enlistment I was required to leave the State, and I left at once by the overland route for Nevada.[18]

He was a little sensitive about his cavalier behavior, yet a charge of desertion is hardly worth arguing about. At least the episode implies no fervent devotion to secession in 1861.

His departure for Nevada with his brother Orion in July of '61 has led to another accusation: that he went out there only to escape military service. Perhaps so, at least in part. According to his niece, Annie Moffett Webster, when Sam arrived in St. Louis on the last boat to get through the Union lines, he was "obsessed with the fear that he might be arrested by government agents and forced to act as pilot on a government gunboat while a man stood by with a pistol ready to shoot him if he showed the least sign of a false move. He was almost afraid to leave the house."[19] She also said that Sam was loyal to the old flag but that, like Robert E. Lee, he could not countenance taking up arms against fellow Southerners who were his friends and neighbors. In Nevada, this divided attitude persisted, yet before the war was over he seemed to have gravitated toward the Union side. Evidence appears in a letter to Billy Claggett from Esmeralda on September 9, 1862. In it Sam says, with genuine concern, that overconfidence threatens the existence of the United States: the North deluded by empty boasting about an easy victory over the Confederacy while an aggressive enemy menaces Louisville, Nashville, Baltimore, and other cities, and while out-maneuvered federal armies continually retreat. The tone of real fear for the survival of the country leaves no doubt of his pro-Union position.[20]

In Washoe, Union men were a strong majority, but Southern sympathizers, variously designated Secesh Democracy,

Jeff Davis Democrats, Douglas Democrats, Peace Democrats, Copperhead Sneaks, made up for their lack of numbers by volubility and nuisance tactics. In Virginia they ran a slate of municipal candidates in March, 1863, made a bid for votes by publishing an address to the people, but lost the election. For a short time they had a newspaper of their persuasion, the *Democratic Standard,* founded in the summer of that year. At their headquarters, the Virginia Hotel, they gathered daily to drink success to the Confederacy. The story goes that a Union man named Lance Nightingill once marched in there, strode up to the bar with a friend, clinked glasses and shouted to the assembled southerners: "Here's to Abraham Lincoln, God bless him, and God damn everybody who doesn't like him."[21]

The Territory had shown its loyalty by sending $20,000 in silver bars to the United States Sanitary Commission. In the 1862 election of a Congressional representative, Mott, Union candidate, defeated Musser, secessionist, by over two to one. Yet a majority of the House in the second Territorial Legislature had been characterized as a dubious group, "passably loyal, at least so far as test oaths go, but like most politicians, they are time-servers" ready to "jump on either side of the fence. . . . God help the Union if its defense were intrusted to the hands of such half-bred patriots."[22] In that session all attempts to pass patriotic resolutions had been frustrated by the opposition. Hal Clayton, leader of the Third House, was arrested for disloyal remarks and sent off to the adobe compound of Fort Churchill for a spell of sawing wood and packing sand around the parade ground, labors from which he was shortly released under bond of $5,000 to refrain from statements offensive to loyal citizens and the United States government. Pro-Southern adherents aired their opinions boldly, generally without molestation unless they became vituperative or boisterous. Police collared fanatics publicly showing off in noisy braggadocio like drinking the health of Jeff Davis, tar and feathers to General Grant; or the loud-mouthed boasting of a man with a thick shock of hair who swore to kill one Yankee for every hair. An Irishman of Gold Hill became an obvious candidate for punitive action when he expressed a heartfelt desire to "kill every Irishman in the Union Army, and . . . to cut Abe Lincoln's throat."[23] Offenders, given a choice between exile to sun-baked Fort Churchill and taking the oath of allegiance to the United States, usually took the oath, for whatever that was worth.

A nervous climate of opinion led to incidents similar to those elsewhere in the country. When a thief, described as "some creature wearing the shape of a human being," stole the flag flying from the summit of Mount Davidson, the Virginia *Union* said: "If he can be caught, and if it were not a profanation of the staff, he ought to be suspended from it in place of the flag."[24] When a Virginia merchant combined patriotism and yuletide cheer by affixing a flag to the top of a tall Christmas tree that rose to the second story, a secessionist lady up there could not stand the sight of the detested Stars and Stripes. With a hatchet she chopped down the holiday flagpole. Johnny Newman hoisted a Confederate flag over his combination store and saloon on A Street, but his partner quickly hauled it down.

The Western press continually circulated stories of thousands of California secessionists migrating to Nevada to take over the government when the Territory became a state. Some did migrate and others came in by emigrant trains from the Middle West, but the numbers were probably not so large as editors supposed. The Knights of the Golden Circle infiltrated Washoe, but they did not blow up anything or otherwise unsettle society except by fomenting rumors. Newspapers did their best to create a reign of terror by publishing sinister tales of guerrillas armed to the teeth, even with batteries of artillery, mobilizing at secret points from which they would descend upon cities, seize power, and set up a Pacific Republic. When five hundred of these irregulars were reported to be gathering near the Sink of the Carson, the *Enterprise* attempted to discount such fanciful yarns by the flippant remark:

We think their numbers are under-rated; it is our firm belief that there are at least 50,000 guerrillas to every acre of ground about the Sink—in the shape of mosquitoes and gallinippers.[25]

Nevertheless, these melodramatic myths, going the rounds, aggravated tension. It is worth noting, however, that in Virginia friction between Unionists and non-Unionists produced little violence. Blood flowed from punched noses in plenty of fights, but the record is remarkably free from shootings over politics. The two factions opposed each other in a cold war that was neither peace nor open conflict, and they somehow made shift to get along with each other. Linthicum, editor of the pro-Southern *Democratic Standard*, might be condemned ideologically, but he was still acceptable as a person and drinking companion. A reporter characterized him as "a vigorous writer, and, socially, a pleasant gentleman," although "politically and patriotically . . . as rotten as a dead mackerel."[26] Mark Twain did not choose his associates on the basis of political bias. He was friendly with Hal Clayton, one of the most positive of the seceshers, also with Jim Hardy, another Democrat, and he was not inclined to shun a man solely on the score of party. Indeed, few in Virginia seemed so stiff-necked that they refused to mingle on any terms with those of the opposite camp.

Citizens avidly followed the war news, which, because of breakdowns in telegraph service, came in spasmodically and inaccurately. In May, 1863, the reported capture of Richmond threw the town into a frenzy. Brass bands paraded, bonfires flared, bells pealed, mill whistles shrieked, the national ensign flew everywhere. The news should have intimidated secessionists, but it only made them arrogant. "During the two days just passed," said the Virginia *Union,*

> many of them have promenaded the streets of Virginia and openly avowed their sympathy with the Southern Confederacy by betting that Richmond had not been captured by the Federals; and upon several occasions they have carried their abuse of Union men and the General Government to such extremes that we confess our surprise that some of them have not been arrested.[27]

Jubilant Union men rashly offered odds of ten to one on the capture of Richmond, and ready takers snapped them up. Hal Clayton was said to have collected $2,500 when word came that General Hooker's Army of the Potomac, far from taking a city, had retreated across the Rappahannock after a bloody four days at Chancellorsville: the 11th Corps shattered in a panicky rout by Stonewall Jackson's men, the whole army badly mauled, Fighting Joe himself knocked out by a falling timber when a shell struck his headquarters. After the jollification, news of another defeat was a bitter pill.

The territorial press was staunchly pro-Union except for the secessionist Virginia *Democratic Standard,* which died after a short life of two months, its brief existence showing the unpopularity of its cause. Of other local papers, the *Union* was one of the most unequivocally pro-Union in the entire West. It began urging the reelection of Lincoln in 1863, and periodically affirmed its position in strong editorials, like this one:

> We are for the Union of the United States—the Union as it was—without equivocation or reserve, and shall break no bread with those who are not, however plausible may be their excuse for treason. We contemn "conservatism" and spurn "moderation" at a time like this, and on a matter so mighty. Hesitation now is half-way treachery! and we'll not brook it![28]

The *Enterprise* was more sensitive, less fervent but still pro, as in its ringing endorsement of Lincoln's Emancipation Proclamation: "Without the shadow of a sympathy with the Abolition aim and sentiment of the past, we rejoice in the edict of emancipation as a just, righteous and necessary measure. . . . We rejoice in it as a speedy means of crushing the rebellion."[29]

Notwithstanding a territorial infusion of Southern sympathizers—as in states predominantly Union like Pennsylvania, Ohio, Indiana, and others—a Carson City correspondent was right in saying: "Secession has no foothold in Nevada. There are a few who have a slight weight of copper on the brain, but they all try to cover it up with the semblance of patriotism."[30] The war came home to Virginia in a striking way in the spring of 1863: gas fixtures for the city, aboard the *Commonwealth* sailing for California, never got there because ship and cargo fell prey to the Confederate raider, *Alabama*. Nobody on the Comstock, whatever his politics, thought highly of that mischance. "Some of our people," said Dan de Quille,

have thought pretty well of Jeff Davis . . . but not a single one of us thought of his wanting our gas-ing machine. We are all down on him! Every time we break our shins in traveling our dark streets, we curse Jeff Davis; when we find our store broken open and our chattels vamoosed, we hang on to one of our useless lamp posts and d—n the whole Confederacy till everything is black and blue.[31]

If the war was never entirely out of mind of Washoe inhabitants, in the boiling town of Virginia they focused much of their attention on mining and speculation, fight and frolic. Eight breweries and numerous saloons ministered to the thirsty: to the discriminating, the Sazerac, Almack's, Mammoth, Golden Age, Occidental, St. Nicholas, and others, their polished mahogany and crystal chandeliers worthy of San Francisco or New York. Territorial directories listed prominent saloons in capital letters. Beckoning the honest miner were snuggeries, neat but not elegant, called Cozy Home, Miner's Retreat, Fancy Free. Luring the unfastidious, murky unnamed dives were also worthy of New York at the drab end of the scale. The saloon was an important community institution, a sort of informal town hall, the center of all celebrations. The opening of a new bar always meant a complimentary news story that described the fixtures and usually characterized the proprietor as "gentlemanly."

An explosive kind of brandy known as Washoe, considered more potent than Minnie Rifle or Chain Lightning, was popular with some drinkers. The effect of "thirty or forty drops" of this "Territorial destruction" upon an unwary taster had once been vividly described:

He first turned white, then red, then round and round, and finally horizontal; his countenance at first depicting the emotions and physiognomical phenomena of a wild cat with her tail in chancery; afterwards his face is said to have assumed that smiling expression peculiar to travellers found in everlasting sleep in the Valley of Sardis. He recovered, however, and described the internal sensation as that of a stomach full of galvanic batteries, yellow hornets, pepper sauce and vitriol.[32]

Straight whiskey was the standard drink. Sophisticated connoisseurs leaned toward whiskey toddies and mint juleps, but whatever the tipple it went down often and late, seldom in an atmosphere of quiet contemplation. A New York *Times* correspondent moaned that after sundown the darkness became hideous with the clamor of caterwauling drunks. Virginia seethed more populously at night, when hundreds of miners, underground all day, emerged from their holes to line the bars and clump over dance floors in small hot cellars with hurdy-gurdy girls. Hearty toping was the fashion of almost everybody, from the very best people down to the riffraff. Temperance was frowned upon and prohibition was unthinkable. To treat and be treated was proper, and no man lost caste if he downed so many treats that he had to be helped home. Mark Twain reflected upon pleasurable vinous habits when he summed up his experience with the variation of etiquette according to locality:

In the mining camps of California, when a friend tenders you a "smile," or invites you to take a "blister," vulgarly called a drink, it is etiquette to say: "Here's, hoping your dirt'll pan out gay." In Washoe, when you are requested to "put in a blast," or invited to take your "regular poison," etiquette admonishes you to touch glasses and say: "Here's, hoping you'll strike it rich on the lower level."[33]

Sociable and noisy drinking was such an established pattern that the Rev. Thomas Starr King, a distinguished San Francisco divine, thus recorded his impressions: "There are but three things at Washoe, Sir: big mines, little mines, and whisky shops; in other words Ophir holes, gopher holes, and loafer holes."[34] Among loafer holes were gambling joints that enticed the gullible with piano and fiddle, sometimes with a small band, to take a fling at High for Luck, Black and Red, or Chuck-a-Luck, then separated them from their cash by all the clever devices known to the crooked gambler. These iniquitous dens made the Virginia *Union* apprehensive over the moral stability of the town:

The presence of her coming disaster broods in any one of half a hundred gambling saloons which line her principal streets, and make her night air impure with the hot discordant steam of vice rising from a hundred open doors.[35]

The *Union,* lacking the humor of the *Enterprise,* was a more earnest sermonizer than its worldly contemporary.

Virginia was a rousing place of spunk and sin that had more metropolitan tone and a more cosmopolitan populace than any other Western city except San Francisco. Nor was the Comstock indifferent to literacy and culture. When the *Evening Bulletin* started up in July, 1863, three dailies circulated about 1,400 copies a day; the *Democratic Standard* made a momentary fourth—better coverage than some large American cities can claim today. In the same month Thomas Maguire opened his fine new Opera House. With a capacity of 1,600, it had a roomy foyer off which were billiard parlors, cigar stand, green-covered gambling tables, and a mahogany bar inlaid with ivory. The only drawback was that, since the basement housed a livery stable, the auditorium smelled noticeably of horse. Julia Dean Hayne and her company gave the premiere performance, and stayed a month. Thereafter traveling thespians put on *Hamlet, Romeo and Juliet, East Lynne, Camille;* and touring celebrities appeared there: young Lotta Crabtree, Modjeska, Adah Isaacs Menken, McKean Buchanan, Mollie Raynor, the Worrell sisters. For the studious, the city library was a going concern in Daggett's brick building on North B.

Everybody expected Virginia to become at least the second in size and importance on the West Coast and very likely the capital of the new state of Nevada. Some cherished the hope of surpassing the metropolis on the Bay. Few questioned such glowing pronouncements as this one: "Our progress has been and will continue to be of such magical rapidity as may well cause the wonder and the admiration of the world."[36]

Mark Twain, on his return from San Francisco early in July, was as ardent a champion of progress as the most determined booster. After a tour of the Savage mine, the Hale and Norcross, the Chollar, and Potosi, he wrote a confident report:

By this trip we found out that the claims upon the Comstock are in a ten times more flourishing condition than they have ever been before since Washoe was discovered; that the amount of ore being excavated is increasing every day; that

to almost every one of them new and costly machinery and
other improvements are being added; that the number of men
employed in these mines is becoming greater and greater
every day, (the Chollar now works sixty-five men,) and that
the first thing you know the cry will be "more mills!" and we
shall have to come down to our work and go to building them.
We are marching on to prosperity at railroad speed, and
Washoe will be a wonderful country yet.[37]

Those statements, in the best Chamber of Commerce manner, coincided with Washoe faith in permanent, continually
expanding, prosperity. The general belief in the inexhaustible
riches of the Comstock Lode fostered the conviction that
munificence for all was just around the corner. Mark Twain's
optimism was genuine as he rode the surge, like everybody
else. Another indication of his attitude appears in a letter to
his mother during this flush year: "I take an absorbing delight in the stock market. I like to watch the prices go up."[38]
He sounds like a speculator of 1929.

Perhaps he had neither the insight nor the inclination to
analyze causes that might interrupt a steadily increasing out-
put of silver bullion. The truth was that ore at 300 to 350
feet was only low-grade to fair. By fall even the Ophir, of
which much had been expected, showed signs of failure at
that depth, and all the mines played out at an average depth
of 500 feet. The general public did not hear about these
unpublicized portents of recession, but the market should
have been illuminating to anybody who read a San Francisco
financial page. Stock values of Virginia mines reached their
peak about July, then slowly declined to the end of the year
and kept on going down thereafter. Newsmen are thought
to have inside information about everything, but Mark Twain
either did not know the whole story of the mines, or did not
choose to believe. A prophet of slowdown and doom was an
undesirable citizen in Virginia. Everybody was convinced,

or at least hoped, that the whole district was rich in silver and gold; whereas the only mines worth anything were on the two miles of the Comstock directly under Virginia. When a correspondent for the San Francisco *Evening Bulletin* contended that flush times could not endure indefinitely because no profitable pay rock had been discovered other than that on the main lode, indignant rebuttals and six-figure statistics snowed him under.

Mark Twain's rosy views were popular wth readers who wanted to be reassured, likewise consistent with the glittering dreams of his own abortive mining adventures, when he had relied on sure things that turned out to be unsure, and when more than once he had been certain he was about to become a millionaire overnight. He had a lifelong ability to conjure fortunes out of vaporous imaginings. Notwithstanding the growing pessimism that marked advancing years, he also retained the booster's faith in material progress. Without the perception to evaluate social and economic effects of change, he did not sense that material progress was partially responsible for some of the very evils that made him bitter. His exposition of the flourishing mines of the Virginia district was entirely in character.

In a spirit equally Twainian he blew off steam about a man named Grub, who had written to "Mr. Twain" from Lake Tahoe, a name Mark Twain detested:

Hope some early bird will catch this Grub the next time he calls Lake Bigler by so disgustingly sick and silly a name as "'Lake Tahoe." I have removed the offensive word from his letter and substituted the old one, which at least has a Christian English twang about it whether it is pretty or not. Of course Indian names are more fitting than any others for our beautiful lakes and rivers, which knew their race ages ago, perhaps, in the morning of creation, but let us have none so repulsive to the ear as "Tahoe" for the beautiful relic of fairyland forgotten and left asleep in the snowy Sierras when the little elves fled from their ancient haunts and quitted the earth. They say it means "Fallen Leaf"—well suppose it meant fallen devil or fallen angel, would that render its hideous, discordant syllables more endurable? Not if I know myself. I yearn for the scalp of the soft-shell crab—be he injun or white man—who conceived of that spoony, slobbering, summer-complaint of a name. Why, if I had a grudge against a half-price nigger, I wouldn't be mean enough to call him by such an epithet as that; then, how am I to hear it applied to the enchanted mirror that the viewless spirits of the air make their toilets by, and hold my peace? "Tahoe"—it sounds as weak as soup for a sick infant. "Tahoe" be—forgotten! I just saved my reputation that time. In conclusion, "Grub," I mean to start to Lake Bigler myself Monday morning, or somebody shall come to grief.[39]

To critics mindful of the emergent style of Mark Twain, that combination of the scurrilous and the lyrical should be instructive. Lake Tahoe always inspired him to rhapsodic prose. The name is not so hideous as all that; Mark's indignation boiled not because of affronted esthetic sensibilities, but because he could not dissociate the name from certain Indians he regarded as too degenerate to be human. In *The Innocents Abroad,* when Lake Como invites comparison with Tahoe, he sputters for several paragraphs in this vein:

Tahoe means grasshoppers. It means grasshopper soup. It is Indian, and suggestive of Indians. They say it is Pi-ute —possibly it is Digger. I am satisfied it was named by the Diggers—those degraded savages who roast their dead relatives, then mix the human grease and ashes of bones with tar, and "gaum" it thick all over their heads and foreheads and ears, and go caterwauling about the hills and call it *mourning.* *These* are the gentry that named the lake.

Newspaper opinion was against him. When the lake was discovered in 1850, Governor John Bigler had allowed it to be named after himself without arousing much protest, but in the eighteen-sixties his Democratic pro-Southern leanings made editors damn the name. They objected to beautiful waters "poisoned by Copperheadism," muddied by the name of "a fifth rate politician," whom they contemptuously called "Bigliar," "John Tahoe" and "this obese apostle of treason." The name was inappropriate, said one rude fellow, because "the lake has no bottom while John is all bottom." He had such a reputation as a drinker that one Virginia citizen said he would "never again call it Lake Bigler until it is emptied of its crystal water and filled with lager beer."[40] Another proposed, as a compromise, that the lake be called "Lago Beergler." The name "Tahoe," suggested by Thomas Starr King, caught on and became so generally used that custom wore Mark Twain down to resigned acceptance; when he wrote *Roughing It,* he used the word without disparaging comment.

At the opening of a new hotel, the Collins House, on July 8, he made his maiden speech in Nevada. It was a festive occasion, as such affairs always were in Virginia, where any inducement sufficed for a celebration. Colonel Collins spoke, Tom Fitch, Rollin M. Daggett, Colonel Turner: but the *Evening Bulletin* said:

Perhaps the speech of the evening was made by Sam Clemens. Those not familiar with this young man do not know the depth of tenderness in his nature. He almost brought the house to tears by his touching simple pathos.[41]

Virginia reporters being the jokers they were, it is impossible to say whether that criticism was meant seriously or as notice that Mark Twain's speech was the opposite of tender. Tenderness was a real part of the nature of this sensitive man, yet, as the *Bulletin* said, few in Virginia suspected softness inside a shell as tough as his seemed to be. Later, when traveling the lyceum circuit, he sometimes showed the tender side, usually in a half-embarrassed way, often dissipating the mood with a joke at the end, as if a public display of emotion were too much for him.

The more familiar roughness appeared when, as fledgling drama critic, he wrote a sort of preview for the San Francisco *Call*:

On Tuesday evening that sickest of all sentimental dramas, "East Lynne," will be turned loose upon us at the Opera House. It used to afford me much solid comfort to see those San Franciscans whine and shuffle and slobber all over themselves at Maguire's Theatre, when the consumptive "William" was in the act of "handing in his checks," as it were, according to the regular program of East Lynne—and now I am to enjoy a season of happiness again, I suppose. If the tears flow as freely here as I count upon, water privileges will be cheap in Virginia next week. However, Miss Julia Dean Hayne "don't take on" in the piece like Miss Sophia Edwin; therefore she fails to pump an audience dry, like the latter.[42]

The Twain technique of waking up the reader with a bludgeon was a forerunner of the manner of some later club-wielders of note: Ambrose Bierce, H. L. Mencken and, in a more urbane but still startling way, G. B. Shaw.

When the *Enterprise*, keeping abreast of the bustling times, moved into a three-story brick building on North C Street in midsummer, enlarged its format, and introduced steam printing, those progressive moves naturally called for the usual demonstration of toasts and speeches. Evidently Mark Twain did not speak this time, but the celebration, coinciding with a bad cold, left him too indisposed to carry on the next day. When he asked the Unreliable to substitute for him, that young man slyly ran in the *Enterprise*, over the name of Mark Twain, a humble apology to all whom the Local had insulted: Mayor Arick, William M. Stewart, Marshal Perry, J. B. Winters, Samuel Wetherill, besides a host of others whom we have ridiculed from behind the shelter of our reportorial position . . . we ask their forgiveness, promising that in future we will give them no cause for anything but the best of feeling towards us. To "Young Wilson," and the "Unreliable," (as we have wickedly termed them), we feel that no apology we can make begins to atone for the many insults we have given them.[43]

The frequency of those insults helps to explain why not everybody looked upon Mark Twain with a friendly eye. On the following day he retorted:

We are to blame for giving "the Unreliable" an opportunity to misrepresent us, and therefore refrain from repining to any great extent at the result. We simply claim the right to deny the truth of every statement made by him in yesterday's paper, to annul all apologies he coined as coming from us, and to hold him up to public commiseration as a reptile endowed with no more intellect, no more cultivation, no more Christian principle than animates and adorns the sportive jackass rabbit of the Sierras. We have done.[44]

In late August a slight check to the onward march of prosperity was a bad fire that ravaged most of Virginia west of A Street and south of Pat Lynch's saloon, and might have destroyed the whole town if the wind had been in another quarter. Of equal news value was a terrific free-for-all battle between Virginia Engine Company No. 1 and Nevada Hook and Ladder No. 1. Those two were such bitter rivals that they always tried to beat each other to a fire; to get there first was more important than putting out the blaze. When Sue Robinson appeared at Maguire's Opera House, she was such a favorite of both that she wore the colors of each on alternate nights, and both companies strove to outdo each other in size of silver bricks presented to her for singing "When Johnny Comes Marching Home."

After the big August fire these firemen collided at the corner of Taylor and C Streets, and at once a wild melee broke out. Fists pounded, faucets and wagon stakes cracked heads, and blood flowed: fifteen men injured, the foreman of the engine company laid out with a trumpet, the city marshal knocked down with a club, one man fatally shot. Mark Twain put this brawl into *Roughing It*, transforming it into an election riot broken up by the peace-loving Buck Fanshaw, who "waltzed in with a spanner in one hand and a trumpet in the other, and sent fourteen men home on a shutter in less than three minutes." The fire seemed to trigger deviltry. All sorts of private fights occurred, some looting by "fiends in human form," and at least two attempts by incendiaries to set the city ablaze again. The city marshal clamped down by closing all saloons and swearing in heavy reinforcements of deputy sheriffs.

Mark Twain was reported to have lost all his clothes, valued at $15, and a great quantity of wildcat stock estimated at ten cents to $200,000. Real losses of merchants were heavy, but a costly fire was only a minor annoyance to Virginia. While embers were still smoking, property owners bargained with laborers to clear away the wreckage, and with carpenters to put up new buildings. Within six weeks scarcely a trace of the disaster remained. For a time, however, the crowding of burned-out inhabitants into the unburned part of town aggravated violence brought on by gamblers, tinhorn sports, and other easily offended people who were temperamentally unable to rub elbows peacefully.

Among gentlemen the fashionable method of avenging affronts was the formal rigmarole of the duello. The ritual was complicated and laborious. An encounter could result from the traditional glove-in-the-face sort of thing, but that was almost unheard-of in the Territory. Generally the insulted party resorted to correspondence. In a letter icy with frozen dignity, but if possible subtly offensive, he asked the insulter for an explanation of his infamous conduct, and implied that the alternative was giving satisfaction by standing up to be shot at. "Go, write it in a martial hand," Sir Toby Belch advises hesitant challenger, Sir Andrew Aguecheek. "Be curst and brief. It is no matter how witty, so it be eloquent and full of invention. Taunt him with the license of ink. . . . And as many lies as will lie in thy sheet of paper . . . set 'em down." The insulter was obligated to reply, and there might be several exchanges of notes of mounting dudgeon, delivered by messenger-boy seconds, one or both parties occasionally invoking "the code."

That word was not merely a manner of speaking. There was a code in print. The most important American treatise on the subject was John Lyde Wilson's *The Code of Honor; or Rules for the Government of Principals and Seconds in Duelling,* first published in Charleston, South Carolina, in 1848, a revised edition coming out ten years later. It is a handy how-to-do-it manual of numbered rules in chapters entitled "The Person Insulted, Before Challenge Sent," "Duty of Challengee and His Second Before Fighting," "Duty of Principals and Seconds on the Ground," "The Degrees of Insult, and How Compromised," etc. Instructions are precise, down to the exact words of the starter who sets off the action: " 'Gentlemen, prepare to receive the word. Are you ready? Fire—one, two, three—halt! nor fire after the word "halt." ' " The author's purpose, he says in his preface, is to discharge a moral duty by adding to the sum of human happiness. In furtherance thereof, he shows a nice concern for the feelings of all parties, urges negotiation before sending a challenge, counsels against opprobrious epithets, and generously allows time for making domestic arrangements and drawing up wills.

Whether or not this text was available to Washoe gentlemen, their duels adhered fairly closely to Wilson's rules, with some variations. Adherents of both sides, eager to arrange subsidiary contests, sometimes became embroiled in their own busy swapping of high-toned indignation, and before long a squad of irascible letter-writers might be snarling at each other, the original cause of controversy becoming somewhat obscured. If, after all this furious penmanship, the insulter continued to delay apology or to avoid accepting a challenge, the insultee published a notice called a "card"— Wilson says that the man may be "posted"—in which he denounced his opponent as liar, coward, sneak, blackguard, poltroon, and other unsavory characters, depending upon the fertility of his imagination. After that the challengee had to accept a challenge or be disgraced forever and ever.

Then a meeting of seconds arranged details of time and place, and the duel proceeded with fantastic punctilio. A principal required two seconds, a surgeon, and an assistant surgeon, though Wilson concedes that the latter functionary might be dispensed with. There were no assistant surgeons at Washoe duels, but the other officials were all present. Seconds carefully measured off the standard ten to twenty paces, like judges of the shotput at a track meet, and meticulously loaded the pistols in each other's presence. Each then presented a weapon to his principal, who grasped it by the barrel with his non-shooting hand. During these solemn rites everybody behaved with the stupefying politeness of ruffled chevaliers in some never-never land as dreamlike as Graustark.

No experienced Washoe duelist became so emotionally lacerated by wounded honor that he failed to keep a weather eye on the Territory's anti-dueling law. It defined sending a challenge or taking part in a duel as a felony; it stated that if one party to a duel died within a year as a result of it, the charge against the killer was murder. This law was not strictly enforced, but it was well to be on the safe side. Old hands instructed neophytes in the gentlemanly pastime to avoid fatalities by aiming, not at the head or heart, but at the legs.

Crippling a man stilled the protest of anguished self-esteem without unduly arousing the constabulary.

In the summer of 1863 Tom Fitch, of the Virginia *Union*, challenged Joe Goodman because of a personal attack in the *Enterprise*. When they met on the field of honor with Navy revolvers at fifteen paces, a crowd of eager spectators hired every hack in town to see the fun. That rabble was a violation of the code. Wilson's rule says that select friends may be invited, but only with the approval of the seconds, and provided that they behave quietly and respectfully—like the gallery around a putting green at a National Open championship. Obviously those Virginians had not read the book; to them a duel was as good as a circus.

Mark Twain was there, of course. When police appeared and arrested both principals, who were put under bond to keep the peace, he grumbled that officious meddling spoiled a good item. He was flippant about the affair, as he also was when he mentioned it briefly in his *Autobiography* over thirty years later. It was unfortunate that his humorous attitude temporarily deserted him when, about nine months after the Fitch-Goodman entanglement, he himself came close to fighting a duel and in the process put on an *opéra bouffe* of behavior that was both sad and ridiculous. Of that, more later.

Not to be deterred, the *Union-Enterprise* contestants went over the line to Ingraham's ranch in Stampede Valley, California, to shoot it out with Colt's five-shooters, one chamber loaded. This time Goodman brought down his man with a shot in the right leg below the knee. Then Major Ferrend, Goodman's second, graciously requested of Captain Rowe, Fitch's second, permission to remove his principal from the scene. Permission granted, with equal grace. Major Ferrend bowed, Captain Rowe bowed in return, and the major and his principal departed.

The brummagem chivalry of the duello, suggestive of

knightly champions assuaging affronted honor in misty Southern dawns, was alien to Washoe. No magnolias bloomed on
Mount Davidson, and when dawn came up over the Sierras
it was magnificent, but it was not redolent of jasmine. The
program of insults and challenges became so frequent that it
excited the derision of sensible citizens. Two men showed
their contempt by staging a sham duel. Faithfully following
the pattern of huffy preliminaries, they attracted a large audience to the field of action, where they faced each other with
pistols loaded with tinfoil. After several rounds, one fell as
if mortally wounded. Police showed up, arrested the supposed murderer, then discovered that the whole thing was a
sell. The joke seems to have had little effect, however, on
touchy persons who believed that their sensitive honor
could be restored to normal only by the old-fashioned method.
Such nonsense introduces childish play-acting into what was
thought to be a man's world.

Earthy inhabitants, ignorant of codified protocol, settled
their differences with five-shooters on the spot, sometimes to
the grave damage of innocent bystanders. The boom year
produced a sharp upturn in the shooting and slashing business. Editors elsewhere commented on Washoe disorder with
an air of horror mixed with shuddery fascination. "Within a
month," said the Stockton, California, *Daily Independent,*

upwards of a dozen men were shot, wounded or killed at
Virginia—exhibiting a bad state of morals in that city. The
Standard says it is absolutely dangerous to venture into a
crowd, as no one knows how soon shooting may commence.[45]

The grand jury of Storey County, N. T. . . . in their late report, September 15th [1863], return the following list of true
bills: For murder, 2; assault with intent to commit murder,
5; assault with deadly weapon to do bodily harm, 5; rape, 2;
dueling, 2. . . . There are beside, burglaries, robberies, lar-
cenies, etc., in still greater numbers.[46]

B Street between Sutton and Union was a favorite outdoor range. So many were cut down there and at miscellaneous other spots that the Virginia *Union* figuratively wrung its hands:

The ghosts of a hundred men surround us, whose murderers walk the streets to-day in contempt of the law through whose fingers they have slipped; our pavements are slippery with the blood of men shot down in open day, and the genius of assassination walks riotant through our crowded thoroughfares.[47]

A spirit of macabre recklessness made life almost as cheap as it is on the modern highway. A diet of whiskey, one reporter observed, caused rowdyism as naturally as turtle soup puts fat on an alderman. With some gun-toters the urge to squeeze the trigger was insistent, like a craving for drugs. A well-known lawyer named Bryan got drunk, wandered into the Jenny Lind saloon, pulled out a derringer and said he wanted to shoot somebody "just for luck." Then he fired at a peaceful, beer-drinking German, but fortunately missed him. Gunplay was so frequent that it ceased to be news. An exchange of shots or a killing, whether by accident or design, got only a few perfunctory lines in Virginia papers.

The *Enterprise*, editorializing on ruffians who molested women, urged the ladies to arm themselves:

We have heard of so many instances, lately, of respectable women being insulted on the streets and in their houses, that we have thought it advisable to warn them to carry weapons and use them when occasion demands. There is no law against killing brutes in self-defense.[48]

The necessity for such feminine militancy is not according to the storybook tradition of Western gallantry. Virginia was different from those fictional mining towns drenched in a stagy glow of sentimentality, like Bret Harte's Roaring Camp.

Of the imaginary characters in these places, the reader's impression, confirmed in recent decades by the astigmatic camera eye of Hollywood, is of rough fellows, crude, sometimes murderous, yet of fundamentally lovable chaps with hearts of gold. Always, so the stories tell us, they preserve so much respect for a chaste woman that she needs no defense against assault other than her own virtue. This pleasant fantasy was not true of Virginia.

Impromptu scuffles were so common as to be almost beneath notice. Josephine Dodge, alias "Buffalo Jo," a prominent trollop, was often in the public eye, bandying obscenities with street corner loafers, and being hauled off to jail dead drunk. Juana Sanchez, known as "Sailor Jack," was a fiery wench who took a pistol away from Jack Butler and shot him dead with it. Teamsters and others continually traded punches, as if for exercise.

In a fist fight about some mail bag arrangement at Silver City yesterday, a stage driver's little finger was broken by his antagonist's nose coming in contact with it. Stage driver threw up the sponge and his opponent turned to the crowd and shouted "Can't we Schoharie boys fight some!"[49]

When Ophir miners blundered into the Burning Moscow, there was a splendid ruckus of drawn revolvers, charges and countercharges, picks and shovels. Police arrested eighteen Ophirs for riotous conduct. The Daly-McGrath prizefight in late summer broke up in a grand row in which five men and three horses were shot, some indiscriminate shooters firing at random into the crowd. These incidents were run-of-the-mill happenings that to some natives were of less importance than the stock market.

Another kind of conflict, more wordy than physical, was a constant procession of lawsuits that made the place a paradise for lawyers. The shrewdest legal brains in the West gravitated to Washoe, and with good reason. Every major mining company was involved, as plaintiff or defendant, in at least fifteen suits; nine companies had 359 cases on the docket, the Ophir leading the field with thirty-seven. The difficulty of establishing clear title to a claim located in 1859 by some old boozer who had disappeared; or of defining a line of demarcation between mines that encroached upon each other, when ore veins had a disconcerting way of changing direction suddenly, and each company naturally wanted the vein on its property; or of unscrambling the facts about a plaintiff who alleged a prior claim to the ground: such problems kept litigious argument going interminably, to the great advantage of counsel skilled in delay, riposte, and chicanery.

Tactics were brazenly cutthroat; bribery was the common practice, accepted and expected by all concerned. Lawyers "handled" judges for a price, and judges also had their price. A litigant out to win made no bones about buying a jury, squaring a sheriff, taking care of deputy sheriffs and prothonotaries, and doling out retainers to anybody else who might be useful. Mining records were suitably altered to assist the case. Hostile witnesses were shanghaied out of the Territory, sometimes assassinated. Friendly witnesses, drilled like rookies by a sergeant, swore to testimony that everybody knew was a tissue of outrageous lies, but exposure of their mendacity had no effect. When the Yellow Jacket Company highhandedly stole mining ground by moving its property line 300 feet to get over the vein, it infringed upon the Union and Princess Companies, which brought suit. Defendant hired a witness to swear that he had many times read the original Yellow Jacket location notice tacked to a nut-pine stump at exactly the point claimed. Cross-examination disclosed that the man could neither read nor write, but the Yellow Jacket won the case just the same. When a jury was paid to deliver a verdict, it delivered regardless of evidence.

Under those circumstances the word "law" had no meaning. Decisions rested not on merit or fact, but on cleverness, power, and money. Suits were commenced without intention of ever bringing them to trial; some were intended only to harass the working of a claim, depreciate its stock, and freeze out discouraged stockholders. Mixed up in these dubious doings were some of the most respected men in the Territory: Judge J. H. Hardy, Thomas B. Reardan, General Charles H. S. Williams, D. W. Perley, and numerous others. A prominent firm was the highly successful partnership of A. W. "Sandy" Baldwin, whom Mark Twain admired, and William M. Stewart, later United States Senator from Nevada, for whom Mark Twain served briefly as secretary in 1867-68. The legal maneuvers of Stewart & Baldwin, and of many other law sharks in Virginia, recall the remark of Washoe historians who say that on the Comstock the only venial sins were cheating at cards and lying. The obvious conclusion is that those Storey County courtrooms, echoing with shameless lies, were packed with notorious sinners.

Legal fraud, besides other sorts of double-dealing, induced a visitor to say that in Virginia

corruption is at a premium, and men's virtue is to be estimated in an inverse proportion to their professions. California in '49 was a kind of vestibule of hell, but Nevada may be considered the very throne-room of Pluto himself. I have seen more rascality, small and great, in my brief forty days sojourn in this wilderness of sage brush, sharpers and prostitutes, than in a thirteen years experience of our squeamishly moral State of California.

The principal occupation of the denizens of this God forsaken angle of creation appears to be the administering to one another of allopathic doses of humbug, which are received with an air of gravity and relish which betokens an abiding and universal faith in their virtue. . . . Mammon is the god of their idolatry, and slavishly submissive to the behests of their demon-lord are all his wretched worshippers.[50]

Above: Gould & Curry mill, 1863, looking down Six Mile Cañon, from a contemporary painting

Left: Weighing a load at Gould & Curry Mine, Virginia City, 1865

Below: Gold Hill, Nevada, about 1870

Above: B Street, Virginia City, 1863-1864; *below*: Firemen on
C Street, Virginia City, about 1863

The habit of administering humbug was hard to resist, for this writer admitted: "If I reside here six months I should turn out a consummate rascal." Also cognizant of idol-worship was the sardonic "Stock Broker's Prayer," published in the *Enterprise* and possibly written by Mark Twain:

Our father Mammon who art in the Comstock, bully is thy name; let thy dividends come, and stocks go up, in California as in Washoe. Give us this day our daily commissions; forgive us our swindles as we hope to get even on those who have swindled us. "Lead" us not into temptation of promising wild cat; deliver us from lawsuits; for thine is the main Comstock, the black sulphurets and the wire silver, from wall-rock to wall-rock, you bet![51]

Outsiders viewed Virginia somewhat as the modern American unacquainted with the Middle West views Chicago: as an unsavory place where the citizenry dodged bullets all day long, and tried to keep its money out of the clutches of thieves. Actually, in Virginia, peaceful inhabitants, law-abiding and reasonably honest, outnumbered their law-breaking fellow townsmen, but the obstreperous ones got the publicity, thus illustrating the truism that upright behavior, however admirable, is too placid to be newsworthy. California editors, delighted to view Washoe with alarm, played up stories of homicide, mayhem, and miscellaneous knavery over there until the impression grew that such performances were universal in the Territory.

Virginia natives put up with their unfavorable reputation, fretting over it somewhat yet at the same time regarding it with pride that became more marked as they grew older. Backward-looking reminiscers are almost invariably mellow. There is much in print about the grand old days on the Comstock, as if Virginia were somewhat like a town in a TV Western, rather cozy except for a few well-known bad men the deadshot sheriff is sure to get soon after the commercial; as if murder and all the trickery men can think of only made

life more gay. Mark Twain was no exception to the habit of
romanticizing. In *Roughing It* he becomes nostalgic over the
rugged vigor of mining camps, praising their "bright-eyed,
quick-moving, strong-handed young giants—the strangest
population, the finest population, the most gallant host that
ever trooped down the startled solitudes of an unpeopled
land." In letters of later years, long after he had left Virginia,
he looks back fondly to those days. Yet he was wise enough
not to put his nostalgia to the test. After his visit to the West
Coast in 1868, he never returned to Nevada or California.

Notwithstanding memories that became more sunny with
age, the usual attitude of those caught up by the hurly-burly
of Virginia at the time was anything but romantic. Joe Goodman was a sort of romanticist and so was Dan De Quille, but
most people were not like that. A correspondent of the Santa
Cruz *Sentinel* spoke for many when he summed up gloomily:
"the work is unhealthy, the climate despicable, living enor-
mously high, the whisky, like the citizens, nearly lightning,
and the water at least forty degrees worse than the washings
of an apothecary shop."[52]

Mark Twain himself, when he lived there, was under no
illusions. In his letters of those days are unflattering remarks
about the country; the satirical description of Washoe in
"Information Wanted" (*The Golden Era,* May 22, 1864) was
scarcely complimentary—the landscape, he said, "looks something like a singed cat." A sketch attributed to the Local of
the *Enterprise* complained of the scenery visible from the
summit of Mount Davidson:

On the north the eye falls on mountains; looking east, the
view is more varied and we see—mountains; turning toward
the south we are again delighted with mountains, and paying
our addresses to the west the monotony of the scenery is
beautifully interrupted by mountains. Washoe Lake, that
has thrown so many romantic young ladies into ecstasy, looks

like a sand-bang about as big as a side of sole leather. In short, whichever way we turn, the eye meets a waste or a Sierra—range beyond range, till they fade away and are lost in the shadows of the distance. We may want poetry, but nobody who ever saw scenery has sincerely praised the view from Mount Davidson.[53]

He was always eager to take off for other places, particularly California, and loath to return when the furlough ended. About the people, the Local's many insults fired at all sorts in the paper showed that he did not regard the populace of this mining camp as gallant young giants.

Despite grubbing and greed and machination, the human touch showed up now and then. Against the blasphemous cynicism of Mammon-worship may be set the tender sentiments suggested by a mining company called "The Orphan Boy and Sweet Alice Consolidated," and of a Gold Hill mine named "The Gentle Annie;" the poetic streak of the Spaniard who called his claim "La Mina del Alto;" or this notice of a wedding: "Eliza Walker and Tom Belcher consolidated on Sunday last. They will soon incorporate and commence an issue of stock."[54] Life in its more homely manifestations somehow went on in Virginia, love existed, and Eros temporarily supplanted Mammon. Once in awhile somebody lifted his sights from stocks and humbug to admire the vast sweep of that empty country. Most observers saw nothing in it but barren desolation. Around Virginia, said one traveler,

The country . . . looks as if the curse of almighty God rested on it forever and ever; long, dreary wastes of sand and alkali, without a green shrub, a bird or anything to break the dreary monotony. I think I did see one bird on the trip here; but the miserable creature had evidently lost all self-respect, and had probably flown out into the wilderness to die.[55]

Another said that the rising sun "tinting the distant mountains of Washoe River with gorgeous Italian hues—similar to the color of a pair of Pike Co. pants," eventually "goes down behind the peaks of the Sierras—evidently disgusted with himself for being obliged to shine on such a country."[56] Occasionally, however, a sensitive spirit responded to the beauty of snow-clad peaks in winter, roseate morning tints changing to the deep purple of evening, the sun shining on the distant Carson River, and the grandeur of tumbling mountains that, visible from C Street, rolled off in ridge after ridge to a far horizon.

Mark Twain remained in town about two months, though taking time out for a week at Steamboat Springs to get over a cold. In early September, shortly after the return of Dan De Quille from his long leave, wanderlust seized him once more. Again he departed for San Francisco, his going this time noted by the pious words of an *Enterprise* colleague, probably Dan: "During his absence the moral tone of this column will be much improved. It could not be otherwise."[57] Tarrying at the Bay about five weeks, he wined and dined as before, viewed Adah Isaacs Menken in her celebrated role of stripper in *Mazeppa*, and became such a social lion that the ladies of the Lick House gave him a complimentary ball. The affair was a great success, he said, honored by the presence of the army and navy, also by "his Grace the Duke of Benecia, the Countess of San Jose, Lord Blessyou, Lord Geeminy, and many others whose titles and faces have passed from my memory."[58]

He began contributing to *The Golden Era*: "How to Cure a Cold," an exaggerated account of his recent stay at Steamboat Springs; "The Lick House Ball" and "All About the Fashions," mostly parodies of elaborate fashion notes in society columns; "The Great Prize Fight," a burlesque exposition, in round-by-round boxing terms, of the political contest between Governor Low and Leland Stanford. Publication in the *Era* showed that he was making headway as a writer.

Outside of San Francisco many people had at least heard of him, but his name was not yet a byword. Since the *Enterprise* staff was as careless about exchanges as other things, the paper did not regularly penetrate remote Nevada and California counties. Country journalists showed their slight acquaintance by enclosing his pen name in quotes. San Francisco editors were better informed, but they did not hail Mark Twain as the coming American genius.

Close to home he was popular with readers who enjoyed his often rough and generally unsubtle humor, but reprehensible to conventional citizens irked by his flippancy, bohemianism, impiety, and scandalous untruths. Nevertheless, he himself had no doubt of his eminence. "Everybody knows me," he cockily told his mother, "and I fare like a prince wherever I go, be it on this side of the mountains or the other. And I am proud to say I am the most conceited ass in the Territory."[59]

Mark Twain, 1862, from an etching by Bicknell

Chapter Four

THAT MASSACRE

❦❦❦❦❦❦❦❦❦❦❦❦❦❦❦❦❦❦❦❦❦❦❦❦❦❦❦❦❦❦❦❦❦❦❦❦❦❦❦

ABOUT the middle of October, 1863, the *Enterprise* Local, reluctantly turning his back upon the enchantments of San Francisco, returned to Nevada sagebrush. On his way home he paused in Carson City to report the first annual fair of the Washoe Agricultural, Mining and Mechanical Society: livestock parade, horse races, possibilities of fruit culture, etc., mostly written up in a humdrum way, as if he were not much interested.[1] By the latter part of the month he was in Virginia, where his doings, as usual, made copy for fellow reporters. The arrival of a new engine for Eagle Engine Company No. 3 meant a liquid celebration, at which Mark Twain made a speech, along with Fire Chief Peter Larkin, Tom Peasley, foreman of No. 3, and Charley Parker, of the *Bulletin*. There were other occasions equally moist. On the 26th the Gold Hill *Daily News* announced: "Mark Twain, Jim Hardy, Judge Leconey, See-Yup, and a lot of other Chinamen at Virginia, are having a series of 'high old' drunks, making as an excuse for their debauchery, the presentation of 'Stars' to Policemen," and went on to scoff at "the vile stuff that forms the staple food of those bummers."

One contemporary greeted him sourly: "Mark Twain again afflicts us by his presence. Tell this to the landlord of the Lick House, who would doubtless like to 'see him.' "[2] Shortly after his return a sally in the *Enterprise* afflicted a large number of people. In the paper of October 28 he published a sensational hoax, possibly inspired by a bottle imp, that vastly enhanced his notoriety among shocked readers for hundreds of miles around.

This one, known as the "Bloody Massacre," told of "a man named P. Hopkins or Philip Hoskins" who lived with a wife and nine children "in the old log house just to the edge of the great pine forest which lies between Empire City and Dutch Nick's." Ordinarily a mild and affable man, Hopkins had shown evidence of derangement when he found out about dividend-cooking in Virginia mining companies in which he had been a heavy investor. Acting upon the advice of a relative, an editor of the San Francisco *Evening Bulletin,* he had put his money into the Spring Valley Water Company, only to discover that the same swindle practiced by this firm debased the value of its stock and shut off the water supply. Whereupon the unstable Hopkins went over the edge into homicidal insanity; in a mad rage he killed his wife and seven of the nine children. Graphic detail elaborated upon blood-spattering ferocity and a horrible harvest of corpses strewn about the house: Mrs. Hopkins lying across the threshold, having been felled with an axe and scalped, her right hand almost severed; Mary, the eldest, fearfully mutilated, a knife thrust into her side; six children, brained with a club, dead in one room; everywhere, as evidence of struggle, a confusion of broken furniture and scattered clothes. Two children, though badly injured, survived. The murderer

dashed into Carson on horseback, with his throat cut from ear to ear, and bearing in his hand a reeking scalp from which the warm, smoking blood was still dripping, and fell in a dying condition in front of the Magnolia saloon. Hopkins expired in the course of five minutes, without speaking. The long red hair of the scalp he bore marked it as that of Mrs. Hopkins.

As in the story of the petrified man, clues to absurdity were plain to the observant. Empire City and Dutch Nick's—so-called after Nicolas Ambrosio (any foreigner was a Dutch-man)—were two names for one and the same place. In that locality were no pine forest, no log house, no large Hopkins family. That a man should ride four or five miles with his throat cut from ear to ear was improbable. A subtle pointer was the juxtaposition of "murderer" and the Magnolia saloon, a well-known Carson bar of which the proprietor was Peter Hopkins. Another hint to the alert was the editorializing con-demnation of San Francisco newspapers, particularly the *Evening Bulletin,* that had

permitted this water company to go on borrowing money and cooking dividends, under cover of which cunning finan-ciers crept out of the tottering concern, leaving the crash to come upon poor and unsuspecting stockholders, without of-fering to expose the villainy at work. We hope the fearful massacre detailed above may prove the saddest result of their silence.

To well-informed editors, these signposts should have pointed clearly toward make-believe. The Virginia *Evening Bulletin* of the same date saw them, labeled the story "as baseless as the fabric of a dream," and reproved the author: "Now we go in for any and all men writing for the press drawing on their imaginations—when they have any—but we are not an admirer of foundationless yarns full of horror, and which by mentioning names and localities, may do much injury without a probability of doing good." The Gold Hill *Daily News* accepted the sensation without question, and put out an extra about it. Tough-minded San Francisco edi-tors, only too happy to publicize the most monstrous atroc-ities in Washoe, seemed half inclined to believe. Small-town papers in distant parts of Nevada and California either re-printed the yarn or a summary of it without comment, or with appropriate shudders over the dreadful things that happened in that territorial no-man's land. In Virginia, the man in the street saw in the tale nothing but blood and dismemberment, which so unnerved him that he could not take his usual drinks with comfort.

The next day the author ran a short notice in the *Enterprise*: "I take it all back." Then, with vindictive fury, the storm burst. For several weeks editors, no doubt disgusted with themselves for having been taken in, and, in San Francisco at least, stung by the accusation of abetting water company fraud, huffed and puffed as they blew up a gale of spleen that buffeted Mark Twain. "The presence of wit . . . in such play upon the public sympathies," said the Gold Hill *Daily News*, "will not be recognized outside of the brain that coined the fabrication."[3] The Virginia *Evening Bulletin* delivered a trenchant rebuke:

> The man who could pen such a story, with all its horrors depicted in such infernal detail, and which to our knowledge sent a pang of terror to the hearts of many persons, as a joke, in fun, can have but a very indefinite idea of the elements of a joke. Is it any joke for a newspaper heretofore of undoubted veracity and reliability permitting itself to spread a story broadcast through the land that disgraces and injures the reputation of the very community that sustains it? If this is a joke we can't see the point where the laugh comes in.[4]

Other papers criticized in tones that varied from temperate to harsh. The Sacramento *Daily Union* said mildly: "It may be considered by the *Enterprise* very pleasant and harmless amusement to trifle with the sympathies of its readers, but many will not see it."[5] The editor of the Grass Valley, California, *National* admitted that he felt "streaked" at having been sold, but consoled himself with the thought that others were in the same boat. "The ass who originated the story doubtless thinks he is 'old smarty'—we don't."[6] The Austin,

Nevada, *Reese River Reveille* was contemptuous: "Some of
the papers are expressing astonishment that 'Mark Twain'
. . . should perpetrate such a 'sell' as 'A Bloody Massacre Near Carson'. . . . They don't know him. We would not
be surprised at ANYTHING done by that silly idiot."[7] A good
many hot shots were fired at "that silly lunatic," "his silly
imposition," "his baseless and worse than idle fabrication,"
"the soul-sickening story," "this miserable creature," "a LIE—
utterly baseless and without a shadow of foundation," and so
forth. In California, said Dan De Quille, "there was a howl
from Siskiyou to San Diego. Some papers demanded the immediate discharge of the author of the item by the *Enterprise*
proprietors."[8]

Battered from all sides, Mark Twain struck back at least
once, chiefly at the Virginia *Evening Bulletin*. His counter-
attack is lost, but he was said to have used such terms as
"picayune papers," "little parson," and "oyster-brained idiot."
No doubt his rebuttal was a choice eruption of heightened
emotions; it is unfortunate that we do not have the full text.
As the critical barrage continued, the shots began to take
effect, for he was reported to be suffering "terrible agony"
over the opprobrium heaped upon him, and particularly over
the possible damage he had done to the reputation of his
paper.

The San Francisco *Journal* emphasized this point when it
said sternly: "We are not fond of hoaxing our readers, and
hereby give the *Enterprise* notice that as long as they keep
the author of that hoax in their employ we shall not trouble
their columns for news matter."[9] Said the Sacramento *Daily
Bee*: "we learn from the Union that the Enterprise now de-
clares that the story was a hoax! . . . Why in this event, the
Enterprise people must be almost as crazy as they falsely
represented Hopkins to be! We shall know how to treat that
journal hereafter."[10] The Auburn, California, *Stars and*

Stripes announced that "in future it will credit nothing from that source which is not corroborated by an 'intelligent contraband.' "[11] The San Francisco *Evening Bulletin,* which had been singled out for special attention in the burlesque, wrote off the *Enterprise* as "famous, or infamous, for its sensational *canards.*"[12] The Gold Hill *Daily News* ironically remarked: "leaving the broad and side-splitting humor of Mark Twain out of the question, the *Enterprise* is a most valuable paper, and has our best wishes."[13]

As such comments showed, the massacre story made editors dubious about the general veracity of the *Enterprise,* and they became doubly cautious if a news item were melodramatic. In late November, when the paper printed a true account of a wild-eyed lunatic who ran amuck in Gold Hill, stabbing four men, the once-fooled Watsonville, California, *Pajaro Times* was too smart to be taken in a second time:

We imagine the whole thing is a hoax, after the style of the bloody massacre at Carson, which we and all other papers throughout the State published in all seriousness. Oh, no, neighbor Enterprise, not twice. You can't play Mark Twain upon us folks in Watsonville. We like the Enterprise—but consider nothing reliable outside of advertisements and puffs.[14]

Another news story, about wolves attacking a miner going to work high up on the slope of Mount Davidson, drew jeers from the Downieville, California, *Mountain Messenger:*

Wolfy, very. This item is now going the rounds of the California press as a genuine occurrence. There is just about as much truth in this story as there was in that of the "horrible massacre of a whole family," and very probably emanated from that same fount of unreliability, the Virginia Enterprise.[15]

San Francisco editors showed their distrust, as one of them had threatened, by not troubling the *Enterprise* very much for news matter. In the *Alta California, Evening Bulletin,* and *Journal,* from this time forth, Washoe items from the Virginia *Union,* evidently considered more trustworthy, far outnumber those from its older contemporary. Mark Twain had reason to be troubled by doubts of journalistic integrity created by his prank.

He was reported to have published a long apology for his misguided humor, but this expression of regret is not extant. According to Paine, he offered to resign because he believed that he had ruined the *Enterprise,* but Joe Goodman waved the offer aside with the encouraging assurance that the turmoil would blow over, and that the massacre story would be remembered long after the hubbub had been forgotten. Dan De Quille soothed his partner with similar counsel. Reminiscing many years later, he said that the persistent and vitriolic attacks

worried Mark as I had never before seen him worried. Said he: "I am being burned alive on both sides of the mountains." We roomed together, and one night when the persecution was hottest, he was so distressed that he could not sleep. He tossed, tumbled and groaned aloud. So I set to work to comfort him. "Mark," said I, "never mind this bit of a gale; it will soon blow itself out. This item of yours will be remembered and talked about when all your other work is forgotten. The murder at Dutch Nick's will be quoted years from now as the big sell of these times."[16]

A man with a conscience as sensitive as Mark Twain's could easily plunge into a pit of self-condemnation. The analogous example of painful soul-searching over another humorous misfire at the Whittier birthday dinner in 1877—when he represented Emerson, Longfellow, and Holmes, those august New England Brahmins, as drunken miners spouting poetry —shows what dire affliction ravaged his spirit when he believed he had made a glaring mistake. After that affair he wrote humbly apologetic letters to the principals, expressed his sense of guilt to Howells, and stewed about it off and on for the rest of his life. His exposition of the harrowing effects of a nagging conscience, as set forth in a facetious essay entitled "The Facts Concerning the Recent Carnival of Crime in Connecticut," is, for all its humorous exaggeration, not an overstatement. The pestilent imp of a conscience described in that paper was his own, always relentless, never satisfied, forever convicting him of choosing the wrong alternative in any course of action.

Still, abased humility over the massacre backfire was temporary, for a counterpoise to mortification was belief in the rightness of his intentions. This belief had strong support in the favorable judgment of his newspaper associates, especially Goodman and Dan De Quille. Their backing restored some of his confidence, and retrospect his balance. Just as, on perennially rereading the broad humor of the Whittier dinner speech, he sometimes concluded that it was top-notch —a 1906 dictation for the *Autobiography* called it "as good as good can be"—so fainter evidence implies that, on reflection, he considered the massacre story not such a ghastly blunder as others said it was. When he wrote about it for the New York *Galaxy* in 1870, he said nothing about an apology, but expressed only surprise that anybody could have taken as fact such an assortment of nonsense.

If he was momentarily distressed by critical attacks upon him, the *Enterprise* was not. In the midst of the firing the paper was reported to be engaged in compiling an anthology called "Lives of the Liars or Joking Justified." As a sarcastic contemporary explained, this project was intended to illustrate the hypothesis that

truth is not an indispensable requisite in the local columns of a newspaper, but that on the contrary, the more outrageous the hoax, the greater the evidence of talent, and the greater the indignation of the papers hoaxed, the more applicable the epithet of "one horse."[17]

To produce this volume, compilers were represented as combing exchanges for examples of what were called "huge Roorbacks," one of them being a burlesque in the New York *Herald* of October 23: a four-column account of a sham banquet at Delmonico's for Private T. E. Miles O'Reilly, 47th New York Volunteers; satirical telegrams from Lincoln, General Grant, Governor Seymour, Count Gurowski, Thurlow Weed, Fernando Wood; malapropos songs and speeches by James T. Brady, Charles P. Daly, and others; and the climactic discovery that the Sub-Committee on Arrangements had forgotten to invite the guest of honor.

It is a pity that this book was not produced, handed down to succeeding generations, and augmented with episodes old and new to show that Mark Twain was neither the first nor the last to fool readers. The massacre contretemps was somewhat like the experience of a famous forerunner, Jonathan Swift. In 1729, when he published "A Modest Proposal," the most grisly of grim jokes, some readers who took it literally denounced the author as a monster. In 1773 Franklin's bitter satire, "An Edict by the King of Prussia," took in some readers, who accepted it as the genuine edict of a petty tyrant. Poe published hoaxes in the *Southern Literary Messenger* and elsewhere.

Hoaxing is not unknown to our day. It appears occasionally on the editorial page of the New York *Times*. In the prohibition days of 1924 one Sanford Jarrell brought off the sell of the century in the New York *Herald Tribune*: a front-page, five-column spread about a 17,000-ton rum ship anchored fifteen miles off Fire Island. The craft was awash with booze, crowded with dizzy flappers, glamorous redheads, and playboys unrestrainedly carrying on to the accompaniment of wild music. Jarrell kept this spurious news hot for a week before his superiors caught on and fired him. Thereafter, wherever he went, he found that his big story had preceded him to confer upon him a blend of fame and notoriety, even as the Carson massacre similarly endowed Mark Twain.

To fire him never entered anybody's head. His burlesque was in accord with Western predilection for tomfoolery, particularly evident in Virginia, where the artful dodge was an old established custom on the *Enterprise*. Dan De Quille was another who preferred the imaginative to the factual. His quaints, which became a Dequillian variety of science fiction, probably owed something to his partner, as in Dan's story of the petrified Washoe Giant of the Comstock Period. His tales also misled readers. One of the best known, "The Traveling Stones of Pahranagat," about rocks drawn together by magnetic power from widely separated spots, got all the way over to Germany, where some solemn Teutons hailed the author as "Herr Dan De Quille, the eminent physicist of Virginiastadt, Nevada." Neither he nor Mark Twain took much interest in straight reporting. As Arthur McEwen said thirty years later:

> The local department of the *Enterprise* . . . was as unlike the local department of a city newspaper of the present as the town and time were unlike the San Francisco of to-day. The indifference to "news" was noble—none the less so because it was so blissfully unconscious. Either Mark or Dan would dismiss a murder with a couple of inches, and sit down and fill up a column with a fancy sketch. They were about equally good in the sort of invention required for such efforts, and Dan very often did the better work.[18]

Well aware of this quirk were some of those very editors who most swiftly mounted their high horses to start tilting at Mark Twain over the massacre story. The ruffled ones could not forgive themselves for their slow-witted failure to read his yarn intelligently; nor, if guilty of connivance at dividend-cooking, could they forbear to respond in the ironical human fashion of toplofty indignation.

The "Bloody Massacre" might have been suggested by a sketch of Artemus Ward's. In the early 1850's he was a compositor on the Boston *Carpet Bag*, to which Sam Clemens contributed "The Dandy and the Squatter" for the issue of May 1, 1852. Several pieces by Ward, who wrote under the name of "Chub," appeared in this magazine. In one of them, entitled "Things From Chub's Knapsack," on October 16, 1852, the wife of an absent-minded Professor Reynolds

was reading aloud from the paper an account of a horrible murder. A man had, so the paper said, deliberately killed his whole family—consisting of some dozen members—with an ax! Mrs. R. laid down the paper with the exclamation, "What a wretch!"

"Yes," said her husband in a quiet tone, looking up from his book, "he should be talked to!"

In the mind of so well-informed a reader of Ward as Sam Clemens the axe murders could easily have taken lodgment.

A more immediate possibility as a source was a news story in the *Enterprise* of July 22 about a Reese River man named Cornell who went on a maniacal tear with an axe, gouging his tentmate, then charged into a crowded saloon, where he slashed an arm, gashed a head, almost cut off a hand, and cut up eight men before he smashed a chandelier and precipitated a tremendous scuffle, punctuated by gunfire, in the dark, the crowd wrecking the place trying to get out. Cornell escaped, after slicing off somebody's ear, then wounded three foot passengers en route to Clifton, two fatally, and the next morning he was found dead with his throat cut from ear to ear. That sort of occurrence supplied ammunition to Mark Twain's critics, who said that, since the Territory furnished so many examples of actual violence, no heavy-handed joker needed to invent fanciful additions.

Details of wholesale bloodletting in the Carson massacre story are similar to those of the lurid Reese River episode. Otherwise, the author maintained that the whole thing was a satire on dividend-cooking in general, on the fraudulent Spring Valley Water Company in particular, likewise on crooked San Francisco newspapers, especially the *Evening Bulletin.* A minor purpose was a mild slap at Pete Hopkins of the Magnolia saloon, a place notorious for forty-rod whiskey, so-called because said to be fatal at that distance. There may have been a muffled implication that this deadly stuff had aggravated the insanity of the murderer. None of these purposes got through to unwary readers. Appalled by cracked skulls, much blood, and a crop of badly cut-up corpses, they missed the underlying satire.

However the boomerang of his elaborate joke may have belabored the conscience of Mark Twain, the misunderstanding and loud condemnation made him gloomy, even sour. A Gold Hill contemporary remarked with some concern:

This favorite writer is "melancholy;" he has got the mulli-grubs. "Where be his jibes now? his gambols? his flashes of merriment that were wont to set Virginia in a roar? Not one now to mock his own grinning? Quite chop-fallen?" (Bully for Shakespeare.) We haven't had a good square joke out of poor Mark these four or five days. He sits behind *that* historic pine table morose and melancholy, and drinking mean whisky to drown his misery. Cheer up, friend Mark; the courier brings the welcome news that all is quiet at Dutch Nick's, the "har" on Mrs. Hopkins' head is coming out like a new "red" shoe-brush; the murderer had *that* gash in his throat caulked and patched, and the blood in *that* pine forest is not ankle deep. Awake, Mark! arise and toot your horn if you don't sell a claim.[19]

Once again he learned, more pointedly this time, how easily the most exaggerated humor may be misunderstood. As he said a few years later: "The idea that anybody could ever take my massacre for a genuine occurrence never once suggested itself to me, hedged about as it was by all those telltale absurdities and impossibilities."[20] The experience may have contributed its mite to the disillusion that, in old age, led him to sardonic reflections upon the stupidity of the damned human race.

Mark Twain, 1864-65

Chapter Five

SEASONED YEARLING

❦❦

AS JOE GOODMAN and Dan De Quille had predicted, the hurricane winds of disapproval blew themselves out within a few weeks. In the vicinity of Virginia Mark Twain's colleagues, who seemed as envious of his impudence as offended by it, soon forgave him, but it was a long time before he heard the last of sly allusions to the Hopkins family. He himself, with a sort of bravado, occasionally made some reference to the story that had caused such a stir. Throughout the uproar the *Enterprise* staff had loyally hung together in support of their embattled comrade.

He and Dan cemented their friendship by setting up a parlor-bedroom suite of bachelor rooms just across the hall from Tom Fitch and family on the third floor of Daggett's new brick building on B Street. The furniture, said Mark Twain, "cost $28,000, in Europe." Upholstery, added Dan, stood them "$15,000 more, in—a horn. . . . Here we come every night and live—breathe, move and have our being, also our toddies."[1] They got on well together. If, after both were settled in bed to read and smoke, one turned out to go downtown for a late snack of oysters, the other became hungry too, got up and went along. In a sketch, "No Head Nor Tail," written for *The Golden Era*, Dan described the cozy domestic arrangement, complained at length of the trouble involved

in borrowing Mark Twain's shirts because none of them had
buttons, and explained his partner's ingenious scheme of
getting supplies by leaving the door open so that men carrying up wood left it there by mistake. In the *Enterprise* and
the *Era* the pair bantered each other with raillery like that
of those sparring bouts between Mark Twain and the Unreliable. Such tactics testified to the genuineness of their friendship. "Never," said Dan, "was there an angry word between
us in all the time we worked together."[2] So serene a relationship was extraordinary for a man as mercurial and unpredict-
able as Mark Twain.

He jogged over to Carson City to report the constitutional
convention, which sat from November 2 to December 11
making a constitution in anticipation of statehood for Nevada Territory. While he was there, one reporter observed:
"Mark Twain's whiskers and moustache are turning red and
gory, like unto ye bloody skulp he once on a time saw in the
gory hand at Dutch Nick's."[3] That was the way those fellows
kept reminding him. The "whiskers" recall his statement in
Roughing It that he arrived in Virginia "whiskered half down
to the waist." This unusual adornment, converting him into
a kind of Rip Van Winkle, would be interesting to see, but it
does not appear in any Western picture of Mark Twain, either
photographic or verbal. For awhile he cultivated luxuriant
sideburns that gave him a look of great dignity, but they
soon came off.

In letters to the *Enterprise* he wrote of convention doings
with reasonable faithfulness. But since he was not a commonplace reporter of politics or anything else, he was often so
bored by prosy proceedings that he digressed to a miscellany
of items about people and places in Carson City, or to giving
his own particular twist to the news, as in this squib:

A teamster was murdered and robbed on the public highway between Carson and Virginia, to-day. Our sprightly

and efficient officers are on the alert. They calculate to in-
quire into this thing next week. They are tired of these daily
outrages in sight of town, you know.[4]

One convention issue aroused his interest and that of
everybody else: a proposed constitutional provision to tax
undeveloped mining property. Out of the debate on that
subject came one of his best efforts, a speech by L. O. Sterns,
delegate from Aurora, who had requested that reporters publish his remarks either verbatim or not at all. Mark Twain
claimed that Sterns' argument on taxation was carefully
transcribed from his own "mysterious short-hand notes," as
follows:

Mr. President, I am opposed, I am hostile, I am uncom-
promisingly against this proposition to tax the mines. I will
go further, sir. I will openly assert, sir, that I am not in favor
of this proposition. It is wrong—entirely wrong, sir (as the
gentleman from Washoe has already said); I fully agree
(with the gentleman who has just taken his seat) that it is
unjust and unrighteous. I do think, Mr. President, that (as
has been suggested by the gentleman from Ormsby) we owe
it to our constituents to defeat this pernicious measure. Incorporate it into your Constitution, sir, and (as was eloquently and beautifully set forth in the speech of the gentleman from Storey) the gaunt forms of want, and poverty, and
starvation, and despair will shortly walk in the high places
of this once happy and beautiful land. Add it to your fundamental law, sir, and (as was stated yesterday by the gentleman from Lander) God will cease to smile upon your labors.
In the language (of my colleague), I entreat you, sir, and
gentlemen, inflict not this mighty iniquity upon generations
yet unborn! Heed the prayers of the people and be merciful!
Ah, sir, the quality of mercy is not strained, so to speak (as
has been aptly suggested heretofore), but droppeth like the
gentle dew from Heaven, as it were. The gentleman from
Douglas has said this law would be unconstitutional, and I
cordially agree with him. Therefore, let its corse to the ram-
parts be hurried—let the flames that shook the battle's wreck,

shine round it o'er the dead—let it go hence to that undiscovered country from whose bourne no traveler returns (as hath been remarked by the gentleman from Washoe, Mr. Stamp), and in thus guarding and protecting the poor miner, let us endeavor to do unto others as we would that others should do unto us (as was very justly and properly observed by Jesus Christ upon a former occasion).[5]

This composition is an excellent example of the creative imagination that made Mark Twain much more than a mere reporter of news events. The "verbatim" transcript is surely a parody yet, like all good parodies, it catches the manner of the original. If Mr. Sterns did not utter those precise words, he undoubtedly delivered an earnest speech similarly gaseous, repetitious, and poetically allusive. The burlesque flourishes give the whole a lift that makes the delegate from Aurora step from the page as a living person. Mark Twain's knack of reproducing the spirit and flavor of talk and situation—demonstrated over and over during his career as writer and speaker—was an important part of his equipment as an artist. That he used this equipment in Washoe shows that his "apprenticeship" there was not a fallow period of merely marking time.

He interrupted his stay in Carson to dash back to Virginia for an event described as a "presentation affair" that occurred either at Harris' saloon in Maguire's Opera House, or in a wine cellar under Kennedy & Malion's store on C Street. It was probably the occasion on which he was given a fake meerschaum pipe. The Visigoths instigated this joke, chiefly C. A. V. Putnam, Steve Gillis, and Denis McCarthy, to get back at Mark Twain for his jokes on them. Charley Pope, then playing at the Opera House, made the presentation speech. Gracefully he dwelt upon the wit and humor, the noble qualities of mind and heart of their esteemed comrade, then presented a pipe with a yard-long cherry stem festooned with ribbon, the bowl decorated with German silver bearing the inscription: "To Mark Twain from his friends." The honored recipient, having been forewarned of what he thought was a genuine testimonial dinner, expressed pleased surprise at the touching tribute, then responded with a prepared speech that, said Dan De Quille, "began with the introduction of tobacco into England by Sir Walter Raleigh, and wound up with George Washington."[6] Frequently interrupted by hearty applause and thunderously cheered at the end, he ordered up sparkling Moselle, at five dollars a bottle, until six bottles had gone around and around. A few days later, when he learned that the pipe was bogus and the whole thing a sell, he was grumpily hostile until Dan calmed him with the assurance that a genuine meerschaum, costing $45, was on the way. It has often been observed that Mark Twain, though fond enough in those days of playing practical jokes on others, did not relish having them played on him.

For the *Enterprise* he wrote an account of his speech:

Mr. Mark Twain being enthusiastically called upon, arose, and without previous preparation, burst forth in a tide of eloquence so grand, so luminous, so beautiful and so resplendent with the gorgeous fires of genius, that the audience were spell-bound by the magic of his words, and gazed in silent wonder in each other's faces as men who felt that they were listening to one gifted with inspiration. [Applause.] The proceedings did not end here, but at this point we deemed it best to stop reporting and go to dissipating, as the dread solitude of our position as a sober, rational Christian, in the midst of the driveling and besotted multiude around us, had begun to shroud our spirits with a solemn sadness tinged with fear. At ten o'clock the curtain fell.[7]

The facetious overpraise of that report is similar to the foolery he put into his self-introductions on the lyceum circuit several years later. In these, referring to himself as "the lecturer of the evening," he extolled "a gentleman whose eloquence, reliability and veracity are surpassed only by his personal comeliness and native modesty," elaborated with highflown words upon the lecturer's talents literary, historical, and linguistic, then casually announced that he was the man. In 1863, however, he was only an amateur speaker groping toward a realization that he had an astonishing aptitude for public performance. His several speeches had been received with considerable praise, and he had successfully competed with veterans, including Tom Fitch, who had a reputation as silver-tongued orator. Such occasions were tentative approaches to Mark Twain's full-scale platforming and after-dinner speaking of later years.

Once again in Carson City, he had a good opportunity to test his speaking powers before the Third House, which unanimously elected him its president. After this body met in a noisy session immediately following adjournment of the constitutional convention, Mark Twain wrote for the *Enterprise* a lively account of its proceedings, headed "Reported by Phonographic Short-Hand." The incoherence, irrelevance, ornate speeches, and stumbling remarks of Messrs. Stewart, Youngs, Ralston, Musser, and others, together with brusque sallies by the worthy president: all that, like the oration of Mr. Sterns, the reporter no doubt embroidered with fanciful additions. Indeed, at this meeting Mr. Sterns was well started on another wordy argument against taxation, agreeing with the gentleman from Storey County, when he was abruptly silenced by the chairman.[8]

Between the constitutional convention and the session of the Territorial Legislature occurred a break of three weeks, which Mark Twain spent in Virginia. The interval was anything but dull, for Artemus Ward came to town. This showman of "wax figgers" from "Baldinsville, Injiany," was so famous as humorous writer and speaker—"the American humorist, *par excellence*," Bret Harte called him—that Thomas

Maguire, San Francisco theater tycoon, backed the venture of bringing him all the way from New York to the West Coast. Landing in the Bay city on November 8, Ward became an instantaneous toast of the town. He met that engaging secessionist tomboy, Lillie Hitchcock, visited a Chinese theater, danced a jig on the gold-paved floor of Ralston's bank, and graciously responded to the overtures of well-wishers who saturated him with his favorite brandy and water. The first recital of his celebrated piece, "The Babes in the Wood," was an occasion of great éclat: Platt's Hall jammed with feverish people who deluged the ticket-taker with silver dollars; the stage crowded with late-comers perched on stools and empty wine cases; the Rev. Thomas Starr King on the platform; the speaker later serenaded at the Occidental Hotel by a brass band. After a second performance at the Metropolitan Theater and much more of San Francisco's open-handed hospitality, he barnstormed for about four weeks among interior California towns: Folsom, Marysville, Nevada City, Drytown, Sonora, Murphy's, and others. Everywhere he ingratiated himself by his humor, witty good nature, and an amiable reluctance ever to decline a drink.

Ward's intention of visiting Washoe alerted Virginia papers. "We understand," said the *Evening Bulletin*, "he has secured the services of Mark Twain and Dan De Quille to personate the babes, and will have a painting of the 'great pine forest' at Dutch Nick's to represent the woods."[9] Mark Twain gave him an advance notice in the *Enterprise*:

We understand that Artemus Ward contemplates visiting this region to deliver his lectures, and perhaps make some additions to his big "sho." In his last letter to us he appeared particularly anxious to "sekure a kupple ov horned todes; alsowe, a lizard which it may be perssesed of 2 tales, or any komical snaix, an enny sich little unconsidered trifles, as the poets say, which they do not interest the kommun mind. Further, be it nown, that I would like a opportunity for to maik a moddel in wax of a average size wash-owe man, with feet attached, as an kompanion pictur to a waxen figger of a nigger I have sekured, at an large outlaye, whitch it has a unnatural big hed onto it. Could you alsowe manage to gobbel up the skulp of the layte Missus Hoppins? I adore sich foot-prints of atrocity as it were, muchly. I was roomina-tin on gittin a bust of mark Twain, but I've kwit kontem-platin the work. They tell me down heer too the Ba that the busts air so kommon it wood ony bee an waist of wax too git un kounterfit presentiment." We shall assist Mr. Ward in every possible way about making his Washoe collection and have no doubt but he will pick up many curious things dur-ing his sojourn.[10]

The invented letter was Mark Twain's imitation of Ward's studied illiteracies, by which he was best known then and remembered today. Although he wrote for the Cleveland *Plain Dealer* a number of humorous sketches in straight Eng-lish, his hallmark is the weird-looking word and the garbled sentence. Modern readers are unlikely to be amused by ridiculous misspellings and fumbled grammar, but such de-vices were a fad at the time, used not only by Ward, but also by other popular funny men like Josh Billings, Petroleum V. Nasby, and Bill Arp. Sam Clemens himself used these tricks in the Thomas Jefferson Snodgrass letters written for the Keokuk *Saturday Post* in 1856-57, but fortunately he gave them up, learning instead to make his humor dependent upon character and situation rather than upon mechanics.

Nevertheless, Ward was a better man than he is generally considered today. Bret Harte, a perceptive critic, justly ob-served that the showman

deserves the credit of combining certain qualities which make him the representative of a kind of humor that has more of a national characteristic than the higher and more artistic standard. His strength does not lie simply in grotesque spell-

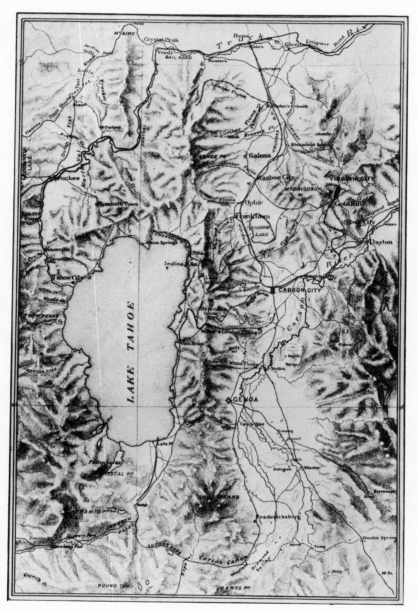

Map of the Comstock area

ing . . . but it is the humor of audacious exaggeration—of perfect lawlessness; a humor that belongs to the country of
boundless prairies, limitless rivers and stupendous cataracts.
. . . "his book" is the essence of that fun which overlies the
surface of our national life, which is met in the stage, rail
car, canal and flat boat, which bursts out over camp fires and
around bar-room stoves.[11]

Beneath the folksy manner and extravagant nonsense were
pointed social criticism, broad satire on human foibles, pretense, sentimentality, hypocritical patriotism. It is not surprising that he was a favorite of Lincoln, who must have relished the "Interview With President Lincoln," an exaggerated account of the President-elect overrun by hordes of of-
fice-seekers, and who once scandalized his Cabinet members
by reading them a Ward sketch as a prelude to a solemn con-
ference. As an adherent of the sensible-lunatic school, Ward
was spiritual ancestor of such twentieth-century zanies as
Robert Benchley, Ogden Nash, and S. J. Perelman. He had a
gift for the homely yet telling phrase, and his jokes—or
"goaks" as he called them—got into newspapers all over the
country. A well-known quip was his answer to Maguire's tele-
gram: "What will you take for forty nights in California?"
Ward wired back: "Brandy and water."

On December 19 Ward and his manager, E. P. Hingston,
set out over the Henness Pass from Placerville, known as
Hangtown, for Carson City and Virginia. Hingston, an Eng-
lishman, was so enthralled by the tremendous landscape that
he was moved to compose a poem, "Pictures in Silver-Land":

On my left a wall of granite—on my right a chasm deep,
Where, in man-untrodden ravines nature sleeps her virgin
    sleep.
Snow and pine trees—pines and snow-drift; mountain peaks
    and glaciers high,
Solemn grandeur, awful stillness—purest air and cloudless
    sky.

Beauteous Tahoe, clear and lucid, glassing in its mirror
  bright,
Every craggy peak around it golden in the morning light.[12]

Pausing in Carson City, Ward spoke in a theater that, he said,
"opens out of a drinking and gambling house. On each side
of the door where my ticket-taker stands there are monte-
boards and sweat-cloths, but they are deserted to-night, the
gamblers being evidently of a literary turn of mind."[13] That
place was only another variety of the curious halls of mining
camps he had performed in on the California tour. In one
town a saloon was his auditorium, the bar itself his platform,
the barkeeper pounding noisy encouragement with a bottle.

Then they went on to Virginia, where they spent a riotous
week in the company of the *Enterprise* staff, particularly of
Mark Twain and Dan De Quille, who were constant companions. Ward made the editorial rooms his headquarters.
Dropping in late at night after a speaking engagement, he
peeled off his coat and helped pull the local columns so that
he and the boys could go out on the town without needless
delay. Once he submitted an editorial with a letter:

Editor, *Enterprise*: I have long noticed the lack of forcible
and stirring editorials in your otherwise excellent journal.
Herewith you will find one of the character designated, which
you are free to accept along with the esteem of
                                            Artemus Ward[14]

Those remarks were mildly satirical, for Goodman's editorials
were anything but flabby. The "Bold chieftain with the vitreous eye," as Bret Harte called him, delighted in the strong
statement of bold attack, and he relished a ding-dong battle.
He printed Ward's editorial, which was a plea of behalf of an
old man named George D. Prentice who had "gone wrong,"
Goodman said, on the breaking out of the rebellion, but
whether personally or politically is not clear.

The famous visitor became as popular in Virginia as he had

been in San Francisco. His solemn visage and his habit of dropping into casual talk Biblical words like "yea," "verily," "prithee," made strangers take a second look, then burst out laughing, Ward doubling them up by looking around in straight-faced astonishment as if asking for an explanation of the joke. Mark Twain borrowed this trick, which he used with never-failing effect on the lecture platform. Ward could also be effusive in what he assumed to be a robust Western manner. When Mark Twain introduced him to the Rev. Franklin S. Rising, Episcopalian rector, without identifying the gentleman, Ward hailed him with great heartiness as "Old Two-Pan-One-Color," and all but slapped him on the back as he shouted, "Is the devil still in your dough pan?"[15]

The showman was all over the place, roaming the streets, seeing the sights, marveling at silver bars in the office of Wells Fargo, dining well and drinking copiously. "Artemus," said Hingston, "spends his spare time with Mark Twain, descending silver mines and visiting the strange places of the city."[16] The trip far down into the depths of the Gould & Curry was the subject of an amusing story in the *Enterprise,* unfortunately lost, by Ward or Mark Twain or both. As much at home hundreds of feet below as on the surface, Ward got on famously with miners, asking the meaning of mining terms and jotting down notes. Miners were so taken with him that they presented him with a heavy gold chain, a splendid gift except that it was too massive to wear with comfort. They "swear by him," said Hingston,

and have named a new mine after him—"The Artemus Ward Gold and Silver Mining Company." President, J. Gleason; Secretary, Mark Twain; Acting Manager, D. Wright de Quille; Treasurer, George Boulden; and Engineer, Joseph F. Lawrence, of San Francisco.[17]

Possibly such an outfit was actually organized, but the names of two *Enterprise* humorists among the officers suggest

that the company was as unreal as Dan De Quille's imaginary
mine, the Pewterinctum. The name does not appear in incor-
poration notices published daily in Washoe and San Francisco papers. Still, since the other officers seem bona fide, and
since the speculative spirit was strong in Virginia, where no
sort of business venture was too bizarre, it would not be
surprising to learn that the Artemus Ward Company issued
and sold a batch of splashily-colored stock certificates.

Poking into those "strange places," Ward and his cronies
visited Chinatown, where they were received with Oriental
courtesy and plied with rice brandy; they explored dance
halls noisy with hurdy-gurdy tunes and the pounding feet of
red-shirted miners. The press rallied around and duly reported. The interviewer for the Gold Hill *Daily News* said:

> We had the pleasure of an introduction to Artemus Ward,
> last evening, in Virginia. He was in company with Dan De
> Quille—the most witty writer in this territory. We never saw
> Artemus before, face to face, but we have often seen him in
> his book, and we confess that in person he is just about what
> we had pictured him out in "our mind's eye." In person he is a
> tall, thin, young man; aged perhaps twenty-seven years; fresh,
> healthy complexion; heavy growth of brown hair on his head,
> heavy mustache; a mouth not as large as a barn door, eyes
> that fairly sparkle with wit, and a soul (you can see it!) evi-
> dently brimful of the milk of human kindness, with a slather
> of creamy wit floating upon the surface. Artemus is a "brick,"
> and socially as social as the jolliest. Dan De Quille and
> Artemus Ward! To see the two tipping glasses together! 'Tis
> worth five dollars to see it.[18]

Of interest in that account is the reference to Dan De
Quille as number one territorial wit. In accord with the
popular estimate, this opinion showed that Mark Twain was
still playing second fiddle, still an uncertain quantity whom
readers considered unlikely to make much of a stir in the
world. It also showed how mistaken contemporary opinion

may be. On the following day the Gold Hill man, as an after-thought, mentioned Ward's nose, "a regular Duke of Wellington proboscis—a kind of inverted town-pump handle—(all great men have such noses)." Mark Twain, in one of his circuit lectures, described that remarkable nose as a promontory that "rambled on aggressively before him with all the strength and determination of a cow-catcher"; the prominent red mustache "seemed not unlike the unfortunate cow."

The flowing bowl overflowed at Chaumond's, Chauvel's, the International Hotel, and elsewhere. Presumably the talk was equally fluent and sparkling, but there is dissenting opinion. George E. Barnes, of the San Francisco *Call*, maintained that Ward was "one of the dullest companions that ever put legs under the mahogany." Mark Twain's conversation, he said, "was not brilliant, nor even interesting" because "he rarely gave tongue to the bright things that were evolved in his brain under the inspiring influence of time and congenial fellowship." Each of the pair, said Barnes, "kept the 'happy thoughts' in his brain till he could print them with profit, and this is the reason that, with both, conversation became nearly a lost art."[19]

Those statements by a contemporary who knew both men cannot be offhandedly dismissed. Still, it is hard to believe that Ward was dull when sufficiently animated by brandy and good company. What Barnes called dullness may have been Ward's way of being witty with an unsmiling air of such intense seriousness that the humor was not immediately apparent. Of Mark Twain, the overwhelming testimony is that he was a voluble conversationalist with friends like Twichell and Howells or with anybody else who stimulated him: for example, his one-time lecture partner, George W. Cable, and their jovial manager, Major J. B. Pond; with Dan De Quille, who never complained that his partner was uninteresting; with Petroleum V. Nasby, with whom he once talked all night; with casual acquaintances met on his travels, especially if they were innocently queer or countrified.

But he also relished the role of monologist fond of the spotlight front and center. Many stories tell of his holding forth at all sorts of gatherings, particularly of impromptu solo performances at Hartford dinner parties, when he rose from the table and strode about the room, waving his napkin while he entertained guests with a great flood of talk. Like all platformers he enjoyed being a prima donna, and Ward did also. Mark Twain emphasized this point when, some years later, he described for Thomas Bailey Aldrich an evening in Barnum's restaurant in Virginia:

present, Artemus Ward, Joseph T. Goodman, (editor and proprietor Daily "Enterprise"), and "Dan De Quille" and myself, reporters for same; remnants of the feast thin and scattering, but *such* tautology and repetition of empty bottles everywhere visible as to be offensive to the sensitive eye; time, 2:30 A. M.; Artemus thickly reciting a poem about a certain infant you wot of ["The Ballad of Babie Bell," by Aldrich], and interrupting himself and *being* interrupted every few lines by poundings of the table and shouts of "Splendid, by Shorzhe!" Finally, a long, vociferous, poundiferous and vitreous jingling of applause announces the conclusion, and then Artemus: "Let every man 'at loves his fellow man and 'preciates a poet 'at loves *his* fellow man, stan' up!—stan' up and drink health and long life to Thomas Bailey Aldrich!— and drink it *stanning!*" (On all hands fervent, enthusiastic, and sincerely honest attempts to comply.) Then Artemus: "Well—consider it stanning, and drink it just as ye are!" Which was done.[20]

On another occasion, at the International, Ward, selecting Mark Twain as a victim, got off one of his characteristic stunts, a baffling rigmarole of nonsense, which he delivered with his usual attitude of intense earnestness:

"Ah,—speaking of genius, Mr. Clemens, now, genius appears to me to be a sort of luminous quality of the mind, allied to a warm and inflammable constitution, which is inherent in the man, and supersedes in him whatever constitutional tendency he may possess, to permit himself to be influenced by such things as do not coincide with his preconceived notions and established convictions to the contrary. Does not my definition hit the nail squarely on the head, Mr. Clemens?"[21]

The puzzled listener had to ask for several repetitions, which became increasingly confusing, before he realized that he was being taken in. The definition of genius is Dan De Quille's version of the story. Mark Twain's is different; in "First Interview with Artemus Ward," he tells of a breakfast preceded by whiskey cocktails that make him believe his brains are addled when Ward embarks upon the same kind of solemn doubletalk about silver mining. Mark Twain himself adopted the device of the nonstop sentence, as in a sketch published in *The Californian* of August 26, 1865, entitled "The Facts Concerning the Recent Trouble Between Mr. Mark Twain and Mr. John William Skae of Virginia City."

The climactic party of the week occurred at Chaumond's on Christmas Eve after Ward's lecture at Silver City. At this one, which lasted most of the night, Ward proposed his well-known toast: "I give you Upper Canada." Why? "Because I don't want it myself." Goodman's big joke of the evening was to present to Ward the bill of $237, which the visitor paid after expressing chagrin over such a trifling tab.

Afterward the puckish showman led his companions a mad dance over Virginia rooftops, not a difficult feat in a town where the tops of houses on one street were about on a level with the next street higher up the slope of Mount Davidson. Skittering like night-prowling cats, they came near being shot by a watchman who took them for thieves. According to Paine, they were saved by Joe Goodman, who identified the roof-hoppers. Another version assigns the role of interventionist to J. B. "Kettle Belly" Brown, a prominent bon vivant who happened along just in time. Whereupon the watchman affably proffered a bottle, and after a sociable drink Kettle Belly joined the revelers in search of further adventures among bars and hurdy-gurdies. Joe Goodman touchingly described the conclusion of that strenuous night:

As the sun rose above the desert range and gilded the Sugar Loaf, Mount Davidson and Cedar Hill it shone likewise upon the porch of Fred Geizler's saloon, where, astride a barrel, sat Mark Twain, whom Artemus Ward, with a spoon, was diligently doping with mustard, while he inquired of the bystanders if they had ever seen a more perfect presentment of a subjugated idiot.[22]

The visiting showman held up under the fast pace with remarkable stamina, considering that he was not a robust man and that he had to pull himself together now and then for lecture engagements. He spoke his piece in Gold Hill, Silver City, Washoe City, and twice in Virginia. At his first performance in Maguire's Opera House he surprised the audience by walking on with a handkerchief held to his eyes as if overcome by grief. Then he announced the sad news that in the great international prizefight between the American, John Heenan, and the Britisher, Tom Sayers, our champion had been defeated. But, added Ward, he believed the nation would survive this disaster and might even experience happy days.

"The Babes in the Wood" pleased everybody except a sour critic of the Virginia *Union*. He contemptuously said that "A. Ward may be a great humorist East, but we can point out a dozen men in this town who can make better jokes and say funnier things, and more of them, in one hour, than Artemus can put into forty lectures upon the 'Babes in the Wood,' or any other subject."[23] That churlish overstatement was no doubt a reflection of pique, since the visiting celebrity was monopolized by the staff of the *Enterprise*. Nobody from the *Union* or the *Evening Bulletin* sat in on those all-night dinner parties or escorted Artemus anywhere around town.

Mark Twain was reported to have listened to the "Babes" with "solemnity of appearance" that gave way occasionally to a delayed "Haw! haw!" He praised its variety and fund of humor: "The man who is capable of listening to the 'Babes in the Wood' from beginning to end without laughing either inwardly or outwardly must have done murder, or at least meditated it, at some time during his life."[24] That comment brought the inevitable allusion to the wholesale slaughter of the Hopkins family.

Artemus Ward was the first writer and speaker with a national reputation to come within the orbit of Mark Twain, and he made the most of it. As an attentive student of Ward's writing, and respectful of its tremendous popularity, he borrowed ideas and phrasing, and imitated devices like tangled syntax and pseudo-seriousness. The showman performing in person was an object lesson in the humorous lecture technique of incoherence, exaggeration, *non sequitur,* and anticlimax. These Mark Twain would adopt and improve upon in his own speaking career. Ward's platform humor had an artlessness that was deceptive; his solemnity so muffled the point of a joke that an audience did not break into laughter until he had gone on. Then he paused, looking surprised and hurt at the unseemly interruption. Mark Twain as a lecturer used exactly the same tactics; with both the manner of delivery was more important than the material. Ward's famous "Babes" and his other standbys, the "Panorama" and "Artemus Ward Among the Mormons," do not seem funny in print, yet spoken they convulsed audiences American and British. Similar comments can be made about Mark Twain. In his development as a figure transcending local limits the visit of Ward to Virginia was of major importance. The likenesses between the two are marked and frequent. A Virginia

correspondent a few years later called Mark Twain "the celebrated 'Artemus Ward' of the Pacific coast."[25]

The visitor was also a valuable counselor in other ways.
Discerning in this sagebrush humorist a spark that others did
not see, Ward advised the *Enterprise* reporter about his writing, urged him to make his name known in the East, and
offered to write on his behalf "a powerfully convincing note"
to the editor of the New York *Sunday Mercury*. In that paper
of February 7, 1864, Mark Twain's humorous short piece,
"For Sale or to Rent," advertising second-hand territorial
officials rejected by the voters, was no doubt the first result of
Ward's assistance. Two weeks later in the *Mercury* appeared
"Those Blasted Children," an essay on the pleasures of suppressing noisy brats, preferably by mayhem. These items, together with "The Jumping Frog" in the New York *Saturday
Press* in 1865, made Mark Twain not entirely a stranger to
Eastern editors when he reached Manhattan in 1867.

Assiduous attention paid to Ward during his Virginia stay,
and the friendly aid that resulted, support the contention that
Mark Twain cultivated people who could be useful to him.
Joe Goodman said that the chief difference between Dan De
Quille and his partner was that the latter had "the commercial
instinct requisite for successfully marketing his talent,"[26] an
essential part of that instinct being an aptitude for knowing
the right people. This behavior was not reprehensible, but it
would appear in a better light if Mark Twain had shown
heartier gratitude for Ward's services. On the contrary, when,
after the great success of *The Innocents Abroad*, he was on
the way to a fame that would eclipse his tutor's, he seemed
half disdainful of the man to whom he owed much. His lecture on Ward, composed for the season of 1871-72, was more
cool than warm, more supercilious than gracious. Nevertheless, such an attitude does not discredit the normality of
Mark Twain's ambition to be somebody and to get some-

where. The urge was in character. It was natural that he should have looked beyond Washoe, unthinkable that, like Dan De Quille, he should have spent his life as a reporter in Virginia.

During the hilarious week the Local, like the visiting speaker, snatched moments from festive dining and drinking to attend to his duties for the paper. When he received a Christmas gift, inscribed "Mr. Twain—compliments of Miss Chase —Christmas, 1863," he acknowledged it in the *Enterprise*:

The handwriting disposed us to suspect treachery, and to regard the box as a deadly infernal machine. It was on this account that we got a stranger to open it. This precaution was unnecessary. The diabolical box had nothing in it but a ghastly, naked, porcelain doll baby. However, we are much obliged—we always had a hankering to have a baby, and now we are satisfied. The mythical "Miss Chase" helped us to do the business, and she has our cordial thanks for her share in it.[27]

The identity of Miss Chase is a mystery, and the point of her joke is lost upon us. She might have been a relative of any of several Chases in Virginia, Silver City, and Gold Hill; she might have been Dan De Quille or some other hoaxer using the name to signify Lizzie A. Chase, one of numerous claimants to the disputed authorship of "Rock Me to Sleep," a sentimental poem Mark Twain delighted to make fun of. There is at least a tenuous connection between the porcelain doll baby and those nostalgic verses about childhood: "Backward, turn backward, O time, in your flight, / Make me a child again, just for tonight!"

Ward's last night in Virginia was a rouser. At a dinner party with Mark Twain and others he got more than usually drunk. Afterward, wandering away by himself, he said, "I went and got drunker, beating, I may say, Alexander the Great in his most drinkinist days."[28] In a mood of alcoholic exuberance he blacked up like an end man and went on stage with the minstrel troupe performing "Three Black Crows" at Niagara Hall. When the audience discovered him, it called for "The Babes in the Wood." He responded with a short talk—"a gibbering, idiotic speech," he called it—and bowed out by saying that he hoped to see them in New York, where he trusted they would all be sober. This escapade raised a few eyebrows. "He made an ass of himself," said the San Francisco *Call*. "Artemus' success in California and the Territory has been so far beyond his expectations that he has been thrown off his poise; and does some remarkable fooling outside of his lecturing."[29]

In Virginia the fooling was superlative; Hingston admitted, with British restraint, that Ward "lived pretty freely" there. Freely enough. He threw himself into experience with such intensity that Joe Goodman's recollection was of a man "bright and handsome as a young Apollo, but exhausting himself by foolish excess and feverish activity, as if aware of his early doom and endeavoring to crowd the utmost into the brief interval of life."[30] For two months after his departure the Virginia *Evening Bulletin* ran the following ad:

Artemus Ward

who is one of the Best Judges of Liquors and Cigars on the Great American Continent, during his sojourn in our city always took his drinks at

WINN & CENTER'S

New Saloon on C Street, next door to McLaughlin & Root's Hardware Store, where he says he was *never better treated—nor oftener—*in his life.

Dissipation in Virginia and elsewhere probably abetted the onset of a nearly fatal attack of mountain fever that shortly afterward laid him low for over a month in Salt Lake City.

On December 29 Ward and his manager set out in a mud wagon for Austin, 180 miles away. Faithful companions gathered to see them off and to bestow going-away presents: a demijohn of whiskey, feet in a mine somewhere behind Mount Davidson, a pouch of tobacco, a bowie knife guaranteed to have killed two men. Mark Twain presented a copy of the *Enterprise*, Dan De Quille a sackful of hardboiled eggs. From Austin, writing to Mark Twain on New Year's Day, Ward called that town "a wild, untamable place, but full of lion-hearted boys," and sent regards to Washoe friends: "I shall always remember Virginia as a bright spot in my existence, and all others must or rather cannot be, 'as it were.'" Mark Twain, publishing part of this letter in the *Enterprise,* said: "I am glad that old basket-covered jug holds out. I don't know that it does, but I have an impression that way. At least I can't make anything out of that last sentence. But I wish him well, and a safe journey, drunk or sober."[31]

Chapter Six

EBBING TIDE

❧❧❧

BY THE END of 1863 the high tide of Virginia prosperity showed signs of gradual ebbing. The symptoms puzzled and aggrieved everybody, as if a retrograde movement could be only a spiteful joke played by malign fate. Yet portents were visible. Street traffic had thinned out, but now and then, particularly on Saturdays, the place came alive with swirling crowds that looked like business as usual. For the time being, momentum generated by months of flush times was strong enough to encourage zealous optimism. On January 3, 1864, the *Enterprise* proudly reported that in eleven days bullion from the Gould & Curry, Ophir, and Savage amounted to $275,000, and that during the previous year the Territory had produced $11,042,458.95, six and a half millions having gone out from the Virginia office of Wells Fargo. Confidently the paper predicted that the total for 1864 would be three times as great. The forecast was an expansive overestimate. The territorial total for '64 was indeed larger than that of the year before, but by only one-third.

News traveling slowly and Washoe still being proclaimed a symbol of silvery promise, the region continued to attract adventurers. The San Francisco *Alta California,* lamenting the annual spring "swarming from the California hive" of thousands of treasure-seekers, mentioned the Territory as one of a dozen destinations. Over the mountain passes to Virginia rode and tramped a steady parade of immigrants, who were about as numerous as the horde of '63. Still potent was the legend of the Comstock Lode as a repository of endless riches. Yet indications of impending decay were apparent to the discerning. In some Virginia business houses appeared the unfamiliar sign "To Let." Among the throngs milling along the streets a good many were idlers who had nothing to do but amble aimlessly and be grateful for the diversion of dogfights. The town had suffered from the exodus of restless people who had drifted away to Boise or Salmon River, and to the latest attraction, the Reese River district around Austin, 180 miles to the east. Soon after this mining region opened up in 1862, a stampede began. From Virginia the rush was so great that stages could not carry them all, but they took off anyhow by mule back or on foot. The road between the two towns, said one traveler, was very bad,

most horrible from dust and "chugholes," and the trip is intensely tiresome; but despite all drawbacks people are rushing over in swarms. Not less than 400 teams are en route, loaded with almost every article needed in a new country. One-half take lumber, one-fourth have dry goods, hardware, etc., while the other fourth is something to eat and drink—whisky predominating.[1]

Chugholes, tiresome journey, and all other hardships attendant upon getting to the makeshift tent and shanty town of Austin did not modify the delirious habit of rushing from place to place, a custom that had been regularly observed since the days of '49. In every mining town were footloose citizens who seemed to have no settled occupation; they toiled not very much, neither did they spin, but hung on somehow until alerted by word of spectacular strikes somewhere else. Then the cry was Ho! for Gold Lake, Gold Beach, Cariboo, Gold Bluff, Kern River, Fraser River, Pike's Peak,

Slate Range, or any of twenty other El Dorados as the nervous
ones pulled up stakes and lit out pell-mell for the new camp.
Then, before long, it was again Ho! as they repeated the
process over and over, lured by one chimera after another,
each imagined to be the longed-for "big thing," complete with
lush meadows, bubbling springs, verdant forests, and nuggets
the size of hens' eggs. The far-off hills were always greener, or
more golden. Virginia was said to have lost a third of its
population in this way.

Mark Twain had taken notice of the furor over the Reese
River district:

Capt. W. Alpheus Smith, formerly of the steamer *Amazonia,* Mississippi river—we recollect the boat pretty well,
and so will others of our citizens—navigated in yesterday,
from Reese river, where he has been taking the bearings of
the country and gobbling up mining claims. He got control-
ling interests in the Barclay & Smith, the Amazonia and the
Ann Smith ledges, and has returned with the impression that
he needs no more. We hope it may prove so; but then twenty-
four hundred feet, in a new country like Reese river, seems a
very small amount for a man to be satisfied with. However,
these ledges are respectively eighteen, ten and twenty-five
feet wide, and the specimens which Capt. Smith brings from
there are exceedingly rich; one from the Amazonia had been
roasted, and was entirely covered with a delicate frostwork
of pure silver. These leads are situated about nine miles from
Clifton. The population of Reese river is steadily increasing,
and Capt. Smith says that trading in town lots, in Clifton
and Austin, is becoming a business among some of the citizens; the ruling price for single lots is $200, and choice ones
range even as high as $500.[2]

It is interesting to note, in passing, that neither that squib
nor any other of his mining items hints at a recurrence of the
mania that had induced him, about two years before, to rush
off to the diggings. Apparently he had had enough of that.

Besides emigration, other signs of retrogression, equally

ominous, were the slipping values of Washoe mining shares, which were the economic barometers of the Territory. In December, 1863, stock of the Gould & Curry was down to $4,950, and within the next five months it dropped to $3,300. In the same period Ophir fell from $1,500 to $760, Savage from $2,750 to $1,500. Chollar, which had nose-dived from $1,200 to $250, made a slight recovery. Within a year after the high point, about the middle of '63, values had declined on an average about thirty per cent. The situation caused unhappy concern, but the best explanations hopeful analysts could offer were that close-fisted San Francisco bankers had created a tight money market, and that rascally operators had rigged transactions.

The major mining companies were paying dividends, varying from the Savage's $5 a foot to the Gould & Curry's $125. Those figures, too, were below the payoffs of flush times. Nevertheless, these companies, though down a little, were not out, and confidence marched with the familiar swagger of bonanza profits. When the Board of Equalization announced to C. L. Strong, superintendent of the Gould & Curry, that the company's improvements had been assessed at $800,000, the news was a minor detail. He shrugged it off with the casual assurance that the company would not grumble if the Board increased the assessment by $300,000, thus showing a debonair indifference to taxes that would no doubt appear eccentric in the board room of a modern corporation. Stocks were depressed, but the old Comstock spirit of reliance upon the full coffer was undiminished.

Yet spirit alone was not enough. Every day Washoe and San Francisco papers published pages of notices of assessments on mining stock, from 20 cents to $5 a share; and notices of assessment sales, with lists of stockholders whose stock would be sold at public auction for non-payment of assessments. Columns of notices showed that a great many mines were unproductive, and that the companies owning them were in financial distress. One happy-go-lucky fellow said philosophically:

Have I not "feet" still? Indeed, I have—hundreds—and were I disposed to ignore the "feet" I could not well do it, for every paper tells me so, compiled with a few appended figures, which, if not rubbed out in the legitimate way, by payment of assessments, will be by sales at public auction. But such advertisements are no disgrace. They apply to almost everybody.[3]

In Virginia and San Francisco, by the end of the year, hysterical trading in feet had become less intense as sober speculators turned to more reliable investments, and reckless plungers had been eliminated because they were cleaned out.

"The times here at present," said a Virginia correspondent in December, 1863,

may be best explained by the words dull, duller, dullest. The contrast between C street of a month ago and the C street of the present, is great. Then, it was so blocked by incoming and outgoing teams, and by crowds of hurrying men, that a passage through it was no easy matter. Now, it is comparatively deserted, and its many saloons lack for patronage. . . . This stringency is in nothing more marked than in the wonderful depression of "feet," and especially such as represent "wild-cat." . . . almost at every corner can men be seen mounted on barrels . . . trying to dispose of stock for non-payment of assessments.[4]

The slacking-off brought increasing unemployment. Men without jobs faced a hard winter, but prices remained high: potatoes six cents a pound, bread twenty-five cents a loaf. According to J. Ross Browne, a veteran traveler,

There are more people now in Virginia than the business of the place requires. . . . My belief is that Virginia City will gradually become what Nature intended it to be—a mere depot for the trade and products of the Comstock lead. . . . It does not possess a single inducement beyond what is based on mineral productions.⁵

The hope was that the coming of spring would cause an upturn, when, in the words of an optimistic reporter, "silver by the million will be disemboweled from mother earth, and enrich the entire population of the country."⁶ Yet another undaunted forecaster predicted a territorial population of five million in ten years:

her alkali plains will be threaded with railroads; she will be connected by rail with the Pacific and Atlantic oceans. Mines, rich as the Ophir, will be successfully worked in all parts of the Territory.⁷

The rosy view bemused many who would not, could not, believe that reaction might ever assail this affluent silverland.

It need not be supposed that, in the face of dull times, the gusty metropolis of Virginia became a ghost town overnight, or that it lost its air of devil-may-care. The slowdown, symptomatic of changes that overtook all mining regions, did not silence subterranean blasts of miners or the spasmodic reports of five-shooters. One January day's record of a suicide, an assault with deadly weapon upon a woman, a husband's attempt to shoot his wife, and a stabbing induced in a California editor familiar reflections upon "an exceedingly bad state of morals in Virginia City. . . . This is worse than Mokelumne Hill in its palmiest days when they had a man for breakfast every Sunday."⁸ Buffalo Jo did her part to keep up the reputation of the town. When she and a gentleman friend walked into the Washington Hotel on C Street and announced their intention of taking over the premises, the landlady promptly put the escort out of action by whacking him over the head with a stool. Then the ladies tangled in a scratching, hair-pulling bout that overturned furniture, smashed the front windows, and filled the air with hoarse cries of battle. Both landed in jail.

The state of Virginia morals was about the same as usual, but when saloon keepers complained of poor business on Sunday, ordinarily their best day, the Gold Hill *Daily News* hailed this development as a victory for righteousness. Business on the other six days was good enough to make up for Sabbath abstention, for the ninth lager beer brewery was under construction, this one being sorely needed, somebody said, because of the permanent Virginia residence of John Tahoe, *né* Bigler.

The flamboyant gesture was still evident. Bally Green, stage driver on the Pioneer Line, was presented with a brass watch big enough to dwarf all other watches: four and a half inches in diameter, two inches thick, weight seven and a half pounds, attached to a chain four feet long and a fob of polished split leather. When a man heard that a barrel of whiskey contained strychnine enough to kill sixteen men, he tried to commit suicide on C Street by drinking a sixteenth of a barrel. Those in the money pursued the policy of free spending. The Virginia *Union* commented on the frequency of extravagant purchases:

The prevailing taste demands the best of everything, and any merchant or mechanic, or artist, will tell you that the most superior articles have the most ready sale. . . . Household economy and bachelor fare present items of expense which would startle the denizens of any other place but this.[9]

As the town headed into a recession, the confident stride may have faltered somewhat, but the pace was far from doddering.

No hint of decrepitude muted the noisy wrangle over the merits of the new constitution that, if adopted, would transform Nevada Territory into a state. This document, having been discussed since the convention had completed its labors on December 11, 1863, would be submitted to the

voters on January 19, 1864. After the first of the year the·
debate became intense.

The Virginia papers plunged into a fierce triangular fight
that filled the air with missiles, the Gold Hill *Daily News*
lobbing bombs over the Divide. Of the principal combatants,
the *Enterprise* was in favor of the constitution; the *Union*,
having started on the pro side, had suddenly switched to the
antis. They traded blows, and both berated the *Evening
Bulletin* as insignificant, contemptible, and stupid. The
Union's abrupt shift of position made it vulnerable, opponents claiming that the paper had changed sides only because
John Church, one of its proprietors, had failed to get the
nomination for state printer. The *Enterprise* called the *Union*
the Weathercock, and Virginia Daily Stultifier, "bartered,
abandoned, unprincipled and daily stultifying itself," and
accused it of secessionism, alleging that Church had once
been heard to cheer for Jeff Davis. The *Union* retorted with a
blast at "Our Treasonable Cotemporary," a paper "published
in this city, and sometimes seen in the saloons about town."
The *Evening Bulletin* called the *Union* "our sore-headed,
tender-souled and incorruptible cotemporary;" the Gold
Hill *Daily News* labeled it a "contemptible, word-eating,
blackmail sheet" that got its straw votes by polling drunken
bummers in groggeries. The *Union* called the *Bulletin* "that
venal purchasable smut-machine," and dismissed the *News*
as only a yapping poodle dog. Everybody accused everybody
else of bribery and corruption: the *Enterprise* of being under
the thumb and in the pocket of "Bill Stewart & Co.;" the
Bulletin of having received $500 from Henry Edgerton to
further his senatorial aspirations, and the same amount from
Judge C. H. Morgan, who had his eye on the supreme court;
the *Union* of being in the pay of the Burning Moscow people
to abuse Stewart, and of having received a substantial re-
tainer from the anti-constitution crowd to defeat the consti-

tution; the Gold Hill *Daily News* of having been bought by
the pro-constitutionalists. All denied the charges and denounced accusers as wanton liars, frauds, poltroons, black-
guards unspeakable.

These fusillades dramatized issues that aroused tremendous interest throughout the Territory. Among voters, Southern sympathizers opposed the constitution because of Article
I, Section 2, which said that "the paramount allegiance of
every citizen is due to the Federal Government," and denied
the right of any state "to impair, subvert or resist the supreme
authority of the Government of the United States;" and because Nevada would enter as a free state with three electoral
votes that would probably be pro-Union. Secesh opposition
led the *Enterprise* to say that all constitutional opponents
were tinged with copperheadism. That statement was extravagant, for objectors included a great many staunch Union
men who complained on grounds economic rather than political. The loudest protests arose over a provision requiring
the taxing of undeveloped mining property. That proviso,
ran the negative argument, meant bankruptcy for mine owners. Another opposition point was that the cost of running a
state government was prohibitive, so far in excess of income
that Nevada would probably go deeply into debt, as California had.

One more objectionable part was Article XVII, Section 5,
which required that state and county officials created by the
constitution, also United States senators and representatives,
be elected at the same time that the constitution itself was
voted on. People believed that this provision opened the door
to second-rate politicians, conveniently forgetting that political hacks are not created by proviso, and that they are
never the exclusive property of one side. In the heated exchange of newspaper opinion voters also appeared to forget
that an editor labored to defeat only those hacks who be-

longed to a clique other than his own. The general feeling, said one reporter, was that, if the constitution were adopted, "the new State will be intrusted to the hands of incompetent men who will act . . . in the interest of a few selfish capitalists—owners in the chief companies, who aver that there is but one ledge in the Territory and that that is the Comstock." Among those considered capitalist henchmen was William M. Stewart, represented as "a high muk-a-muk," who "lives in the most showy residence in town, excepting perhaps that of Charley Strong, Superintendent of the Gould & Curry."[10]

Sharp criticism concentrated on Stewart, or "Billstewart" as he was sometimes called. Said the Washoe City *Old Pah-Utah*:

Wonder if Bill Stewart, Sandy Baldwin, Jil Hardy, and a few more "intensely loyal" gentlemen like themselves, have got an order from Jeff Davis to support the State Constitution?[11]

That was probably a reflection of the fear that ratification would somehow permit secessionists to take over the state government—a curious point of view considering strong secesh opposition. The Visalia, California, *Delta*, reporting Stewart's threat to move the capital from Carson City if Ormsby County did not vote right, resorted to Biblical analogy:

Our Saviour was taken up into a high mountain by the devil, who told him he would give unto him all the land he saw for his possession if he would fall down and worship him, when the d——d old scoundrel hadn't even a squatter's right to a foot of it.[12]

Actually, Stewart's position was not very clear. Having endorsed the constitution at the outset, he later took an equivocal position, as if to undermine the document. On the critical taxation issue he straddled by arguing that the courts could use discretion in determining whether or not an excavation was a mine, and that it was not a mine if no minerals had been dug out of it. Mark Twain, having fun with Bill Stewart's "construing" the constitution to demonstrate that a hole in the ground was not necessarily a mine, cited "The Great Gould & Curry Hole-in-the-Ground."

Determined opponents formed a vigorous Anti-State Organization that, by means of county executive committees, put its case before the people with campaign tactics: band music, posters, newspaper propaganda, mass meetings, forceful speakers. The Storey County committee, with headquarters in Virginia, was an able body composed of David S. Turner, William A. M. Van Bokkelen, Almarin B. Paul, and others. Its motto was "No Constitution!" and it offered a prize of a twenty-four-foot American flag to the county polling the largest majority against on voting day. When the *Enterprise* published letters of William Higby and John Conness, sent to Goodman from Washington, D.C., saying that the administration urgently desired statehood for Nevada, the antis placarded Virginia streets with a reply:

Editor of *Old Piute*—My Dear Sir: I understand that bogus dispatches are in circulation in your Territory, purporting to come from Chase, Conness and Higby. Permit me to say there is nothing in it. We don't care a d——n about it, whether you become a State or not.

Yours, truly,
A. Lincoln

N.B. Bill Seward is with us.[13]

Joe Goodman was in his element. He loved a fight and, like other outspoken members of his staff, he had no qualms about making enemies. Trouncing dissenters with great energy, he defended his position vigorously and, since he was a poet, at times rhapsodically. "Our destiny," said he on the eve of decision, "hangs upon the result—bright and beautiful as the Bow of Promise if the Constitution be adopted; but dark and gloomy with portents of evil, if it be rejected."[14] In the same issue he addressed a fervent appeal to

Union Men of Nevada!—Would you vote against the adoption of the constitution if you knew you were opposing the wishes of the Administration? Would you oppose Old Abe? We think not.

The conflict naturally embroiled Mark Twain. Having reported the constitutional convention, he had praised its "large proportion of men of distinguished ability," and concluded: "We shall have a Constitution we need not be ashamed of, rest assured."[15] Standing with his paper in advocating adoption, he seemed at first confident, then became doubtful as opposition gathered head. From Carson City he wrote on January 4 that the constitution was

an excellent piece of work in some respects, but it had one or two unfortunate defects which debarred it from assuming to be an immaculate conception. The chief of these was a clause authorizing the taxing of mines. The people will not stand that. . . . I am satisfied they will refuse to ratify our constitution on the 19th inst.[16]

Therefore, as if giving up the fight, he said in the same letter: "when men say, 'Let our constitution slide for the present,' we say Amen." Yet forceful remarks in a later dispatch, on January 12, muttered no spineless Amens:

As I said before, the people of Ormsby will oppose the Constitution. O, certainly they will! They will if they are sick—or sentimental—or consumptive—or don't know their own interests—or can't see when God Almighty smiles upon them, and don't care anyhow. Now if Ormsby votes against the Constitution, let us clothe ourselves in sackcloth and put ashes on our heads; for in that hour religious liberty will be at an end here—her next step will be to vote against her eternal salvation.[17]

That outburst, cryptic in its reference to religious liberty, implies his own strong endorsement of the constitution and consequently of statehood. Seven years later in *Roughing It,* however, he records his belief that the Territory could not have supported a state government,

since it had nothing to tax that could stand a tax, for undeveloped mines could not, and there were not fifty developed ones in the land . . . and it did seem as if nobody was ever going to think of the simple salvation of inflicting a money penalty on murder.

Those statements make his position, in retrospect, seem uncertain, but the *Roughing It* point of view does not appear in his *Enterprise* letters of 1864. His contemporaries had no doubts about where he stood; they considered him, along with Stewart, a constitutional supporter.

Voting day was a carnival in Virginia. Business houses closed, and the holiday spirit brought on a number of good fights, one of the best being a brisk encounter in which a butcher attempted to decapitate his adversary with a cleaver. His aim was poor, and he succeeded only in gashing his man from forehead to chin. Band wagons, representing both sides, rolled around town all day, musicians playing "John Brown's Body," "Hail Columbia," "Yankee Doodle." Decorating the wagons were garish slogans: "Vote the Constitution and Union," "Vote Down the Constitution and Taxation," "Down with the one lead party, Bill Stewart and the other Politicians," "White Men vote anywhere—Niggers can't." At night a huge transparency opposite Stewart's law office depicted the burial of the constitution.

Throughout the Territory voters rejected statehood by an impressive majority of five to one, Humboldt County winning the Storey Executive Committee's prize flag for polling the best negative percentage. Western secession papers hailed the result as a victory for anti-Unionism. Said the

Marysville, California, *Express,* a noted copperhead journal: "All manner of means were resorted to by the vile Abolitionists to cram the Constitution down the throats of the people, but all to no avail."[18] Said another equally rabid sheet, the Grass Valley, California, *National*: "Our folks put it up to help slaughter that free nigger Constitution, and may be they didn't succeed! 'Oh, no!' "[19]

Pro-Union opponents of the constitution were uncomfortable at finding themselves voting on the same side as secessionists, but Washoe editors unfavorable to statehood ignored that awkward misalliance as they cheered the outcome. John K. Lovejoy, the salty character who ran the Washoe City *Old Pah-Utah,* let go:

Forty thousand guns and several hundred anvils for Nevada Territory! Let the mountain torrents leap for joy and the sagebrush emit doubly their perfume. May all the lambs, young widows and jackass rabbits joyfully gambol together on our sunny plains. . . . Bill Stewart & Co. are busted out, and some of the balance of us are busted in. Whoop! We'll all be happy yet. If we have wounded the feelings of anybody in the campaign, we'll allow him to forgive us "in a horn" of whisky.[20]

The San Francisco *Alta California* congratulated the people of the Territory on their triumph over the "professionals—the men who labored for the establishment of a State Government, solely for the purpose of becoming Senators and Governors, and living in luxury at the expense of the masses."[21]

On the day after the voting the Gold Hill *Daily News,* pro-constitution during the campaign, took its defeat like a sportsman by running an announcement under the heading "All Aboard!":

The good old ship "Constitution," Captain Bill Stewart, master, and George W. Bloor, pilot, will leave the wharf in front of the Bank Exchange, Gold Hill, at sunrise to-morrow

morning, for the head of Salt River. . . . Mark Twain is expected to get aboard at Carson City, with the seat of government in his breeches.

The next day the *News,* reporting the sailing on schedule and
the distribution to each passenger of "a bottle of Constitution peppermint, a copy of the Union Platform . . . and a
clay pipe," again said that the ship would stop a few hours
at Carson City "to take on board several gentlemen who are
entitled to a passage, not the least of whom is Mark Twain,
Esq., the historian of the Hopkins family; Sandy Baldwin,
and several others."

The reverse at the polls deferred statehood for about nine
months. Another convention met in July to frame a new constitution. This body revised the objectionable mining tax
proviso to make it apply only to the proceeds of mines, not the
property; and rejected the pleas of romanticists to make the
name of the state officially Washoe. On September 7 voters
approved the second document by a majority as large as that
by which they had killed the first. Both convention and voting
occurred without fuss or bitter controversy in an atmosphere
of public calm that looked like apathy compared to the combative mud-slinging of eight months before. The January
argument that a state government was too costly was much
stronger in September, when values of stocks and real estate
had depreciated, but nobody fulminated about that point.
It was as if the ammunition locker were empty, all the fire-
works having been shot off the first time. On October 31
Lincoln proclaimed Nevada the thirty-sixth state, just in time
to vote in the critical presidential election. The infant responded nobly by rolling up a plurality of 3,000 for Lincoln.

The defeat of the first constitution also defeated the slate
of candidates put up by the Nevada State Nominating Committee. Out of that rejection came Mark Twain's facetious
"For Sale or to Rent," which, as already noted, introduced

him to Eastern editors via the New York *Sunday Mercury*. Among the discarded officials advertised there was "One Secretary of State," who was his brother, Orion. The ad described him as

An old, experienced hand at the business. Has edited a newspaper, and been Secretary and Governor of Nevada Territory —consequently is capable; and also consequently will bear watching; is not bigoted—has no particular set of religious principles—or any other kind.

The *Enterprise* noted differences between the brothers when it characterized Orion as "a gentleman beloved by all who know him. In addition to all his positive recommendations, he is a brother of that 'moral phenomenon,' Mark Twain."[22]

Those comments are illuminating. Love, like that of Ben Jonson for Shakespeare, infused those few associates of Mark Twain who succeeded in penetrating his inner defenses. There was no question about the steadfast regard of Dan De Quille, Joe Goodman, and Steve Gillis. According to Paine, Steve's last message was: "Tell Sam I'm going to die pretty soon, but that I love him; that I've loved him all my life, and I'll love him till I die."[23] Such affection is remarkable and enviable—but it was far from the emotion he inspired in all who knew him. They were as likely as not to be puzzled over how to take him, or to be rubbed the wrong way as to feel good will. Unlike Orion, Mark Twain was not generally regarded as a lovable person in Washoe.

In Carson City to report the third Territorial Legislature, which sat from January 12 to February 20, he sent to the *Enterprise* day-by-day summaries of doings in the House. In addition, he wrote his usual mixture of comments political, social, and personal. The topics—Miss Clapp's school, Mr. Lawlor's school, Theodore Winters' new house, the extortionate prices charged by Carson City undertakers—made his dispatches something like the miscellanies of the columnist who has a free hand to fill his space with whatever takes his fancy. One of his best stories ridiculed the many applications for notarial appointments. The legislature having revoked all existing notaries' commissions and limited the number of new ones for each county—eight for Storey, ten for Lander, four for Ormsby, and so on—there was a great scramble among applicants. Mark Twain, professing surprise at having found a man who had applied to the governor for a notary's commission, kept up the pretense:

Think of it. Ponder over it. He wanted a notarial commission—he said so himself. He was from Storey county. He brought his little petition along with him. He brought it on two stages. It is voluminous. The County Surveyor is chaining it off. Three shifts of clerks will be employed night and day on it, decyphering the signatures and testing their genuineness. They began unrolling the petition at noon, and people of strong mining propensities at once commenced locating claims on it. We are too late, you know. But then they say the extensions are just as good as the original. I believe you.[24]

This news, he found, "does not amount to much as a sensation item, after all," because he discovered "seventeen hundred and forty-two applications for notaryships already on file in the Governor's office. . . . as much as eleven cords of petitions stacked up in his back yard." On the street, he said, would-be notaries buttonholed him, among them Chief Justice Turner, William M. Stewart, Judge Baldwin, Judge North, Washoe Jim, Ah Foo, Hong Wo, Wells Fargo, and "seventy-two other prominent citizens of Storey county, with a long pack-train laden with their several petitions." This burlesque, "Concerning Notaries," appeared in *The Golden Era* of February 28.

One significant event of the Carson stay was Mark Twain's delivery, before the Third House and others, of what was called his Third Annual Message. Given at the request of the trustees of the local Presbyterian Church, this speech, on January 27, attracted a large audience at a dollar a head to the district courtroom of the Ormsby County courthouse. Hal Clayton presided, and everybody of any consequence was there. The text of this message has not survived, but it was said to have been humorous and satirical at the expense of Governor Nye, the Third House, and territorial officers. The speaker was pleased to have drawn a bigger crowd than Artemus Ward, and he was gratified by the congratulations of various notables. When he heard that Judge Sandy Baldwin and Theodore Winters had each sent $100 to San Francisco to buy a watch for "Governor Mark Twain," he was set up: "a pretty good result," he said, "for an incipient oratorical slouch like me, isn't it?"[25]

On this speaking performance, his first before a mixed audience that had paid to hear him, a judicious estimate of whether or not he was really an "oratorical slouch" would be useful, but little criticism exists. A correspondent named "China," of the Gold Hill *Daily News,* promised to send a phonographic transcript, but it did not appear. Clement Rice, the Unreliable, mentioned the "effervescing spirit" of the message of "Mark Two," but that was partly hearsay because he also said that, after squirming awhile in a room heated to suffocation by a roaring fire and tightly closed windows, he walked out. The most comprehensive remarks came from a stern critic of the Virginia *Union,* called "Meriden," who reprehended Twainian humor in a sweeping condemnation:

San Francisco has its "Norton First." The City of Virginia has its "Mark Twain." The first has anointed himself Emperor of all the United States of America .   the second has constituted himself the burlesque Governor of Nevada Territory. . . . The burlesque Governor is grotesque in his manner, and studious . . . for high attainments as a satirist and humorist. The burlesque Emperor is grotesque in appearance and has none of that cunningness of egotism which distinguishes his contemporaneous potentate. . . . The burlesque Governor has several *fortes*, all of which are indulged in through a vulgar estimate of ordinary occurrences. A true satirist will ridicule the follies of the times, in direct and polished terms, and will separate his subjects from the grave details of matters undeserving . . . harsh and flippant expressions. He will never attempt to affect a neuralgic contempt for himself and all human relations, that he may succeed in bringing a matter, displeasing only to himself, into contempt; or that he may assert a privilege of playing loosely with moral and serious points; or, that he may exhibit a noticeable style of "peculiar wit." The style of the burlesque Governor is . . . disconnected from genial originality and variation. His originality is like that of the literary bubble known as "Artemus Ward," whose assumed name, even, is not, as some may suppose, a quaintly original conception. It was stolen from the times of 1775, when it was honorably borne by one of the first generals appointed by the Continental Congress.[26]

This reviewer went on to complain of the disgusting clownishness of Ward and Twain, and to disapprove, justly, of the latter's belief that wit was implicit in the frequent and tiresome "as it were" and "so to speak," likewise in the wearisome reference to something as "an infernal humbug." Then he concluded with a slap at vulgarities "contemptible in the literary sense, and equally scandalizing to the reportorial profession."

That diatribe was another round in the continuous running fight between the *Union* and the *Enterprise*. Of the two, the *Union* was the more serious-minded, more solemn, more preachy. It was successful with readers who preferred the humdrum pace of the plodder to the other's sometimes erratic impulses, but it lacked the virility of the *Enterprise* because, though not devoid of capable writers like Tom Fitch and Rice, it had no array of talent to match the versatility of Mark Twain, Joe Goodman, Dan De Quille, and Rollin

Daggett. Meriden's harsh criticism was in part deserved, but it also shows that not all Westerners had for breezy Western humor the appreciation that has generally been assumed. Even so careless a place as Virginia had its genteel people who, like Meriden, were offended by unpolished language. Mark Twain's only retort to the *Union's* damning indictment was a slurring reference in a Carson letter of February 5 to "one of our Miss Nancy 'Meriden' Prosecuting Attorneys."

Back in Virginia by the latter part of February, the political reporter became again the Local. Of city news in the *Enterprise*, miscellaneous items seem written in the spirit of Mark Twain, if not always precisely in his style. There was the story of a man hauled into court, who said that his business was "Rough gambling":

We looked sharply at the man who claimed so singular a trade. A pair of small black eyes, scarcely bigger than peas, twinkled under . . . heavy, black eyebrows, each hair of which appeared to project straight in the direction to which the eyes underneath were directed. A heavy, black, sailor like beard encircled his chin and covered his cheeks. The mouth was the only redeeming feature. There rested a sort of rude, defiant frankness. He swung back and forth against his legs a dilapidated Peruvian hat.

When the judge asked him to explain rough gambling, defendant replied: "I means, yer Honor, that my style is, where the run o' the cards doesn't fetch me a feller's money, I knocks him down and takes it anyhow."[27]

Another story once again brought into the news that indestructible townswoman, Buffalo Jo:

About 12 o'clock last Sunday night, a woman rushed out of the National Saloon . . . on C street, just opposite the Sazerac, yelling murder, and pursued by two men. Now, it so happened that just in front of the Sazerac was standing one of our "Brave Volunteers," and the woman ran toward him as though to seek his protection. When almost across the street to where the soldier was standing, one of the men overtook her and struck her a blow that knocked her down. The woman fell almost at the soldier's feet, when the men took to their ʾheels. Not knowing who the woman was, our soldier boy drew his revolver and fired at the man who had knocked her over, but without hitting him, as the man was running. On picking up the prostrate woman she was recognized at once as Buffalo Jo, a well-known character in this city. She was not very badly hurt. The soldier boy was arrested, but on hearing the facts in the case the Police Judge at once discharged him.[28]

There was the sad tale of Betsey and Peter, sweethearts in the mountains of California:

One day Betsey's mother died, and the respectful neighbors followed in solemn procession to the burial. As the coffin was lowered into the grave, overcome by her grief, Betsey swooned. Pete sprang forward, endeavoring to revive her by such plaintive entreaties as "Betsey, speak to your own dear Peter!" Vain attempt! Gazing on the pale lids which lay on the sweet eyes as lifeless as if they had closed forever, he heaved a deep sigh, and turning to the bystanders said in a tone of tenderest anguish, "I'll bet any man four bits she never speaks again!"[29]

In addition, the usual outbreaks of violence made copy, the *Enterprise* of March 8 conveniently lumping the record of several days in one account: of P. H. Dowd and William Janes, who started out by throwing glasses at each other in the Gem saloon and ended by shooting, Patrick Cox joining the fray and Dowd being drilled through the chest; of a stranger in the Clipper saloon who amused himself by guying a harmless character known as "Drunken Jimmy" until Jack McNabb remonstrated with a revolver, peeling a strip from the stranger's head and getting his own vest ruined in the exchange of shots; of Mike Haley, who, in cocking his derringer to polish off an opponent during a dispute over a chicken fight, accidentally shot a large hole through his left hand; of John

Boyd, a woodchopper in Newton Canyon, who had been cut to pieces with an axe; of a wild man, crazy drunk, rushing about the streets with a long knife, threatening to carve up anybody in his way; and of the trifling doings of a midnight robber, a woman whipper, and an Irishman and a Mexican who pounded each other in a hurdy-gurdy row. All these events, given about a half column, were reported with a *sang-froid* that verged on boredom.

The big news of late winter was the arrival, on February 27 from San Francisco, of Adah Isaacs Menken. She was the sensation of the hour. A woman of intense temperament who was not merely the adventuress or immoral exhibitionist of popular legend, she was a puzzling combination of worldly wisdom and naïveté. Volatile, fearless, and uninhibited, she yet had a sort of innocence that made even so accomplished an amorist as Alexander Dumas swear that his relations with her had been only avuncular. Meeting many prominent writers and painters during her short life—Dickens, Swinburne, Charles Reade, Rossetti, Burne-Jones, Gautier—she was naturally suspected of numerous love affairs. One such imputation she refuted and by implication all others when she said: "I never lived with Houston; it was General Jackson and Methusaleh and other big men."[30]

Growing up in New Orleans, familiar with several languages by the age of twelve, translating the *Iliad* from the Greek, she began her dramatic career there in 1857. An aspiring writer, she became a regular contributor of poems to the Cincinnati *Israelite*. Then she moved on to New York, where she left her first husband, Alexander Isaacs Menken. Without making certain that she was legally divorced, she shortly afterward married the heavyweight champion prizefighter, John Carmel Heenan, who was granted an annulment on allegation of bigamy. As a frequenter of Pfaff's café on lower Broadway, she knew Walt Whitman, Ada Clare, Fitz-James

O'Brien, George Arnold, and the other habitués of that beery Bohemia. She was perceptive enough to see genius in Whitman long before many others saw it, and his influence appears in the rhythms of her own poetry. When the Civil War began, she was a fiery Southern sympathizer, who was once arrested for waving a rebel flag in Baltimore. For her New York stage appearances she insisted that her dressing room be decorated in Confederate gray.

Her chief claim to fame, or notoriety, rested on her performance in the title role of *Mazeppa*, a drama based on Byron's poem. In the climactic episode of the play she was disrobed in full view of the audience, her theoretical nudity covered by tights, then strapped on the back of a snorting steed that galloped up a ramp simulating a mountain. After her first appearance in the role, at Albany on June 3, 1861, *Mazeppa* immediately became the great successful shocker of the day. The public undressing never failed to win the noisy acclaim of enthusiastic males, as well as the dour disapproval of the prudish. Criticism ranged from the ribald to the stern. Waggish reporters had a good time with "this most manifest female," "the great unadorned," "the great bare;" they joked about her "spreading herself," said that she "outstrips all competitors," and described her luggage as "two immense cigar boxes filled with clothing." Tight-lipped fellows condemned "a scandalous obscene exhibition," "an exhibition without restraint and without shame," a performance lascivious, lewd, indecent, and so on. Sober critics, without going to either extreme, conceded that she had talent as an actress, acknowledged her earnestness and intensity, but sometimes complained of unevenness because of exaggeration.

Mazeppa was a good enough show for Thomas Maguire, who again engineered the importation of a celebrity to San Francisco. Leaving New York in the midst of the draft riots of July, 1863, she landed in California several weeks later with a third husband, Robert Henry Newell, a humorist who wrote under the name of Orpheus C. Kerr. Like Artemus Ward, she was a favored visitor who met everybody, social and literary: Joaquin Miller, Bret Harte, Lillie Hitchcock, Charles Warren Stoddard, Ina Coolbirth, Charles Henry Webb, and others. For some strange reason, however, she apparently did not meet Mark Twain, who was in the city during her stay. Writer as well as actress, she contributed to *The Golden Era* a number of poems, all of them very subjective and often on the theme of hopes unfulfilled, as in "El Suspiro" in the issue of January 3, 1864:

> Where is the promise of my years,
> Once written on my brow?
> Ere errors, agonies and fears
> Brought with them all that speaks in tears,
> Ere I had sunk beneath my peers—
> Where sleeps that promise now?

On August 24 she opened in *Mazeppa* before a packed house in Maguire's theater, with a distinguished cast, including Junius Brutus Booth, and a production well staged down to the horse itself. Byron describes this "Tartar of the Ukraine breed" as "Wild as the wild deer, and untaught, / With spur and bridle undefiled." Miss Menken did her best to stick to the text by choosing her horses and collaborating with a trainer to school them in the difficult business of combining some docility with pawing impatience. In San Francisco the fiery steed was a full-blooded California mustang.

The audience was brilliant. Governor Leland Stanford occupied a box, dress circle and parquet shone with San Francisco's best in beauty and fashion. The entire assemblage glittered. Thereafter for sixteen nights she played the piece before 30,000 people, who whooped and howled and stamped, perhaps because, as a mark of special regard for the West

Coast, she discarded tights in favor of very short close-fitting shorts—"the little end of a dimity nothing," one reporter observed. In a letter to the *Enterprise*, on September 13, Mark Twain said:

She appeared to me to have but one garment on—a thin tight white linen one, of unimportant dimensions; I forget the name of the article, but it is indispensable to infants of tender age— I suppose any young mother can tell you what it is, if you have the moral courage to ask the question. With the exception of this superfluous rag, the Menken dresses like the Greek Slave.

The bare Menkenian thigh, which disturbed him somewhat, did not unsettle sophisticated San Francisco critics. Charles Warren Stoddard said rapturously: "Garments seemed almost to profane her, as they do a statue."[31]

On her acting, opinion varied. Mark Twain, in that letter of September 13, described her technique as athletic:

Here every tongue sings the praises of her matchless grace, her supple gestures, her charming attitudes. Well, possibly, these tongues are right. In the first act, she rushes on the stage, and goes cavorting around after "Olinska"; she bends herself back like a bow; she pitches headforemost at the atmosphere like a battering-ram; she works her arms, and her legs, and her whole body like a dancing-jack: her every movement is as quick as thought; in a word, without any apparent reason for it, she carries on like a lunatic from the beginning of the act to the end of it. At other times she "whallops" herself down on the stage, and rolls over as does the sportive pack-mule after his burden is removed. If this be grace then the Menken is eminently graceful.[32]

Another critic, brushing off the indignation of moralists with the remark that "Prudery is obsolete," took a more favorable view:

She fences with a strong wrist and Bowery dexterity. She attitudinizes, sometimes extravagantly, sometimes with statuesque effect. . . . The Menken is a beauty, and believes that "beauty unadorned is adorned the most."[33]

The San Francisco *Alta California,* approving without reserve, called her

quite an actress—calm, considerate, careful and judicious—of the modern natural school. . . . She reads well, has a fine voice, is fully self-possessed. . . . she is all grace—a model for the sculptor and the painter, every action being the "poetry of motion."[34]

These mixed judgments leave her acting skill in doubt, but nobody questioned her tremendous drawing power. After a triumphant San Francisco run, Washoe was an inevitable destination for this exciting woman. When news of her coming wafted over the mountains, one hundred dozen photographs of the lady were sold in and around Virginia. The Gold Hill *Daily News* said:

Mark Twain is writing a bloody tragedy for her, equal to Mazeppa—and which will excel Mazeppa in many respects. It is to be called "Pete Hopkins; or, the Gory Scalp." Mark is now training one of Balaam's Arabian steeds especially for this play. Those who have attended the performances of Ada, admire her very much—"what they have seen of her."[35]

On February 27 she arrived in Virginia with her husband, Orpheus C. Kerr. That gentleman, said a reporter, "occupied a decidedly lively and conspicuous position on top of the hind boot. He was dressed in a black moustache, a plug hat, and a gray blanket, and looked either like a troubadour or a Georgia major just returned from the war."[36] Such a notice was unusual attention for Orpheus. Generally he tagged along, sulky and querulous at the end of the procession, like a baggage-handler ignored by everybody, most of all by his glamorous wife. What the attraction was that induced her to marry him can only be wondered at, for she gave him much less attention than she lavished upon the many dogs under-

Adah Isaacs Menken

Adah Isaacs Menken in the
title role of *Mazeppa*

foot in her room at the International Hotel. Although he was a humorist, he appeared to find no humor in his role of forgotten man.

The press was on hand to greet her, the *Enterprise* staff being out in force and at once taking charge of the lady as it usually did of visiting men and women of distinction. Having been tipped off by Artemus Ward that Joe Goodman and his boys were good people to know, she cultivated their favor. At Maguire's Opera House the front row was reserved for the *Enterprise,* and she played to Goodman, Mark Twain, Dan De Quille, and the rest of them. The Virginia debut on March 2 was not entirely successful, for she chose to open in *The French Spy.* In that one she took another male role, of a young Arab page boy. A petite creature, she made an appealing boy —"a thing of beauty and a boy forever," some wit said—but she did not lose any clothes, hence disappointed the audience.

By the 7th she reverted to the favorite *Mazeppa,* and the house was crammed, the *Enterprise* solidly in front; Julie Bulette, the highly esteemed madam, regal in sables, occupied a stage box. Joe Goodman went all out in unrestrained praise:

It is only in intensely emotional situations that Miss Menken displays those remarkable qualities which prove her claim to the title of great actress. . . . In these she stands peerless as a speechless but eloquent delineator of human passions. . . . When you have watched the dawn of a fresh emotion in her soul, which rises and glows till her whole being is suffused with its spirit, and trembles in her countenance with more than voiceful intelligibility, finding its ultimate expression in some action whose grace and significance scorn interpretation, you feel that words would be a miserable, meaningless mockery. It is no abstract conception of passion that Miss Menken delineates. It is the passion that springs from a profoundly emotional and womanly heart—a heart with all the finest sensibilities, quickest instincts, generous impulses, and noblest purposes, that ever animated or actuated mortal being.[37]

When Dan De Quille chimed in, and the pair kept up this laudation for several days, a California editor dryly remarked: "Both the editors of the *Enterprise* have gone crazy —but they didn't have far to go."[38] After a week or so, when the fervor had subsided somewhat, an oafish reporter derisively observed: "The local of the Enterprise doesn't pile it up quite so steep onto her this week. Guess Dan has discovered that she wears drawers."[39]

The Virginia *Union,* as might have been expected, was grimly disapproving. With a sternness worthy of John Calvin, it condemned a shocking spectacle:

Taking the name of Mazeppa for the style of the scandalous obscene exhibition now nightly on display at the Maguire—which, as public journalists, we have thought proper once to attend and to endure to its close—is a defamation of an historical name, and of some noble historical incidents. . . . what we say is that an exhibition without restraint and without shame of the most lascivious nature that lewd imaginations can invent, ought to meet with the public reprehension.[40]

That criticism gave Goodman an opening and he leaped into battle. Defending Miss Menken's decency, he raged that any prig like the *Union's* critic "should blush that he is made in the image of his God—if, indeed, he is. He should rail against painting and sculpture, and the other arts which have developed their most beautiful and divine conceptions in ideal likenesses of the human form."[41] The next day he fired a thunderous salvo at the *Union's*

wanton depravity, an instinctive scurrility, a spirit of low envy, to which aught that is grand or beautiful or admirable is a rebuke as scornful and withering as the contempt with

which God must look down on such a miserable miscreation
—a venomous hate which stings because despised—a reptile
revenge, which knowing how it is loathed and hated, would
trail its slimy form over all that is good and lovely in this
beautiful creation.

The editor of the *Enterprise* was in fine form. In the jaded
twentieth century, when female bareness has long since
ceased to be a controversial novelty, we may envy him his
readiness to roar about it.

Mark Twain's part in this contest is not clear. Paine says
that, fascinated like all men who met her, he vied with Dan
De Quille in singing praises of Miss Menken. Bernard Falk,
one of her biographers, says that Mark Twain fell under her
spell: "To speak her praises in the Virginia City *Enterprise*
became the humorist's solemn and chivalrous duty."[42] No
contemporary evidence attests this bedazzlement. None of
the extant Virginia favorable criticism is identifiably his, and
the fascination is questionable. Dan De Quille, who should
have known what he was talking about, said that Mark
Twain did not care much for the lady. At best he was more
wary than enthusiastic, more nearly disapproving than
charmed. There is an uneasiness in his remarks about her, a
tongue-in-cheek, half ribald attitude very different from Joe
Goodman's fervent exaltation of womanly heart and soul. No
fascination appears in Mark Twain's uncomplimentary criticism of her acting, or in "A Full and Reliable Account of the
Extraordinary Meteoric Shower of Last Saturday Night,"
published in *The Californian* of November 19, 1864. In that
one, the combination of drinking and telescopic observations
produces remarkable sights, one of them being a resplendent
spectacle:

the whole constellation of the Great Menken came flaming
out of the heavens like a vast spray of gas-jets, and a glory
spread over the universe as it fell! [N. B. I have used the term

"Great Menken" because I regard it as a more modest expression than the Great Bear, and consequently better suited to the columns of *The Californian*, which goes among families, you understand.]

Although he did not admit that the strip act disturbed him, the inference is that it made him so uncomfortable that he had to dismiss it with a snigger. Emotionally, he was more nearly of the party of the upright Virginia *Union* than of the enlightened Goodman, for he had the prude's squeamishness about nudity. A good example is his shocked horror over Titian's painting of Venus, in Florence, as expressed with denunciation of lewdness in *A Tramp Abroad*. In his San Francisco letter of September 13 he had observed of Miss Menken that "some of her postures are not so modest as the suggestive attitude" of the Greek Slave. If that innocuous sculptured nude struck him as suggestive—meaning improper—it implied a psyche that was Comstockian. In Washoe days he still possessed, also, remnants of the belief that any woman on public display, in whatever fashion, was suspect. That belief would disappear in time; nevertheless, despite his railing at Victorian mores, Mark Twain himself was partly a Puritan. Considering the decorum of Olivia Langdon, the one woman who really fascinated him, he was not likely to have been attracted by the actress.

Still, in Virginia he did his part in entertaining the enticing visitor, even taking her some of his writing for criticism. "She is a literary cuss herself," he said. "She has a beautiful white hand, but her handwriting is infamous. . . ."[43] Remaining in town over a month, Miss Menken did not suffer for lack of attention. When Engine Company No. 2 serenaded her at the International Hotel, she appeared on the balcony, clad in gold satin, causing a near riot that called out police reserves. The firemen made her an honorary member of the company —one of "Two's fellers"—and gave her a red morocco fire belt.

"Adah," said a California editor, "can man a brake or break a man, as well as any of 'em."[44] Miners gave her a two-thousand-dollar brick of silver, and named a mine the "Mazeppa Mounting Ledge." A newly-organized Menken Shaft and Tunnel Company issued stock certificates decorated by the picture of a naked lady on a galloping stallion. Presented with 100 shares, she sold them a year later for $50,000. That windfall, together with the $36,000 she was reported to have made by the Western theatrical venture, shows that she was not merely an impractical romantic.

There are vague stories of dinner parties in Virginia, but not much detail. Years later Dan De Quille wrote about a small affair at the International at which Miss Menken was hostess, Ada Clare co-hostess, he and Mark Twain the only guests. Orpheus, uninvited, made the gentlemen uneasy by prowling up and down the corridor outside, occasionally poking his head into the doorway to scowl upon the company. The purpose of the dinner was to discuss a novel Miss Menken was thinking of writing, but apparently they never got around to talking about it. The atmosphere seems to have been somewhat strained, but all might have gone well enough had there not been in the room, according to Dan,

about nineteen dogs of as many breeds, "mongrel," puppy, whelps and hound . . . some Ada Clare's pets and others belonging to the Menken. These pampered beasts she continually fed upon cubes of sugar soaked in brandy and champagne. This kind of provender made the animals howlingly hilarious, to the great delight of their mistress, but to the great disgust of Twain, who was seated on Menken's side of the table, where the canine carnival was most rampant.[45]

When one of these pets nipped Mark Twain, he aimed a kick at the offender under the table, but unfortunately hit Miss Menken, "causing her to bound from her seat," Dan said, "throw herself on a lounge and roll and roar in agony."

This mischance put a damper on the party. Mark Twain grew sullen, and the two men left shortly, braving the dark looks of Orpheus, still on sentry duty in the corridor. If Dan put any truth into that account, it is another indication that Mark Twain was not fascinated.

On the night of March 31 she suddenly left Virginia without saying goodbye to anybody, and returned to San Francisco. On her departure for Australia in April, *The Golden Era* gave her over a column of affectionate farewell, and homespun poets produced verses serious and saucy. Said one:

> Benevolence adorns thine hand,
> And Cando graces thy fair brow:
> A thousand grateful creatures stand
> To crown thee with their blessings now.[46]

In a parody of that touching tribute, another, styled "Jimpson," wrote:

> And am'rous eyes now gloat on thee
> Nor note the pit's obscene delights,
> While greedy vision sees thy form,
> And revels 'round thy matchless tights.[47]

In Panama she parted from Orpheus, having become enamored of a horse-trainer named Barclay whom she had met in Virginia; then she went on to England and the continent to scandalize and to charm. By 1868 her brief and turbulent life had ended. Mark Twain took no further notice. He did not mention her in *Roughing It* or in the miscellaneous reminiscences dictated for his *Autobiography*.

Mark Twain, 1865

Chapter Seven

"THE WEEKLY OCCIDENTAL"

ℑℑℑ

IN CHAPTER fifty-one of *Roughing It,* Mark Twain says that two unfailing signs of prosperity in a mining region were vice flourishing in saloons, gambling dens, and brothels; and the birth of a literary paper. Then he gives over the entire chapter to the story of a Virginia literary paper, *The Weekly Occidental,* published there by Thomas Fitch and Company. This publication has received little more than casual mention by Mark Twain commentators, but the neglect is not surprising, for no copy has yet been discovered of the first, last, and only number, which came out on March 6, 1864. There are no data on subscribers or number of copies sold.

Something like *The Golden Era,* the *Occidental* was an ambitious eight-page journal of musical, dramatic, fire, and military departments, local gossip, "Musings and Gleanings," editorials, poems, essays, and stories. Although its columns were open to anybody, whether amateur or professional, the experienced Virginia press corps furnished most of the material in the first issue. Joe Goodman contributed a patriotic poem, and Dan De Quille was represented by at least two pieces. His "Lost in the Sierras" is a tragic tale of a man losing his way in heavy snow, and freezing to death high in the mountains. He flounders, thinks of his wife and children, then lies down to drift off into a benumbed and fatal sleep.

Cold are the nights on the mountain heights—cold the stars and blue sky. The stiffened form of the lost gold hunter still lies in the snow on the side of the great white mountain; we are sad to know how many nights have passed since he went to sleep with his face on his arms and his breast against the snow, dreaming of the white cloth spread on the table in the little brown cabin, far below among the foothills.[1]

In a different vein is Dan's satirical letter from "A. Bilk" to "Bobby" about "A Promising Mine and a Model Superintendent." Bilk says they have struck it richer than ever. "We are now getting out rock that very much resembles the Comstock; indeed, when compared with the Comstock ore that presents the same appearance as ours, the very best judges can but admit they do look alike." The superintendent is so affable that he is not above chatting with shareholders, if they "address him with proper deference." His forte is spending money judiciously.

He is never easy except when constantly engaged in making judicious expenditures. . . . Ah, you would adore him! He has just bought a splendid pair of horses—dappled greys—and a magnificent carriage. . . . he has several times actually invited some of us stockholders to ride with him. Ah, just to see him handle those horses and at the same time gracefully smoke a two-bit cigar! . . . Our tunnel is in about three thousand and ten feet—it will be full that much when we get in three thousand feet further. As to location, there is no more promising location in the country than ours; there are only six companies working under us in tunnels. . . . Our machinery has not yet arrived, but our Superintendent thinks there is no doubt but it will come if we send for it, and send the money with our order.[2]

Dan was a versatile writer. His pathos might be a little soft, but Washoe readers liked it that way, and his humor had a twinkle in its eye. These examples suggest why Joe Goodman and others considered him a man of great promise.

"Climatic Influences of Washoe," by Dr. R. Eichler, is a learned exposition of the effect of atmospheric pressure in Virginia, about 7,000 feet above sea level, on the human organism: a discussion of respiratory troubles induced by lack of oxygen at high altitudes, effect on heart and lungs, headaches and bleeding of newcomers, etc.[3] An anonymous narrative entitled "A Sensation Yarn of the California Fever of 1850" is another sad tale of death overtaking an emigrant train near the Platte River, "the broad swath of the grim reaper," cholera, cutting down half the complement, thirteen men and one woman.[4] An unidentified sketch, "The Early Miners of the Comstock Lead," sensitively recreates adventures of the first prospectors in 1850.

Do not imagine, ye who have been taught that the settlement of Washoe dates no farther than 1858, that for the five years preceding, the cañons which skirt the Comstock were unpeopled. Do not believe the oft repeated flourish that we are inhabiting a city of twenty thousand souls—a city of churches and school-houses—a city of saloons and graveyards —a city of banks and gambling houses—a city of brokers, of preachers, of saints, of sinners, of vice, of virtue, of wealth, of poverty, of heaven, of hell, of everything good and bad, social and physical, which constitutes the pride and shame of great cities elsewhere—and that the streets we frequent were unmarked by the foot of the Saxon six years ago.[5]

An unsigned editorial, probably by Fitch, on "Food for the Gallows," predicts a bad end for teen-age Virginia ruffians who persecute citizens, make life especially miserable for the Chinese, maim animals, and amuse themselves by shooting at inoffensive pedestrians. These juvenile delinquents, says the editorial,

will be hanged before attaining their majority—some of them are orphans, a few runaways, and the children of drunken parents; but they all talk "feet," chew tobacco, carry weapons, and swagger most insufferably.[6]

Mrs. Fitch and Rollin M. Daggett were also contributors and, with a good deal of space to fill, there were undoubtedly others. Fitch was the prime mover in this venture, but he had plenty of assistance from eager volunteers, chiefly of the *Enterprise*. Mark Twain was an associate, apparently in a sort of unofficial advisory capacity, like three or four others, all of whom offered gratuitous counsel in the traditional manner of literary editorship. Nothing of his was in the first number, but he was supposed to have been in the second one, which, alas, never appeared. His contribution was "The Aged Pilot Man," a parody of Erie Canal songs—"Ho! lighten ship! ho! man the pump!/Ho, hostler, heave the lead!"— which he put into *Roughing It*, where, he says, "it will answer in place of a tear dropped to the memory of the lost *Occidental*."

The new weekly got polite, if brief, notices in San Francisco and elsewhere. Said the Marysville, California, *Daily Appeal*:

The external and typographical face of the *Occidental* is excellent, and we have no doubt that its literary reputation will be soon established. The pens and the experience of such writers as Thomas Fitch, R. M. Daggett, Dan de Quille, J. T. Goodman, Mrs. Fitch and others, must make it a popular paper. We wish it success.[7]

Even the Virginia *Union* condescended to approve, no doubt because Fitch was on the staff of that paper. "We are pleased to observe," it said, "that the proprietors of 'The Occidental' have totally eschewed that 'flash' literature which is so apt to be the staple of Sunday papers, and have started their paper with a high tone."[8]

The several contributions rescued from other columns, and mentioned above, show that the tone was at least not trashy. Nevertheless some of the content of the paper, had it continued, would have been peculiar. The chef-d'oeuvre of the

Occidental was to be a continued novel, at a chapter per number, written by half a dozen collaborators, one of whom was Mark Twain. In *Roughing It* he elaborates for several pages upon the bewildering details of this yarn concerning a duke, a blonde, and a Rosicrucian alchemist involved in extravagant escapades and incredible coincidences. He says that Mrs. Fitch, described as "an able romanticist of the ineffable school," did the first instalment. Tom Fitch was to write the second, then Rollin Daggett, called "a dark and bloody editor of one of the dailies," then an unknown characterized as "a dissolute stranger with a literary turn of mind —rather seedy . . . but very quiet and unassuming," and finally Mark Twain. He says that the absurd complications introduced into the story by the stranger caused so much disagreement and delay that the *Occidental* died.

Dan De Quille recalled a different version of this business. His order of collaboration was: Rollin Daggett, Mrs. Fitch, Mark Twain, Joe Goodman, Tom Fitch, Dan DeQuille. Daggett, starting off with a beauteous heroine and a hero who was a pupil of the Rosicrucian alchemist, injected much mystery and left the hero in great peril at the end of the instalment. Indeed, Dan remarked, each writer, after getting the young man out of the predicament created by the previous collaborator, planned to maneuver him into such a tight spot that extricating him would have been "a sort of literary game of chess." He and Mark Twain intended to harass Daggett's favorite character, the Rosicrucian hermit, with a demon fiddler, but they never got the chance to do it.[9]

Tom Fitch remembered yet another arrangement. According to him, he chose the title of the novel, "The Silver Fiend, a Tale of Washoe," and wrote the first chapter. He began, he says, with "a thrilling description of a runaway team on a mountain road in the Sierras, stopped by a lariat in the hands of a college athlete, who while on a prospecting tour had camped on the mountain side."[10] Then Daggett was to have stepped in. He planned to tell how the athlete was jerked three miles over the mountain into a valley, where he landed in the middle of an Indian camp. Mrs. Fitch, who followed, dwelt upon the home life and education of a beautiful Vermont girl, compelled by loss of fortune to go West. Presumably she was supposed to meet the agile lariat-thrower, but Mark Twain, the fourth collaborator, had other ideas. After the paper had collapsed, he told Tom Fitch:

"I should have kept the compact, but I intended to place that Vermont girl in a situation that she would have found difficult to explain to the satisfaction of her friends. I had her dealing monte in 'Dandy Pete's' saloon in Virginia City."[11]

After each collaborator had taken a turn, they would go around again, and yet again if necessary. According to Dan and Mark Twain, there was much discussion and not a little wrangling over story line and treatment, and no wonder. The substance, as remembered by some of the principals, is enough to render a critic speechless. Considering the fragmentary outlines of this weird unpublished novel, its failure to be born was no great loss. Dan De Quille observed: "nothing was ever said about how it was to be ended, and had the story been carried forward in accordance with the original plan, it would have been one of the curiosities of literature, and probably running yet."[12]

The *Occidental* died, said Dan, because its writers used all their powder for the first shot. That is hard to believe of experienced newspapermen, fertile of imagination, and accustomed to daily writing. Still, a more modest format—say four pages instead of eight—might have prolonged its life. Mark Twain believed that the cultural soil of Virginia was too arid to nurture literature. He said bitterly: "I'm sorry the literary paper stopped before my turn came, but you couldn't expect that kind of a paper to be permanent here, could you?

Can a lark sing in a cellar? Can summer abide on Mont Blanc? Will flowers bloom in hell?"[13] In *Roughing It* he says more softly: "I was sorry enough, for I was proud of being connected with a literary paper—prouder than I have ever been of anything since, perhaps."

Mark Twain, 1870

Chapter Eight

THE ARMY OF THE LORD

❧❧

$\mathbf{A}$S 1864 moved on into spring, indications of economic strain became manifest in Virginia, but a steady influx of new arrivals created a deceptive bustle. Reporters strove mightily to make the most of the illusory stir. The Gold Hill *Daily News* described the Saturday jam of people and traffic:

negroes, Sandwich Islanders, Chinamen and Indians mingling promiscuously with those wearing whiter skins. Ladies of easy virtue are met and jostled on the walks by ladies of uneasy virtue, and bare-legged Indian women rumple the proud circumferences of both as they meet in the throng. Chinamen, driving before them asses laden with faggots, Mexicans with trains of mules packed with merchandise, and Americans with vehicles of every kind, and bearing every kind of freight, crowd along the street, while the air vibrates the dull roar of a busy city.[1]

The Virginia *Union* commented on a feverish tearing down of old buildings and replacing them with new, on brick yards and lumber dealers swamped with orders. "The owners of vacant lots hold them at a high figure as the suburbs of the city gradually expand, and there can be no doubt that the next few months will witness a revival of business, equal, if not superior, to that of the past season."[2] One of those unquenchable optimists put in his reassuring word:

The future of Nevada is under no cloud. There is nothing in our circumstances, to create alarm, or apprehension. The whole world cannot rival us in substantial resources. Our mines are unequaled in productiveness, and the prospect is that our riches are inexhaustible.[3]

Territorial production of bullion for the first quarter was $3,930,724, an increase of 62½ per cent over the corresponding period of the year before. Virginia accounted for almost two-thirds of this total, but shipments from there were below the best rate of 1863. Mining stocks, still slipping downward, showed no signs of climbing back toward the highs of flush times: by June, Gould & Curry was quoted at $1,560, Ophir at $760. Assessments heavily overbalanced dividends. A great many stockholders in the 200 companies in and near the Virginia district—Honest Abe, Mary Ann, Oro Fino, Morning Star, Nightingale, etc.—relinquished their shares by default to the public auctioneer.

A correspondent of the San Francisco *Call* said that a scarcity of money in circulation, combined with high interest rates, sometimes 10 per cent a month, made Washoe

duller than ever before; duller even than in the tight times of 1860, when the country was almost wholly abandoned by disappointed prospectors and frightened (by Indians) adventurers. . . . Upon many claims work has ceased, and as a consequence, hundreds of men are out of employment. . . . the two Stock Boards (a few weeks ago there were five) . . . are gasping for life. In the County Recorder's office, where one year ago ten scribes were kept constantly busy, one man is sufficient to record all the conveyances of real estate.[4]

Another observer, discerning little commercial well-being behind a superficial front of dash and vigor, reiterated the theme of "intensely dull." Virginia, said he, was on the downswing of a cycle that invariably affected a region dependent solely on mining for economic health.

Did it not . . . ever strike you that all mining towns . . . go up like a rocket and come down like a stick? Such is the fate of this place. Real estate high, rents high, but not as of last year, and lower and lower must they come until they find that level which necessarily arrives to all communities based and founded on fictitious capital and imaginary wealth.[5]

Business was depressed but, as usual, no visible depression of Virginia spirits lessened enjoyment of the unusual event and the quirk pleasurably mad. A citizen named John A. Dougherty got into the news by walking 108 hours without stopping, all in O'Connor's saloon. A lamb on B Street attracted attention by chewing tobacco; a cat on the Divide by drinking coffee laced with cognac. A stimulating morale-booster arrived when John K. Lovejoy, Washoe City editor of the *Old Pah-Utah,* moved himself and his paper to Virginia in April, renaming his paper the *Old Piute.* This sheet, which once more gave the town four dailies, was a natural for the place. Lovejoy was an earthy character who had a knack for the telling remark in homely language that amused editors all over the West. "We calculate," said he in his Virginia salutatory,

to concentrate in the Old Piute all of the bravery of the Enterprise, the consistency of the Union, the egotism of the Gold Hill News, the conceit of the Carson Independent, the stupidity of the Bulletin, the waggery of the Humboldt Register, the dryness of the Aurora Times, and the utter worthlessness of the Reese River Reveille.[6]

He succeeded fairly well in that difficult assignment by the use of wit, ribaldry, guacherie, barnyard humor, and blunt personalities, all delivered with the genuine or assumed naïveté of the semiilliterate countryman. From time to time he came forth with sallies like this:

A lady friend of ours, married just four months, has produced a fine boy, weighing four pounds. What do you think

of that, hey? Why, sposen she'd went on four or five years
at the rate of a pound a month, wouldn't it have been a
whopper?[7]

The gusty Lovejoy, in addition to the equally gamesome
gentlemen of the *Enterprise,* provided for Virginians reading
vivacious enough to take their minds off the sagging market.
For the paper of April 1 Mark Twain wrote a hoax entitled
"Another Traitor—Hang Him!" about a purported complaint
entered in the court of Judge Davenport by Thomas Fitch
against W. F. Myers. Complainant alleged that, "on the 30th
day of March, 1864, in the office of Myers & Daggett, in the
City of Virginia," defendant said

that negroes were inferior to white men, and were designed
by God Almighty to be the servants of white men, and defendant also used other language derogatory of the character
of our fellow-citizens of African descent, and calculated to
damnify them and bring them into contempt and ridicule.
And complainant further says, that prior to the slanderous
and wicked language of the defendant aforesaid, our colored
fellow-citizens enjoyed a good reputation, and that by said
slanderous language the colored race aforesaid were greatly
scandalized, and the Government of the United States
brought into disrepute and the Southern Confederacy encour-
aged, and Uncle Abe greatly maligned, and the public peace
jeopardized and all Union men injured and traitors bene-
fited. Now, therefore, this complainant prays that a warrant
may issue against the defendant for misprision of treason,
and that defendant's body be taken into custody, and that
defendant be punished either by hanging, or by being compelled to pack sand-bags at Fort Churchill, and that he also
be compelled to take the oath of allegiance, and be otherwise
dealt with according to the statutes in such case made and
provided.

No doubt that legal jargon was intended as a satire on
superpatriots who were quick to scent treason in every casual
word, and were ever ready to howl for the scalps of suspected

offenders. (We of the twentieth century have become familiar with these overheated self-appointed guardians of liberty; it is interesting to note that they were also known to Washoe.) Mark Twain's piling up of grave damages to the government, to Uncle Abe and Union men, likewise the horrendous prayed-for penalties, are an obvious burlesque of the tactics of the misguided zealot. There may have been, too, some personal joke on Fitch and Myers, but the point of it is lost to us.

This story attracted no attention comparable to the windy turmoil stirred up by the massacre hoax, but it caught the eye of the Virginia *Evening Bulletin,* which delivered a tart rebuke:

Mark Twain, who is notorious for constantly lying—under a mistake—made another mistake by perpetrating the . . . supposed-to-be sensational item as a "goak," but we can't for the life of us see where the laugh comes in. We suppose our neighbor thinking because this is April Fool's Day, he had a greater license than usual. But we don't see it. He who is a fool all the rest of the year, has no special rights on this particular day.

The Fitch vs. Myers invention, more obviously satirical than the Hopkins sell, if not screamingly funny, hardly deserved such a dense reception and so stiff a reprimand. The criticism showed the wide difference between the gayety of the *Enterprise* and the stodginess of the *Bulletin,* which all its local contemporaries regarded as a thick-headed paper.

The *Bulletin's* comments are also illuminating in that they aid in putting Mark Twain's Nevada reputation into proper perspective. Some twentieth-century admirers convey the impression that after about twenty months on the Comstock, he was a universal favorite who had won unanimous recognition as the leading writer and chief wag of the region. Paine says that when he hurriedly departed for San Francisco only a jump ahead of the sheriff, as he thought, he left "with a new name and fame—elate, triumphant, even if a fugitive." Effie Mona Mack remarks that "he *was* the recognized humorist of Washoe." It was not quite like that. The Virginia *Union* seldom gave him so much as a pleasant nod; the Gold Hill *Daily News* was as likely to be gruff as to be agreeable when it mentioned him; the attitude of the *Bulletin,* as reflected in the criticism above, was contemptuous. His name was anathema to the San Francisco *Evening Bulletin* and the Austin *Reese River Reveille,* and an object of suspicion, if not distaste, to some small-town California editors. Papers had called him hard names: miserable wretch, ass, fool, liar, idiot. Far from being a general favorite, he was, in popularity, still no better than second best to Dan De Quille. It is significant that the instigators of the *Weekly Occidental,* who surely wanted to put their best foot forward in the first number, included two contributions by Dan but nothing by Mark Twain.

Within five years book and magazine publishers would be bidding for his favor with attractive offers, but he was not that kind of literary property in 1864. Nevertheless, the slings and arrows of outrageous damnation served a useful purpose in developing the thick skin that is a prime requisite of a writer. Mark Twain was not then, or ever, permanently crushed by critics. The disapproval of the serious-minded did not appear to slow him down, or to convert him to a right-thinker devoted only to the truth and nothing but the truth. When Dan De Quille fell off a horse, his partner threw facts overboard in a lunatic account of a "Frightful Accident to Dan De Quille":

He was coming down the road at the rate of a hundred miles an hour (as stated in his will, which he made shortly after the accident), and on turning a sharp corner, he suddenly hove in sight of a horse standing square across the channel;

he signaled for the starboard, and put his helm down instantly, but too late, after all; he was swinging to port, and before he could straighten down, he swept like an avalanche against the transom of the strange craft; his larboard keel coming in contact with the rudder-post of the adversary. Dan was wrenched from his saddle and thrown some three hundred yards (according to his own statement, made in his will, above mentioned), alighting on solid ground, and bursting himself open from the chin to the pit of the stomach. His head was also caved in out of sight . . . one of his legs was jammed up in his body nearly to his throat, and the other so torn and mutilated that it pulled out when they attempted to lift him into the hearse which we had sent to the scene of the disaster, under the general impression that he might need it; both arms were indiscriminately broken up until they were jointed like a bamboo; the back was considerably fractured and bent into the shape of a rail fence. Aside from these injuries, however, he sustained no other damage. . . . His first remark showed that the power of his great mind had not been impaired by the accident, nor his profound judgment been destroyed—he said he wouldn't have cared a d——n if it had been anybody but himself. . . . Dan may have exaggerated the above details in some respects, but he charged us to report them thus, and it is a source of genuine pleasure to us to have the opportunity of doing it. Our noble old friend is recovering fast, and what is left of him will be around the Brewery to-day, just as usual.[8]

Dan's reply accused Mark Twain of misrepresenting the facts, of showing false grief by tying crape on his hat, and of stealing the De Quille estate, consisting of shares in the Pewterinctum mine, and of coat, shirts, and shoes, some of which were traded for "a bottle of vile whisky." Then, said Dan,

when the police were about to snatch him for drunkenness, he commenced blubbering, saying that he was "overcome for the untimely death of poor Dan." By this dodge he escaped the lock-up, but if he does not shortly give up Pewterinctum stock—which is of fabulous value—shell out our tooth-brush and take off our socks and best shirt, he will not escape the Territorial Prison.

P. S. We have just learned that he stole the crape he tied about his hat from the door-knob of Three's engine house, South B street.[9]

Later Dan said that he forgave his partner because of the sad disaster that had befallen him during a boxing lesson. The instructor, in an offhand way, "let one fly straight out from the shoulder and 'busted' Mr. Twain in the 'snoot,' sending him reeling—not exactly to grass, but across a bench—with two beautiful streams of 'claret' spouting from his nostrils."[10] This episode actually occurred at a gymnasium called Chauvel's Fencing Club, where it was the fashion among newspapermen to exercise with the foils and put on the gloves. When Mark Twain playfully squared off in front of George Dawson, a skilled boxer, the latter landed on Mark's nose about as Dan said, with the further result of enraging Mark Twain to the point of looking around for a club with which to assault Dawson murderously. Dan made capital of that red and bulbous nose for some time after.

Some local items of this spring have a Twainian tone. One concerned two men named Gashwiler and Charley Funk, of the Virginia and Gold Hill Water Company. They rushed into the *Enterprise* office "in a state bordering on lunacy," and full of indignation over an advertisement in the *Evening Bulletin.* In the ad were several Scriptural quotations: "If any man thirst, let him come unto me and drink;" "Whosoever drinketh of the water that I shall give him shall never thirst; but the water that I shall give him shall be in him a well of water springing up into everlasting life;" "The lamb, which is in the midst of the throne . . . shall lead them unto living fountains of waters. . . ."

We ask, now, in all candor, if there is a man in all Virginia who is competent by reason of his extraordinary natural or acquired stupidity, to guess what these gentlemen found in the above extracts to fill their souls with rage? As we hope for mercy past and present, they thought it was an attempt to ring in an opposition water company on the people! We call that infernal ignorance—and if we could think of a stronger term Gashwiler and Charley Funk should have the benefit of it. When men get so far gone that they do not know the Sermon on the Mount from a bid for a water franchise, it is time for them to begin to reform and stop taking chances on the hereafter.[11]

A discourse upon the weather is in his manner, aided by tongue-in-cheek literary flourishes he knew how to affect as a parody of the genteel style. Dropping out of the rhapsody with a thump at the end is a typical device.

The weather still continues cloudy, misty and rainy. The clouds wrap themselves lovingly about the neighboring mountain peaks even at noonday, while as the shades of evening approach they descend to similar liberties with all the little hills in the country, lingering fondly over them till shamed by the glaring eye of old Sol to a reluctant retreat to the more staid and elevated society of the hoary-headed granite peaks. Though some folks may not like this sort of weather, it is admitted by all to be much bullyer for the country than what dry weather is—as for us, give us rain or give us lager beer![12]

Local news being less plentiful than previously, Virginia reporters found themselves pushed to fill their columns in the spring of '64. Gun-toters, heretofore dependable sources of items, were lackadaisical, disinclined to start shooting. The Gold Hill *Daily News* made the extraordinary comment that "Virginia is more quiet than ever before in its history. Places that were once the most disorderly in town are the most orderly and peaceable. Oil has assuaged the troubled waters —the surface of Virginia society is calm, scarce a ripple disturbs the quiet."[13] Undoubtedly Mark Twain was aware of this sagging behavior. As an ambitious man, unwilling to remain in a place that was running downhill, he had surely speculated on the attractions of greener pastures somewhere beyond the mountains. Although he did not know it at the moment, his Comstock career was moving toward a climax and a precipitate departure. In May, the auctioning of the famous sack of flour not only gave him and other reporters material for their papers, but it also had repercussions that forced him out of Washoe.

On April 19, at a city election in Austin, Ruel C. Gridley, merchant, Democrat, and an old schoolfellow of Mark Twain's, bet on the outcome with Dr. Herrick, County Assessor and Republican: the loser to carry a fifty-pound sack of flour from Austin to Clifton, a mile and a quarter distant. Gridley started the next morning with the sack of flour, decorated by ribbons, on his shoulder, preceded by the flag and the Austin band, and accompanied by Dr. Herrick and others of the two parties. The band, honoring both contestants, alternated "John Brown's Body" with "Dixie." At the Bank Exchange saloon in Clifton, Gridley delivered the sack, he and others making speeches described as "most appropriate and graceful." Then they paraded to Grimes & Gibson's saloon, where the proprietors generously set up free drinks for everybody who could squeeze in, and where Gridley proposed that the sack be auctioned for the benefit of the Sanitary Fund.

The United States Sanitary Commission, which had the blessing of the government but no connection with it, was a private undertaking organized by physicians and philanthropists in 1861. As a forerunner of the American Red Cross, it looked after soldiers' health and comfort in ways that army surgeons were not able to do. The Commission inspected camps, aided in running down lost leave or discharge papers, provided transportation for the sick and wounded, assisted the needy families of soldiers, and published pamphlets to improve camp sanitation. The organization subsisted on voluntary contributions.

In large cities a popular fund-raising method was the Sanitary Fair, which ran for a week or more. It was a huge bazaar accompanied by devices like auctions, lotteries, and raffles, although in New York and Brooklyn that gambling was stopped by the pious protests of clergymen. The New York fair displayed a sword to be awarded to the Union general who received the most votes at one dollar each, General Grant winning by 15,782 votes over General McClellan. At Boston, one California pear was raffled for $20. By such means, these fairs netted substantial sums: Brooklyn, $400,-000; Cincinnati, $250,000; Boston, $145,000; Albany, $60,000; Cleveland, $50,000. On May 17 a great Mississippi Valley Fair was to open at St. Louis in a series of buildings covering several acres. Washoe had a Sanitary organization, which operated by means of county commissions. They solicited contributions at all times, but especially on occasions when the public turned out, as on an election day.

Gridley's auction suggestion found immediate favor. The first buyer bid in the flour at $350, then turned it back to be sold again. The second, Gridley himself, who paid $305, also put up the sack again; it was sold and resold all day, the crowd wildly cheering every successful bidder. As people became infected with the excitement of the occasion, they tossed twenty-dollar gold pieces into the pot until the auctioneer had a bagful of double eagles. The selling and reselling continued the next day under a rule that opening bids should be not less than $100. Saloon keepers contributed champagne and cigars to be auctioned, clothiers neckties and shirts, one firm donating a complete set of account books, a property owner giving eight lots in Watertown and a block in Austin. Total receipts were $5,335 for the Sanitary Fund.

This unusual feat of making money-raising a stimulating game gained wide publicity throughout the West. At Virginia, a combative desire to outdo Austin resulted in an invitation to Gridley to bring his flour sack over there. After an enthusiastic Sanitary meeting in Maguire's Opera House on May 15, the auction brought $580, but since the citizenry was not yet properly aroused, that modest sum was only a faint hint of what was to follow on the great day ahead.

On the morning of May 16 a noisy parade escorted Gridley and his flour to Gold Hill: waving flags, the Metropolitan Brass Band, and a rabble of cheering citizens, the now famous sack having been enclosed in buckskin as a protection against weather and rough handling. " 'Tone' was given to the procession," said the Gold Hill *Daily News,* "by the presence of Gov. Twain and his staff of bibulous reporters, who came down in a free carriage, ostensibly for the purpose of taking notes, but in reality in pursuit of free whiskey."[14] Mark Twain had his share of free drinks, which flowed plentifully at all stops, but he did not neglect his duty. For the *Enterprise* of the 17th he reported the adventures of "The Army of the Lord" in two long stories that, in detail and coverage, are far superior to those of any other papers in Nevada and California. His account of this episode in Chapter XLV of *Roughing It* is vivid impressionism, but its details often vary from those of his newspaper narrative, which, as spot news, may be accepted as a true report.

At Gold Hill the silver-tongued Tom Fitch made a stirring speech; then Marshal Sam Arnold took the stand as auctioneer, and the bidding began. Mining companies bid generously, mill companies, local business houses, private citizens; some tossed money into a hat. "The greatest enthusiasm reigned throughout," said Mark Twain, "and the heavy bids were received with tremendous cheering by the crowd." As the sum mounted, he overheard one jubilant fellow say:

"We're beating Virginia all to pieces." And another: "Good! we always *do* do it!" After several hours, when the total had reached $6,062, "The announcement was made . . . that Gold Hill had distanced Austin and taken the flour, and Mr. Gridley mounted the rostrum and threw up a sponge according to promise."

Carriages, band, speakers, and flags moved on to Silver City. Arriving there in the rain in the middle of the afternoon when many people were at work, they met a less spirited reception, but, thanks again to Fitch and Arnold, collected over $800 anyhow. On leaving town, they were hailed by Mrs. Eliza Elliott, proprietress of the Sierra Nevada hotel, who contributed $40. "The boys," said Mark Twain, "gave her three hearty cheers and took a drink. Further down the cañon, Klein & Boub called the party in to moisten themselves, and contributed $25. All these parties are citizens of Silver City."

About four o'clock the Army of the Lord, "with flags flying and music blasting," reached Dayton and halted before the Occidental saloon. Judge Hayden, who, said Mark Twain, "has not his equal as an auctioneer on the bench of this or any other country, stood up in the rain and made sales." To add variety, somebody tossed the judge's old hat to the auctioneer, who knocked it down to himself for $10, remarking that it was the cheapest old hat he had ever bought. Another man captured a bug, placed it on the Occidental bar, named it the "Great Sanitary Bug of Washoe," and called for bids. One ignorant bidder, when informed what the auction was about,

showed strong symptoms of disgust. "Damn the Sanitary Fund!" he cried, "is that all?" At this Captain Close confronted him with—"My friend you must not damn the Sanitary Fund here!" But the man—who had been going it altogether on the merits of the bug—insisted upon damning the

Sanitary Fund, whereupon Captain Close turned loose upon him and gave him a beautiful thrashing, blacking his eyes handsomely. During the confusion incident to this slight digression from the programme, the Great Sanitary Bug was swept away and lost, or his bugship might have sold for thousands of dollars, and might have had the honor of a glass case and a trip to the Mississippi Valley Fair, labeled— "The Great Sanitary Bug from Washoe."[15]

The take at Dayton was $1,835. Said Mark Twain: "Welly good, John, notwithstanding the rain."

Backtracking to Silver City, the Army paused to allow Tom Fitch to tell the story of the Sanitary Bug and the damnifier properly rebuked, a recital that gained an additional $650. A second stop at Gold Hill produced close to another thousand. Then the destination was Virginia. By this time, said Mark Twain, the procession was several hundred yards long, made up of "the National Guard and regulars from the Fort, the music wagon, carriages, horsemen and a multitude of citizens on foot, and the old original army thus augmented, moved upon Virginia's works and stormed them." The night-time auction there was wildly hysterical, the populace being determined to beat Austin and Gold Hill. They did, handily, by the aid of many large bids: Gould & Curry, $3,500; Potosi, $550; Chollar, $500; Bajazet, $500; Empire Mill, $500; Stewart & Baldwin, $500; in addition to many modest donations of five and ten dollars. All were duly listed, with names attached, by the Local of the *Enterprise,* who showed that he knew how to get the facts and to report them straight. He announced the total for the evening as "a fraction less than *thirteen thousand dollars!* We saw Gold Hill's $6,500, and went her $6,500 better. Glory to Virginia! . . . The cheering was not altogether light."

There were amusing contretemps. When the Sons of Temperance bid $100, auctioneer Charley De Long yelled:

"Where are you now, you whiskey men? Come on, you saloon keepers! It's cold water against whiskey!" Some one here cried out: "One hundred dollars for the whiskey interest." "Who from?" asked Charley. "Asa L. Waughsman," was the reply. Cheer upon cheer followed, and the drums joined in the applause. Asa keeps a fashionable two-bit drinking saloon, and because he is not distinguished for his liberality, but has the reputation of being a Copperhead, the crowd cheered the more lustily. Mr. De Long praised Asa's liquor, pointed out his saloon, recommended that he should be patronized—and he was, most liberally. But lo, and behold! to-day, after all his honors, Asa comes out and asserts that the party who used his name for one hundred dollars had no authority to do so, and is unknown to him, and that he (Waughsman,) cannot, in justice to himself, contribute one hundred dollars or one dollar to the Sanitary Fund![16]

The auction sharpened the keen rivalry between the *Union* and the *Enterprise*. In a letter of May 16 to his mother and sister, Mark Twain commented upon home office tactics for keeping ahead in this race:

The other day the *Daily Union* gave $200, and I gave $300, under instructions from the proprietors always to "go them a hundred better." To-night the *Union* bid $100, and I bid $150 for the *Enterprise*. I had to go to the office to make up my report, and the *Union* fellows came back and bid another $100. It was provoking, because I had orders to run our bid up to $1,000, if necessary, and I only struck the *Union* lightly to draw them on. But I guess we'll make them hunt their holes yet, before we are done with them.[17]

According to his own record, the *Union* outbid the *Enterprise* by $200 to $150. Probably the failure to keep his paper out in front rankled, for in a few days he tried so violently to make those fellows hunt their holes that the effort rebounded upon him with calamitous effect.

Late contributions brought the Sanitary grand total for all Washoe up to about $30,000. "Altogether," said Mark Twain in his *Enterprise* story, "yesterday was the greatest day the Sanitary Fund ever saw in Nevada Territory." Joe Goodman suggested that the flour be made into thin flapjacks, 500 to the pound, and sold for $500 each. Editorially, he said proudly:

Notwithstanding the dull times at present prevailing in almost every branch of industry in the Territory, Nevada has, in spite of this adverse state of affairs contributed more generously to the Sanitary Fund than ever before. The times may pinch the people of Nevada, but their patriotism cannot be pinched out of them.[18]

Lovejoy, of the *Old Piute*, contributed his own variety of entertaining observations:

In connection with the estimated value of that Sanitary sack of flour that was so frequently bought yesterday, we are requested . . . to make an estimate of the amount of lager beer drank by Marshall, of the *Union*, Clemens, of the *Enterprise*, and Gillespie, of the OLD PIUTE, while on their travels with *that* sack. We have taken immense trouble to obtain correct statistics of the breweries on the route, and with the assistance of Dan De Quille, have ascertained that the amount consumed by the three gentlemen above mentioned, is as follows: Paid for by the above reporters, 1 quart; paid for by the public—a sufficient quantity to make Clemens good natured, Marshall communicative, and Gillespie to get into our bed with his boots on, and attempt to say the Lord's prayer.[19]

Mark Twain's inebrious state, which was not entirely good-natured, was partly responsible for the nonsensical melodrama that followed hard upon the triumphant march of the Army of the Lord.

Gridley went on, with his buckskin burden, to Sacramento, which staged a turnout of military companies, of bands and auctions of all sorts of things from lager beer to one strawberry; then to San Francisco for a rousing program at the Metropolitan Theater. Actors performed a comedy, "Love

R. C. Gridley and his sack of flour

and Champagne," a flag-bearer recited Joseph Rodman
Drake's "The American Flag," and the audience rained silver
upon a one-legged nineteen-year-old youth introduced as a
veteran of Fredericksburg, who later confessed that he had
never been in the army. Enthusiasm ran high in both cities,
but neither came close to matching the record of Virginia.

As Gridley's travels continued, the news filtered back to
the Middle West, sometimes with permutations—the Chicago
Tribune reporting that he had paid the election bet by carrying the sack from Sacramento to Clifton, over 300 miles. At
any rate, the sack became famous or, in the same sense as
reporters generally used the word, "notorious." The Rev. Dr.
Henry W. Bellows, President of the United States Sanitary
Commission and something of a quipster, said that it promised to become more renowned than any other in history since
the sack of Troy. A San Francisco haberdasher made capital
of the current excitement: "The Gridley Sack is a new style
Coat just received by Houston, Hastings & Co."[20]

Amid the general approval, sour notes sounded in the dire
forebodings of some editors who could not forget that the in-
stigator of this ingenious auction scheme was a Democrat,
hence suspect. "Gridley," said a California paper,

is a Copperhead. This fact cannot be denied by any man at
all acquainted with him. . . . It is perfect nonsense for newspapers in the interest of the Union party to deny the fact of
his Copperheadism. He may, however, act honestly in this
matter, though we think it is a doubtful case.[21]

Another hinted more strongly that, since he was a Democrat,
he must naturally be a thief and a scoundrel:

We notice with much regret that Gridley . . . is a Copperhead! and that he is also the custodian (?) of the funds. . . .
Surely there is some mistake in this? . . . How patriotic contributors would stare, were they to find one of these mornings,
that Mr. Gridley and the funds were *non est!*[22]

Sweet are the uses of partisanship. Gridley was obliged to publish testimonials from good Republicans, who stoutly affirmed his loyalty and probity. Union editors leaped to his defense as a patriotic "War Democrat," and hotly denounced his detractors as ungenerous, unjust, slanderous, sickly, narrow-minded, and contemptible.

Silver bars, the number variously reported as three to eleven, were transported free of charge by Wells Fargo to St. Louis. At the Mississippi Valley Sanitary Fair, installed in a glass case, they attracted much attention from the curious, who paid an admission fee of ten cents a head to look at them. To Almarin B. Paul, of the Storey County, Nevada, Sanitary Commission, the Treasurer of the Fair sent greetings: "Well done Storey County! . . . We of St. Louis salute you of Storey County fraternally."[23] That brought a growl from the *Reese River Reveille* of Austin, where the whole thing had started: "The narrow selfishness of the Virginians is exhibited in every possible instance. The liberal donations of Austin and other places in the Territory are ignored."[24]

Chapter Nine

COFFEE AND PISTOLS
FOR SEVERAL

❦❦❦

THE GREAT flour sack auction started a chain reaction of rapid events that resulted in Mark Twain's abrupt departure from Washoe within two weeks. Because he and Dan De Quille found the spirit of the Sanitary occasion too exhilarating to give up, they kept the spree going, and that friskiness led to trouble. While they were chatting in the office after the big doings of May 16, and putting the paper to bed, Mark Twain, in a far from sober mood, wrote an insulting squib based on remarks he had overheard, made jokingly by unidentified drunks in the crowd:

the reason the Flour Sack was not taken from Dayton to Carson, was because it was stated that the money raised at the Sanitary Fancy Dress Ball, recently held in Carson for the St. Louis Fair, had been diverted from its legitimate course, and was to be sent to aid a Miscegenation Society somewhere in the East; and it was feared the proceeds of the sack might be similarly disposed of.

Dan counseled against publishing this affront to the ladies of Carson City—one of whom was Mollie Clemens, Mark Twain's sister-in-law—who had sponsored the fancy dress ball on May 5. Mark Twain heeded this advice, agreed that his so-called joke was in poor taste, and tossed the item aside. Then they went off to the theater, forgetting the squib left on a table, where the composing room foreman, finding it, assumed that it was copy. Thus it appeared in the *Enterprise* of the 17th, together with a mitigating statement that the story was a hoax, "but not all a hoax, for an effort is being made to divert those funds from their proper course." The explanation did not stay the storm.

The most offensive part of the joke was the reference to miscegenation. That word had been bandied about the country for months after the publication, by a New York publisher in December, 1863, of an anonymous pamphlet entitled *Miscegenation; the Theory of the Blending of Races, Applied to the White Man and the Negro.* Among other points the author made these: that since the rebellion had been caused less by slavery than by color prejudice, peace could be restored by removing the color line in a blending of black and white; that advocating the mingling of races was the duty of all anti-slavery men; that anybody who helped to unite the races was doing his bit for a millennial future when the highest form of mankind would be neither black nor white, but brown.

In a long review, Theodore Tilton, editor of *The Independent,* complained of a too dogmatic tone. He also said he was not convinced that "the writer is in earnest. Our first impression was, and remains, that the work was meant as a piece of pleasantry—a burlesque upon what are popularly called the extreme and fanatical notions of certain radical men named therein."[1] Still, he subscribed to the spirit, if not the letter, of the thesis. Commenting editorially, he said:

we shall have no permanent settlement of the negro question till our haughtier white blood, looking at the face of a negro, shall forget that he is black, and remember only that he is a citizen.[2]

As Tilton suspected, the book was a hoax. By a Democratic writer, it was intended to serve as anti-Republican propaganda by implying that the Lincoln administration favored miscegenation. Nevertheless, as often happened with these elaborate mockeries, most people took the work seriously. Horace Greeley approved of its theories, likewise Henry Ward Beecher and that oratorical firebrand, Anna Dickinson. Wendell Phillips, the perennial agitator, said: "I have no hope for the future but in that sublime mingling of races which is God's own method of civilizing and elevating the world."[3] Far more plentiful than sincere endorsement, however, were scurrilous jokes about intermarriage, and savage attacks upon the author's "nasty doctrine."

As "miscegenation" got into paper after paper, its intended implications experienced a metamorphosis that confounded the original intention. By the time the word reached the Far West in the spring of 1864, the press out there interpreted the term, either by accident or design, as a Democratic slogan and the password of a Copperhead. Union editors in Nevada and California pinned the label of racial amalgamationist on everybody in the opposing party, denounced "purblind apostles of the . . . damnable system of American slavery," and pointed out that Southern Democratic slave-owners had practiced miscegenation for a long time with their female chattels, then profited from it by selling the offspring.

Hence the imputation of Copperheadism in that unfortunate Mark Twain item was invidious. In a stiff note to the editors of the *Enterprise,* four officers of the Carson City organization—Mrs. W. K. Cutler, Mrs. H. F. Rice, Mrs. S. D. King, Mrs. H. H. Ross—entered a strong rebuttal:

In behalf of the ladies who originated and assisted in carrying out the programme, let us say that the whole statement is a *tissue of falsehoods,* made for *malicious* purposes, and we demand the name of the author. The ball was gotten up in aid of the Sanitary Commission, and *not* for the St. Louis Fair. At a meeting of the ladies, held in this city last week, no decision was arrived at as to whether the proceeds of the ball should be sent to St. Louis or New York, but one thing *was decided,* that they should go to the aid of the sick and wounded soldiers, who are fighting the battles of our country, *and for no other purpose.* The only discussion had upon the subject was whether the funds should be forwarded to St. Louis or New York, and this grew out of a circular received from St. Louis, by one of the members, stating "that a portion of the proceeds of the St. Louis Fair, were to be applied to the aid of the Freedmen's Society." In order to have no mistake in the matter, and that the funds should all be applied to the Sanitary Commission, it was proposed by some of the ladies that the money be sent to New York, but no final decision was arrived at. In conclusion, let us say that the ladies having the matter in charge, consider themselves capable of deciding as to what shall be done with the money, without the aid of outsiders, who are probably desirous of acquiring some *glory* by appropriating the efforts of the ladies to themselves.[4]

The *Enterprise* did not publish this letter, which appeared in the Virginia *Union* of May 26 and 27, nor did Mark Twain immediately acknowledge the protest. It caught him in the midst of what he called "trouble & vexation," with at least two other rows on his hands, as will shortly appear. Since the ladies had called him a liar, which he was, he felt bound to demand the duelist's satisfaction from somebody, but felt frustrated because he could not honorably call out any of the ladies. In a letter to his sister-in-law, Mollie, he said distractedly:

Now, Mollie, whatever blame there is, rests with me alone, for if I had not . . . had just sense enough to submit this article to Dan's better judgment, it would have been published all the same, & not by any mistake, either. Since it has made the ladies angry, I am sorry the thing occurred, & that is all I can do, for you will see yourself that their communication is altogether unanswerable. I cannot publish that, & explain it by saying the affair was a silly joke, & that I & all concerned were drunk. No—I'll die first.

Therefore, do one of two things: Either satisfy those ladies that I dealt honorably by them when I consented to let Dan suppress that article upon his assertion that its . . . publication would wound their feelings—or else make them appoint a man to avenge the wrong done them, with weapons in fair & open field.

They will understand at a glance that I cannot submit to the humiliation of publishing myself as a liar (according to the terms of their letter) . . . so long as I have the other alternative of either challenging or being challenged.[5]

We may wonder why, of a sudden, Mark Twain had become pugnacious over being called a liar. More than one editor had called him that without incurring threats of a challenge. Had he insisted upon "weapons in fair & open field" to avenge the humiliation of every insult flung at him, he would have had little time for anything else. As for conceding that he was an untruther, he had done that. His announcement the day after the sensational massacre yarn—"I take it all back"— amounted to an admission of fancy lying. Yet here he was with a chip on his shoulder, his sense of humor in abeyance as trouble and vexation began to assume the color of disaster mixed with the ludicrous guise of farce.

Mollie's diplomatic intercession softened one of the ladies, Mrs. Cutler, who wrote him a forgiving letter. To her he replied:

I address a lady in every sense of the term. Mrs. Clemens has informed me of everything that has occurred in Carson in connection with that unfortunate item of mine about the Sanitary Funds accruing from the ball, and from what I can understand, you are almost the only lady in your city who has understood the circumstances under which my fault was committed, or who has shown any disposition to be lenient with me. Had the note of the ladies been properly worded, I would have published an ample apology instantly—and possibly I might even have done so anyhow, had that note arrived at any other time—but it came at a moment when I was in the midst of what ought to have been a deadly quarrel with the publishers of the *Union,* and I could not come out and make public apologies to any one at such a time.[6]

He thanked her for her consideration, and deplored the ostracism Mollie had suffered on his account.

On May 24, admitting that the miscegenation item was only a rumor, he said in the *Enterprise:*

We cannot quarrel with ladies—the very thought of such a thing is repulsive; neither can we consent to offend them—even unwittingly—without being sorry for the misfortune, and seeking their forgiveness, which is a kindness we hope they will not refuse. We intended no harm, as they would understand easily enough if they knew the history of this offense of ours, but we must suppress that history, since it would rather be amusing than otherwise, and the amusement would be at our expense. . . . One lady complained that we should at least have answered the note they sent us. It is true. There is small excuse for our neglect of a common politeness like that, yet we venture to apologize for it, and will still hope for pardon, just the same. We have noticed one thing in this whole business—and also in many an instance which has gone before it—and that is, that we resemble the majority of our species in the respect that we are very apt to get entirely in the wrong, even when there is no seeming necessity for it; but to offset this vice, we claim one of the virtues of our species, which is that we are ready to repair such wrongs when we discover them.

Privately he grumbled to Orion that the ladies "got out of me what no *man* would ever have got, & then—well, they are ladies, & I shall not speak harshly of them."[7] Although he did not precisely retract the miscegenation slander or label himself a liar, that apology should have been adequate. Mark Twain called it "sufficient," and it was, even winning, but it did not satisfy Mr. Cutler. In a letter now lost he communicated his sense of insult, apparently in strong terms, to Mark Twain, who drafted a red-hot reply that called Cutler names and urged him to issue a challenge if so minded.[8] Thanks to the restraining counsel of faithful Dan De Quille, this incendiary missive was not mailed. In its stead went a less inflammatory draft, but no violence resulted from this exchange of choler. It was just as well, for Mark Twain had involved himself in more altercations than he could cope with.

A day or so after the flour sack auction, while Joe Goodman was temporarily absent on business over the mountains, the *Enterprise* published an editorial by Mark Twain, entitled "How Is It?— How It Is." He boasted of the superior liberality of his paper, and accused Virginia *Union* employees of paying their subscriptions to the Sanitary Fund only because they were forced to do so by the upright gentlemen of the *Enterprise*. The *Union* replied by asserting that its people had given $515 in gold to the Fund, and by denying all unpatriotic imputations. Then, when the *Enterprise* kept up the nagging attack, its rival loosed a terrific barrage:

We showed the utter and unprecedented meanness of the Enterprise . . . and that paper yesterday returned a string of despicable stuff knotted so full of lies that there was not left a space sufficient for the smallest thread of truth. Never before, in a long period of newspaper intercourse—never before in any contact with a contemporary, however unprincipled he might have been, have we found an opponent in statement or in discussion, who had no gentlemanly sense of professional propriety, who conveyed in every word, and in every purpose of all of his words, such a groveling disregard for truth, decency and courtesy, as to seem to court the distinction of being understood as a vulgar liar. Meeting one who prefers falsehood; whose instincts are all toward falsehood; whose thought is falsification; whose aim is vilification through insincere professions of honesty; one whose only merit is thus described, and who evidently desires to be thus known, the obstacles presented are entirely insurmountable, and whoever would touch them fully, should expect to be abominably defiled.[9]

That was as thorough a drubbing as Mark Twain had ever received, but it was not all. In the same issue an equally irate communication, signed "Printer," bitterly resented the insidious accusations of the *Enterprise* as an unwarranted slur upon all printers. Claiming that a receipt from the Secretary of the Sanitary Fund attested a donation of $315 from the *Union's* typesetters, freely made under no pressure from anybody, Printer said:

We can only view his blackguardism as an attack upon the members of our craft. In asserting that we "Had not intended to pay the bill, but on secondary consideration, and for the sake of saving an entirely imaginary reputation for virtue and honesty, concluded to do so," he has endeavored to misinterpret the generous, patriotic promptings of laboring men who gave their little mite willingly; and in so doing he has proved himself an unmitigated *liar*, a *poltroon and a puppy*.

The evidence cited in both protests indicated that the facts were on their side. That continued Sanitary jag of Mark Twain was surely a beauty if it induced him to tamper with the truth in a manner that was reckless even by his own elastic standards. Evidently Dan's better judgment was not at hand, this time, to suppress the wild assaults upon the *Union*.

Again called a liar, in eight or nine different ways, and now decorated with the additional citations of poltroon and puppy, Mark Train reacted in accordance with his current bellicosity. The upshot was the widely-publicized duello correspondence between him and James L. Laird, proprietor of the *Union*. The industrious letter-writing began the morning the *Union* and Printer came out with their damning indictments, and continued all day. Six notes, packed with spleen by several people, traveled back and forth before midnight.

As the insulted party, Mark Twain opened the exchange with a sharp order, properly delivered by Steve Gillis, already nominated as his second. After referring to the *Union's* abuse and acknowledging authorship of the "How is it?" editorial, the insultee said: "Some time since it was stated in the Virginia Union that its proprietors were alone responsible for all articles published in its columns. You being the proper person, by seniority, to apply to in cases of this kind, I demand of you a public retraction of the insulting articles I have mentioned, or satisfaction. I require an immediate answer to this note."[10] His only reply to that demand was a brief note from J. W. Wilmington, who admitted that he was the author of the letter signed "Printer," and who said that he had nothing to retract.

Whereupon Mark Twain, in a letter to Laird longer than his first one—the time getting on toward evening now—again fixed responsibility for the insults upon the proprietor:

Mr. Wilmington is a person entirely unknown to me in the matter, and has nothing to do with it. In the columns of your paper you have declared *your own* responsibility for *all* articles appearing in it, and any further attempt to make a catspaw of any other individual and thus shirk a responsibility that you have previously assumed will show that *you* are a cowardly sneak. I now *peremptorily* demand of you the satisfaction due to a gentleman—without alternative.[11]

One may imagine the spirit of John Lyde Wilson, author of that manual on dueling, hovering about as he diligently thumbed a ghostly text to run down "without alternative," a term unknown to him. It meant that, the time for apologetic retraction having gone by, the only recourse was to render "the satisfaction due to a gentleman."

Laird responded with an even wordier screed in which he

endorsed the character of Wilmington, and acknowledged responsibility for editorials and communications in the *Union.* Then he said:

The editorial in the *Enterprise* headed "How is it?" out of which this controversy grew, was an attack made upon the printers of the *Union.* It was replied to by a *Union* printer, and a representative of the printers, who in a communication denounced the writer of that article as a liar, a poltroon and a puppy. You announce yourself as the writer of that article . . . and demand "satisfaction"—which satisfaction the writer informs you, over his own signature, he is quite ready to afford. I have no right, under the rulings of the code you have invoked, to step in and assume Wilmington's position, nor would he allow me to do so. You demand of me, in your last letter, the satisfaction due to a gentleman, and couple the demand with offensive remarks. When you have earned the right to the title by complying with the usual custom, I shall be most happy to afford you any satisfaction you desire at any time and in any place. In short, Wilmington has a prior claim upon your attention. When he is through with you, I shall be at your service. If you decline to meet him after challenging him, you will prove yourself to be what he has charged you with being, "a liar, a poltroon and a puppy," and as such cannot of course, be entitled to the consideration of a gentleman.[12]

As these gentlemen became more edgy, they became less gentlemanly, forgetting Wilson's injunction to avoid derisive epithets. Both showed a nice skill at penning insufferable churlishness with an air of lofty dignity; Laird's repetition of the liar-poltroon-and-puppy theme was a neat thrust between the ribs.

In the longest letter yet, Mark Twain came back with a third assertion of Laird's fundamental responsibility, quoted the paragraph on falsehood from the *Union*'s fierce editorial, referred to his opponent's "craven carcass," and returned to the business at hand:

You assume in your last note that I "have challenged Wilmington," and that he has informed me, "over his own signature," that he is quite willing to afford me "satisfaction." Both assumptions are utterly false. I have twice challenged you, and you have twice attempted to shirk the responsibility. Wilmington's note could not possibly be an answer to my demand for satisfaction from you; and besides, his note simply avowed authorship of a certain "communication" that appeared simultaneously with your libelous "editorial," and stated that its author had "nothing to retract." For your gratification, however, I will remark that Wilmington's case will be attended to in due time by a distant acquaintance of his who is not willing to see him suffer in obscurity. In the meantime, if you do not wish yourself posted as a coward, you will at once accept my peremptory challenge, which I now reiterate.[13]

There may have been a misunderstanding here. Mark Twain assumed that when Laird said "the writer," he referred to Wilmington, but he could have meant himself—not that clarifying such a minor ambiguity could have improved the flavor of this stew. The "distant acquaintance" supposed to attend to the upstart Wilmington was Steve Gillis, who put in his oar with a note conveyed by *his* second, a man named Millard. To Wilmington, Steve said:

You are, perhaps, far from those who are wont to advise and care for you, else you would see the policy of minding your own business and letting that of other people alone. Under these circumstances, therefore, I take the liberty of sugesting that you are getting out of your sphere. A *contemptible ass and coward* like yourself should only meddle in the affairs of *gentlemen* when called upon to do so. I approve and endorse the course of my principal in this matter, and if your sensitive disposition is aroused by any proceeding of his, I have only to say that I can be found at the *Enterprise* office, and always at your service.[14]

Since Wilmington had taken no part in this imbroglio beyond his one brief unwarlike statement, the pugnacious

Gillis was going out of his way to pick a fight. Wilmington's only response, made orally to Millard, was that he had no quarrel with Gillis, and the matter ended there. Considering the gutter antics of those so-called gentlemen, the reluctance of that *Union* printer to meddle with them deserves approval. He was at least one sensible man among this gaggle of lunatics. Washoe Hotspurs they were, each eager to kill some six or seven dozen of Scots at a breakfast.

All day seconds kept the trail hot between offices of the two papers, and at the *Enterprise* building the preparation of peremptory demands and the search for odious names went on until nine o'clock at night. Steve Gillis, according to his own story, assisted in putting bite into the letters of Mark Twain, and otherwise urged his fellow gladiator on toward the field of battle. On such a momentous day the Local doubtless had little time or desire to be reporter.

After so much furious letter-writing, a calm of one day ensued, no notes from anybody. Then Laird replied to Mark Twain's latest outburst. Again stating that Wilmington was the proper antagonist, as the author of the "liar, poltroon and puppy" communication, he said:

Any attempt to evade a meeting with him and force one upon me will utterly fail, as I have no right under the rulings of the code to meet or hold any communication with you in this connection. The threat of being posted as a coward cannot have the slightest effect upon the position I have assumed in this matter. If you think this correspondence reflects credit upon *you* I advise you by all means to publish it. In the meantime you must excuse me from receiving any more long epistles from you.[15]

The continued evasion, as Mark Twain considered it, resulted in his "posting" Laird in the *Enterprise* the following day:

I denounce Laird as an unmitigated liar, because he says I published an editorial in which I attacked the printers employed on the *Union,* whereas there is nothing in that editorial which can be so construed. Moreover, he is a liar on general principles, and from natural instinct. I denounce him as an abject coward, because it has been stated in his paper that its proprietors are responsible for all the articles appearing in its columns, yet he backs down from that position; because he acknowledges the "code," but will not live up to it; because he says himself that he is responsible for all "editorials," and then backs down from that also; and because he insults me in the note marked "IV," and yet refuses to fight me. Finally, he is a fool, because he cannot understand that a publisher is bound to stand responsible for any and all articles printed by him, whether he wants to do it or not.[16]

At the same time the *Enterprise* also published the letters of both parties, the collection showing that on the score of insults the contestants were about neck and neck. Laird had implied that the correspondence would reflect no credit on Mark Twain, and he was right. Nothing in that eruption of high-flown invective conduces to a feeling of pride in the author, but only to a sad dismay that he should have fallen into so absurd an aberration—or possibly have been pushed into it by friends like Steve Gillis with a misguided sense of humor.

The Western press pounced upon these letters, some with solemn disapproval, others with hoots and jeers. "Hoity! Toity!!" said the Gold Hill *Daily News,* which called the affair "emphatically a bad egg" because the cause of the quarrel was unlikely to gain public sympathy, and which reprehended the unseemly language of both opponents. Then, scoffing at "A Falstaffian Duel," the paper said:

As we go to press, a rumor is rife in town that Pete Hopkins, of Carson, having heard that his friend Mark Twain was about to enter into a contract to be killed, has come to the rescue and assumed the dying part. Pete has had no rest since that terrible massacre at Dutch Nick's, and is desirous of dying a savage death; besides, he thinks he would make a better target than Mark, in which opinion we coincide. Blood, or *something else,* is likely to grow out of this difficulty, unless the parties can be made to believe, in the language of Bulwer, that "the pen is mightier than the sword." The duel will perhaps come off in the pine forest at Empire City. Horrible! most horrible![17]

The Carson *Independent,* reporting receipt of a strong letter from 200 butchers protesting against a story that accused them of using dog meat in sausages, said:

We want it distinctly understood that we are not responsible for anything that appears in the local columns until after we ascertain how that celebrated newspaper fight is going to terminate in Virginia. If the editors there conclude to allow the "prints" to fight their battles for them, why then we'll be responsible for everything that appears in every column of the *Independent* . . . and in the event of anybody's feeling aggrieved at us, they can call in at most any hour of the day, and talk to the gentleman who sets up the "locals." He will satisfy them to their heart's content, and no matter which gets killed we shall write a first class obituary for the sufferer.[18]

A California editor called the affair "Coffee and Pistols for Several," another "Knights of the Quill." A third concluded that "the easiest and most honorable way they can end the trouble is to go to a cheap grocery, take a little 'tarantula juice,' and say no more about it. After so much wind they must need some stimulus."[19] The San Francisco *Evening Bulletin* briefly referred to "a column of duello correspondence, in which certain valiant men, whose names are unknown here and therefore need not be mentioned, throw dirt at each other." Quoting a number of choice epithets from the letters the paper remarked: "The writers who thus parade their griefs before the public, may think this is 'strong' language, but it really costs nothing to the weakest and most foolish of men to utter it."[20] The San Francisco *Call* sensibly observed:

It is well, perhaps, that only ink instead of blood has been shed in this affair, but it would have appeared better if neither had been spilt. The day has gone by when duels can give any man credit for bravery or honor, wisdom or truth; and to call people fools, cowards, poltroons, liars, puppies, and other flattering names, does not make them so, nor prove them so. It simply shows that passion and not good sense has been for a time the master.[21]

After the posting of Laird, events moved swiftly. Mr. Cutler had issued a challenge, and other Carson City husbands had made threatening noises, but Mark Twain heeded them not: "this flour sack business," he said, "may rest, as far as Carson is concerned."[22] As for the main bout, it fizzled. Whether or not the seconds of the principals arranged a meeting is not clear, but no duel occurred. As Mark Twain and Steve Gillis some years later told the story, which was repeated by Paine, Laird was scared off when his seconds gave him the misinformation that Mark Twain could hit a small target, like a bird, four times out of five at thirty paces. No contemporary evidence supports that account. The testimony shows, rather, that Mark Twain and Steve Gillis themselves planned a hasty exit, inspired by fear of being gathered in as violators of the anti-dueling law, and bundled off to the territorial prison. Dispatching to Orion an emergency request for $200 to take him far away from Virginia, Mark Twain said on May 26:

Steve & I are going to the States. We leave Sunday morning per Henness Pass. Say nothing about it, of course. We are not afraid of the grand jury, but Washoe has long since grown irksome to us, & we want to leave it anyhow.

We have thoroughly canvassed the Carson business, & concluded we dare not do anything, either to Laird or Carson men without spoiling our chances of getting away. However, if there is any chance of the husbands of those women challenging *me*, I don't want a straw put in the way of it. I'll wait for them a month, if necessary, & fight them with *any* weapon they choose. I thought of challenging one of them & then crossing the line to await the result, but Steve says it would not be safe, situated as we are.[23]

He was belligerent to the last. On May 29, when he and Steve set out for San Francisco, the Virginia reaction appeared to be: good riddance. The Gold Hill *Daily News* implied the feeling of general relief in an editorial entitled "An Exile":

Among the few immortal names of the departed—that is, those who departed yesterday per California stage—we notice that of Mark Twain. We don't wonder. Mark Twain's beard is full of dirt, and his face is black before the people of Washoe. Giving way to the idiosyncratic eccentricities of an erratic mind, Mark has indulged in the game infernal—in short, "played hell." Shifting the *locale* of his tales of fiction from the Forest of Dutch Nick's to Carson City; the *dramatis personae* thereof from the Hopkins family to the fair Ladies of the Sanitary Fair; and the plot thereof from murder to miscegenation—he slopped. The indignation aroused by his enormities has been too crushing to be borne by living man, though sheathed with the brass and triple cheek of Mark Twain.[24]

The *News*, reporting that a meeting of the Carson Ladies Sanitary Society gave "three groans for the *Territorial Enterprise*," remarked that this mark of disesteem was for the paper "as the vehicle of Mark Twain's abominations." The bad boy, having "*vamoosed*, cut stick, absquatulated," it was to be hoped that the *Enterprise* "will become purified, and by the united efforts of Goodman and Dan De Quille once more merit the sweet smiles of the ladies of Carson."

On the abrupt departure, the *Union* maintained a discreet silence. Only Lovejoy, of the *Old Piute*, came forth with an affectionate farewell:

Left yesterday for bluer skies and more verdant hills, S. L. Clemens, Esq., alias "Mark Twain." Yes, Mark has gone, and amid our fragrant sage brush, quartz-crowned hills and alkali hydrants we repose solitary and almost alone. The world is blank—the universe worth but 57½, and we are childless. We shall miss Mark; his bosom friend De Quille will miss him; Marshall will do ditto; every lunch house in the city, every brewery and every woman (who knew him)—and to know was to love him—will miss him. We can't dwell on this subject; we can only say—God bless you, Mark! be virtuous and happy.[25]

Thus ended, anti-climactically, one of the most depressing episodes in Mark Twain's career, and one that at the same time ended his career in Washoe. The conclusion was inglorious. In that hasty, half-furtive take-off it is impossible to see, as Paine insists, a triumphant exit, nor is there anything to cheer about in the silly performance that led up to it. Mark Twain cut the ground from under a defense of his conduct by being in the wrong from the start; a detached observer can only deplore an entanglement that became less excusable as it grew more snarled.

He himself, recovering from the combative fit that made him eager to do battle with everybody in sight, told the dueling story in after years in a humorous way that suggested regret for such folly. In "How I Escaped Being Killed in a Duel," written for *Tom Hood's Comic Annual for 1873*, he says, referring to his opponent as "a Mr. Lord":

I was young and foolish when I challenged that gentleman, and I thought it was very fine and very grand to be a duellist, and stand upon the "field of honour." But I am older and more experienced now, and am inflexibly opposed to the dreadful custom.

If a man were to challenge me *now*—now that I can fully appreciate the iniquity of that practice—I would go to that man, and take him by the hand, and lead him to a quiet, retired room—and kill him.

He did not mention the episode in *Roughing It,* telling instead a curious story of leaving the *Enterprise* because, having been editor during the temporary absence of Joe Goodman, he could not endure demotion to the status of mere reporter again. "I could not," he says, "serve in the ranks after being general of the army." Yet at the same time that that book was coming out, he often put the duel into his lecture on Nevada, composed for the American lyceum season of 1871-72, and given in London in 1873, generally concluding with a frivolous moral; he used it on the round-the-world speaking tour of 1895-96. Elsewhere he implied, indirectly, that the brief pugnacity of that Virginia fiasco seemed in retrospect distressing. In *A Tramp Abroad,* a chapter on "The Great French Duel" is a burlesque account of an affair of honor between M. Gambetta and M. Fourtou, Mark Twain posing as Gambetta's second and proposing various weapons, from axes to brickbats at three-quarters of a mile. In *Life on the Mississippi,* he condemns Sir Walter Scott's approval of the duel as part of the "Middle-Age sham civilization" that entrapped southerners in reactionary romanticism.

A version of the Washoe conflict similar to that in *Tom Hood's Comic Annual* got into Mark Twain's *Autobiography.* He says there: "I had no desire to fight a duel. I had no intention of provoking one." Those testy notes to Mr. Laird, their haughty spleen and studied insults, indicated a strong intention of provoking hostilities, but let it pass. The mistaken recollection in old age of what he believed he had not intended in Virginia does credit, at least, to the sanity of afterthought. That abortive duel was on his mind to the end of his days, and the inference is that he was ashamed of it. Mark Twain was often thoughtless, but he was not heartless or insensitive.

ENVOY

ALTHOUGH Mark Twain hurriedly left the Territory under a cloud that seemed blighting at the time, his stay of about twenty-one months in Washoe was more beneficial than otherwise. Offering a robust variant of the life he had known on the river, Virginia was the right place for a young man who, like the same man when older, relished stir and action. A berth on the *Enterprise* was admirable for him because it allowed him to write as he pleased, more or less. As a result, the authentic Mark Twain tone began to appear soon after he became a reporter. A number of his items for the paper show the makings of that casual and brilliant American style that he learned how to handle better than anybody else, and that he brought to full flower in *Huckleberry Finn*, parts of *Roughing It* and *Life on the Mississippi*, and elsewhere. The rough-and-tumble of that Nevada newspaper milieu was good conditioning for a writer, a good test of his stamina. Mark Twain not only survived, but also took initial steps toward the cultivation of a national audience.

In Washoe he found his *nom de plume*, no inconsiderable discovery in the light of what that pseudonym became and what it means today. It was more valuable than all the treasure he lamented not having found in the mines, or than all his feverish schemes for making fortunes out of those unwise business ventures of later years.

Association with Joe Goodman and Dan De Quille, the latter particularly, gave Mark Twain the advantage of their good judgment, literary and social. Some of his sallies were wild enough, but they could have been more so without Dan's sensible advice. It is too much to say that his critical appraisal of his own writing improved markedly in Virginia; to the end of his days it was never very good. Yet the counsel of level-headed Dan, whom Mark Twain respected, surely had some effect.

Finally, in spite of occasional bad judgment and bad taste, egregious errors like the duel business, mistakes that brought down upon him wrath and curses, he did acquire a reputation as a humorous fellow with a talent that was both lively and sardonic. In San Francisco, whither he went after running away from Washoe, his status became better than it had been in Virginia, and he improved upon it by contributions to *The Golden Era* and *The Californian*. By the time he left California in 1866—after a trip to the Sandwich Islands, reported in popular letters written for the Sacramento *Union*; and a lecture tour that took him back to Virginia, where all past sins were generously forgiven—San Francisco editors conceded that he was the best-known writer on the Pacific Coast. This hard-won eminence he reached only after some five years, in which experience as a reporter for the *Enterprise* played a salutary part.

In an 1895 interview he remarked: "You have heard it said, I suppose, that I was not a success in newspaper work. What more success could I have had? I was a reporter and then city editor of a paper in Virginia City, and I gave satisfaction."[1] That conclusion was substantially correct. As advancing age made the memory of Washoe years glow ever more radiantly, his fervent eulogy had the warmth of affectionate nostalgia. "Those were the days!—those old ones," he said. "They will come no more. Youth will come no more. They were so full to the brim with the wine of life; there have been no others like them."[2]

NOTES

ABBREVIATIONS IN NOTES
(full references in Bibliography):

Autobiography—Mark Twain's Autobiography
*Biography—*Albert Bigelow Paine, *Mark Twain: A Biography*
*Enterprise—*Virginia City, Nevada, *Territorial Enterprise*
Letters—Mark Twain's Letters
MTBM—Mark Twain, Business Man
MTE—Mark Twain of the Enterprise
MTN—Mark Twain in Nevada
MTP—The Mark Twain Papers, University of California
S.L.C.—Samuel L. Clemens

1. Miner Becomes Reporter

1. Letter from Aurora, May 30, 1862, Sacramento *Daily Bee,* June 6, 1862.
2. Fragment of letter to Orion Clemens, in Carson City: Esmeralda, May 11, 1862, by Mark Twain, in *Mark Twain's Letters,* I, 73-74, edited by Albert Bigelow Paine, copyright 1917 by The Mark Twain Company, renewed 1945 by Clara Clemens Samossoud. All quotations from this volume are reprinted with the permission of Harper & Row, Publishers, Inc.
3. S.L.C. to Orion Clemens, May 17, 1862, *MTBM,* 68.
4. Nevada City, California, *Nevada Democrat,* July 24, 1862. The editor remarks: "They have some brave orators out West . . . if we admit that the reporters translate them aright, and of course they 'don't do anything else.' "
5. San Rafael, California, *Marin County Journal,* July 26, 1862.
6. S.L.C. to Orion Clemens, August 5, 1862, *Letters,* I, 83.

7. *Biography,* I, 204.
8. Rollin M. Daggett, "Daggett's Recollections," San Francisco *Examiner,* January 22, 1893.
9. J. Ross Browne, "A Peep at Washoe," *Harpers New Monthly Magazine,* Vol. XXII, No. CXXVIII (January, 1861), 151.
10. Letter from W.C.P., Virginia City, n.d., Austin, Nevada, *Reese River Reveille,* October 21, 1863.
11. San Francisco *Daily Alta California,* July 10, 1862.
12. San Francisco *Evening Bulletin,* n.d., reprinted in Marysville, California, *Daily Appeal,* May 30, 1862.
13. *Enterprise,* n.d., reprinted in Marysville *Daily Appeal,* May 15, 1862.
14. *Enterprise,* October 1, 1862.
15. *Ibid.,* n.d., reprinted in San Francisco *Daily Alta California,* October 20, 1862.
16. *Enterprise,* September 19, 1862.
17. Red Bluff, California, *Beacon,* October 16, 1862.
18. *Enterprise,* n.d., reprinted in Oroville, California, *Weekly Butte Record,* November 15, 1862.
19. Mark Twain, "Memoranda," *The Galaxy,* Vol. IX, No. 6 (June, 1870), 858.
20. Letter from Neb, Virginia City, September 17, 1862, San Francisco *Herald and Mirror,* September 22, 1862.
21. Letter from V., Virginia City, October 29, 1862, Suisun, California, *Solano County Herald,* November 15, 1862.
22. *Enterprise,* n.d., reprinted in San Francisco *Evening Bulletin,* July 24, 1862.
23. Letter from Rambler, Virginia City, September 12, 1862, San Francisco *Daily Alta California,* September 17, 1862.
24. *Enterprise,* n.d., reprinted in Nevada City *Daily Gazette,* April 29, 1864.
25. S.L.C. to the California Pioneers of New York City, October 11, 1869, Jackson, California, *Amador Dispatch,* October 30, 1869.
26. S.L.C. to mother and sister, February 16, 1863, *MTBM,* 77.
27. G.E.B., "Mark Twain," San Francisco *Morning Call,* April 17, 1887.
28. Letter from Tule, Carson City, November 14, 1862, Sacramento *Daily Union,* November 18, 1862.

29. Letter from Tule, Carson City, December 2, 1862, *ibid.*, December 4, 1862.

30. *Enterprise*, n.d., reprinted in Sacramento *Daily Bee*, December 18, 1862.

31. Letter from Tule, Carson City, December 17, 1862, Sacramento *Daily Union*, December 19, 1862.

32. *Enterprise*, n.d., reprinted in Sacramento *Daily Bee*, December 18, 1862.

33. Letter from Nevada, Carson City, December 17, 1862, San Francisco *Evening Bulletin*, December 22, 1862.

34. Washoe City, Nevada, *Times*, n.d., reprinted in Unionville, Nevada, *Humboldt Register*, May 2, 1863.

35. See letters from Carson City, December 5, 12, 1862, *MTE*, 35-41.

36. See letter from Carson City, December 23, 1862, *MTN*, 224-27.

37. *Enterprise*, n.d., reprinted in Marysville *Daily Appeal*, December 21, 1862.

38. *Enterprise*, n.d., *ibid.*, December 31, 1862.

39. *Enterprise*, January 6, 1863.

40. *Ibid.*, n.d., reprinted in Stockton, California, *Daily Independent*, January 14, 1863.

41. *Enterprise*, n.d., reprinted in Santa Cruz, California, *Sentinel*, January 31, 1863.

42. *Enterprise*, February 19, 1863.

43. *Ibid.*, n.d., reprinted in Stockton *Daily Independent*, February 26, 1863.

44. Dan De Quille, "Reporting With Mark Twain," *California Illustrated*, July, 1893, 171.

45. *Enterprise*, n.d., reprinted in Oroville *Weekly Butte Record*, May 2, 1863.

2. Enter Mark Twain

1. See letters from Carson City, January 31, February 3, 6, 1863, *MTE*, 49-61.

2. S.L.C. to unidentified correspondent addressed as "Dear Sir," June 24, 1874. Facsimile in *The Eighteenth Year Book 1919* (The Bibliophile Society, Boston, 1919), 124.

3. See Ernest E. Leisy, "Mark Twain and Isaiah Sellers," *American Literature*, Vol. XIII (May, 1942), 399; Ivan Benson, *Mark Twain's Western Years*, 81.

4. Eureka, Nevada, *Sentinel*, May 8, 1877.

5. Nevada City *Transcript*, February 22, 1866.

6. See "Mark Twain's Pipe," San Francisco *Chronicle*, n.d., reprinted in Cleveland, Ohio, *Herald Supplement*, November 2, 1872.

7. See *Biography*, IV, Appendix C II, 1599-1600.

8. Como, Nevada, *Sentinel*, June 4, 1864.

9. S.L.C. to A. Arthur Reade, March 14, 1882, *Study and Stimulants*, 120.

10. See Paul Fatout, "Mark Twain's *Nom de Plume*," *American Literature*, Vol. XXXIV, No. 1 (March, 1962), 1-7.

11. *Enterprise*, February 25, 1863.

12. *Ibid.*, February 19, 1863.

13. *Ibid.*, n.d., reprinted in Marysville *Daily Appeal*, February 28, 1863.

14. *Enterprise*, March 7, 1863.

15. *Ibid.*, March 20, 1863.

16. S.L.C. to mother and sister, April 11, 1863, *Letters*, I, 89. Reprinted by permission.

17. *Enterprise*, n.d., reprinted in Oroville *Weekly Butte Record*, May 2,' 1863.

18. *Enterprise*, May 3, 1863.

19. Arthur McEwen, "In the Heroic Days," San Francisco *Examiner*, January 22, 1893.

20. *Enterprise*, n.d., reprinted in Eureka, California, *Humboldt Times*, April 18, 1863.

21. Fremont Older, "Russell K. Colcord," San Francisco *Call-Bulletin*, September 12, 1929.

22. G.E.B., "Mark Twain," San Francisco *Morning Call*, April 17, 1887.

23. Arthur McEwen, "In the Heroic Days," San Francisco *Examiner*, January 22, 1893.

24. San Francisco *Examiner*, April 22, 1910.

25. *Enterprise*, n.d., reprinted in Unionville *Humboldt Register*, May 16, 1863.

26. See Pamela Moffett to S.L.C., March 6, 1863, MTP.

27. Columbus, Ohio, *Daily Ohio State Journal*, January 6, 1872.

3. Flush Times

1. *Enterprise*, May 3, 1863.

2. *Biography*, IV, 1386.

3. *Enterprise*, February 5, 1870.

4. Gold Hill, Nevada, *Daily News*, October 28, 1863.

5. *Enterprise*, June 21, 1863.

6. George Lyman, *The Saga of the Comstock Lode*, 198.

7. Letter from Virginia City, May 26, 1863, San Francisco *Evening Bulletin*, June 14, 1863.

8. Santa Cruz *Sentinel*, n.d., reprinted in Colusa, California, *Weekly Colusa Sun*, May 30, 1863.

9. San Francisco *Journal*, n.d., reprinted in Gold Hill *Daily News*, October 31, 1863.

10. Sacramento *Daily Union*, n.d., reprinted in Suisun *Semi Weekly Solano Herald*, March 2, 1864.

11. Unionville *Humboldt Register*, n.d., reprinted in Suisun *Solano County Herald*, June 13, 1863.

12. New York *Leader*, n.d., reprinted in Oroville *Weekly Butte Record*, August 8, 1863.

13. San Francisco *Daily Alta California*, July 14, 1863.

14. New York *Tribune*, June 19, 1863.

15. Jane Clemens, "To All in the Territory," October 14, 1862, *MTBM*, 73. She was persistent about that debt. In a letter of September 28, 1864, she says: "About two weeks ago Bixby paid me $235.00 the full value of Sam's note, intrust and all." See *MTBM*, 81.

16. *Congressional Record*, Vol. 86, Part 1, 698, 699.

17. New York *Times*, February 7, 1940.

18. San Francisco *Chronicle*, March 30, 1919.

19. Reminiscence of Annie Webster, *MTBM*, 60.

20. See S.L.C. to W. H. Claggett, September 9, 1862, MTP.

21. Miriam Michelson, *The Wonderlode of Silver*, 206.

22. Letter from Tule, Carson City, December 15, 1862, Sacramento *Daily Union*, December 18, 1862.

23. Nevada City *Daily Gazette*, July 18, 1864.

24. Virginia City *Union*, n.d., reprinted in Marysville *Daily Appeal*, July 18, 1863.

25. *Enterprise*, n.d., reprinted in San Francisco *Evening Bulletin*, September 20, 1862.

26. Letter from Argentoro, Virginia City, October 24, 1863, San Francisco *Morning Call*, October 28, 1863.

27. Virginia City *Union*, n.d., reprinted in Sacramento *Daily Union*, May 15, 1863.

28. Virginia City *Union*, n.d., reprinted in Sacramento *Daily Bee*, May 9, 1863.

29. *Enterprise*, n.d., reprinted in Marysville *Daily Appeal*, January 16, 1863.

30. Letter from An Occasional Correspondent, Carson City, November 27, 1863, San Francisco *Evening Bulletin*, December 1, 1863.

31. San Francisco *The Golden Era*, September 27, 1863.

32. San Leandro, California, *Alameda County Gazette*, June 23, 1860.

33. Downieville, California, *Mountain Messenger*, September 28, 1867.

34. Columbia, California, *Tuolumne Courier*, September 5, 1863.

35. Virginia City *Union*, July 18, 1863.

36. Letter from S.M.D., Virginia City, May 14, 1863, Austin *Reese River Reveille*, May 23, 1863.

37. *Enterprise*, n.d., reprinted in Marysville *Daily Appeal*, July 12, 1863.

38. S.L.C. to mother and sister, February 16, 1863, *MTBM*, 77.

39. *Enterprise*, n.d., reprinted in *The Golden Era*, September 13, 1863.

40. *Enterprise*, n.d., reprinted in Sacramento *Daily Union*, September 4, 1863.

41. Virginia City *Evening Bulletin*, July 9, 1863.

42. San Francisco *Morning Call*, n.d., reprinted in Virginia City *Evening Bulletin*, July 17, 1863.

43. *Enterprise*, August 1, 1863.

44. *Ibid.*, August 2, 1863.

45. Stockton *Daily Independent*, September 30, 1863.

46. *Ibid.*, October 6, 1863.

47. Virginia City *Union*, n.d., reprinted in San Jose, California, *Mercury*, November 26, 1863.

48. *Enterprise*, n.d., reprinted in Eureka, California, *Humboldt Times*, October 17, 1863.

49. *Enterprise*, n.d., reprinted in Marysville *Daily Appeal*, October 1, 1863.

50. Austin *Reese River Reveille*, November 11, 1863.

51. *Enterprise*, n.d., reprinted in Jackson *Amador Weekly Ledger*, October 31, 1863.

52. Santa Cruz *Sentinel*, n.d., reprinted in Colusa *Weekly Colusa Sun*, May 30, 1863.

53. *Enterprise*, n.d., reprinted in Gold Hill *Daily News*, October 16, 1863.

54. *Enterprise*, n.d., reprinted in Stockton *Daily Independent*, October 6, 1863.

55. Letter from Latrobe, Clifton, Nevada, April 4, 1863, Suisun *Solano County Herald*, April 18, 1863.

56. Letter from Latrobe, Virginia City, June 30, 1862, Suisun *Solano County Herald*, July 5, 1862.

57. *Enterprise*, September 6, 1863.

58. Mark Twain, "The Lick House Ball," *The Golden Era*, September 27, 1863.

59. S.L.C. to mother and sister, August 19, 1863, *Letters*, I, 92. Reprinted by permission.

4. That Massacre

1. See letter from Carson City, October 19, 1863, *MTE*, 81-86.

2. Letter from Argentoro, Virginia City, October 24, 1863, San Francisco *Morning Call*, October 28, 1863.

3. Gold Hill *Daily News*, n.d., reprinted in Sacramento *Daily Union*, November 2, 1863.

4. Virginia City *Evening Bulletin*, n.d., reprinted in Sacramento *Daily Union*, November 2, 1863.

5. Sacramento *Daily Union*, October 31, 1863.

6. Grass Valley, California, *National*, November 3, 1863.

7. Austin *Reese River Reveille*, Supplement, November 7, 1863.

8. Dan De Quille, "Reporting With Mark Twain," 172.

9. San Francisco *Journal*, November 2, 1863.

10. Sacramento *Daily Bee*, October 31, 1863.

11. Auburn, California, *Stars and Stripes*, n.d., reprinted in Marysville *Daily Appeal*, November 7, 1863.

12. San Francisco *Evening Bulletin*, December 18, 1863.

13. Gold Hill *Daily News,* October 30, 1863.
14. Watsonville, California, *Pajaro Times,* November 21, 1863.
15. Downieville *Mountain Messenger,* November 28, 1863.
16. Dan De Quille, "Reporting With Mark Twain," 172.
17. Gold Hill *Daily News,* November 21, 1863.
18. Arthur McEwen, "In the Heroic Days."
19. Gold Hill *Daily News,* November 2, 1863.
20. Mark Twain, "Memoranda," 861.

5. Seasoned Yearling

1. Dan De Quille, "No Head Nor Tail," *The Golden Era,* December 6, 1863.
2. Dan De Quille, "Reporting With Mark Twain," 171.
3. Gold Hill *Daily News,* November 27, 1863.
4. San Francisco *Morning Call,* December 2, 1863.
5. See letter from Carson City, December 5, 1863, *MTE,* 94.
6. Dan De Quille, "Reporting With Mark Twain," 175.
7. *Enterprise,* n.d., reprinted in *The Golden Era,* December 6, 1863.
8. See letter from Carson City, December 13, 1863, *MTE,* 102-110.
9. Virginia City *Evening Bulletin,* December 19, 1863.
10. *Enterprise,* n.d., reprinted in *The Golden Era,* November 29, 1863.
11. "Artemus Ward, by Bret Harte," *The Golden Era,* December 27, 1863.
12. *The Golden Era,* January 31, 1864.
13. Charles Farrar Browne (Artemus Ward), *To California and Back,* 25. A sweat cloth was a green cover used for dice games.
14. Joseph T. Goodman, "Artemus Ward," San Francisco *Chronicle,* January 10, 1892.
15. William C. S. Pellowe, *Mark Twain Pilgrim From Hannibal,* 84.
16. Edward P. Hingston, *The Genial Showman,* 418.
17. New York *Spirit of the Times,* n.d., reprinted in *The Golden Era,* March 27, 1864.
18. Gold Hill *Daily News,* December 23, 1863.
19. G.E.B., "Mark Twain," San Francisco *Morning Call,* April 17, 1887.

20. S.L.C. to Thomas Bailey Aldrich, January 28, 1871, *Letters,* I, 183. Reprinted by permission.

21. Dan De Quille, "Artemus Ward in Nevada," 404.

22. Joseph T. Goodman, "Artemus Ward."

23. Virginia City *Union,* n.d., reprinted in Suisun *Semi Weekly Solano Herald,* January 16, 1864.

24. *Enterprise,* n.d., reprinted in Virginia City *Evening Bulletin,* December 28, 1863.

25. Mokelumne Hill, California, *Calaveras Chronicle,* November 10, 1866.

26. Joseph T. Goodman, "Artemus Ward."

27. *Enterprise,* n.d., reprinted in Marysville *Daily Appeal,* December 30, 1863.

28. Artemus Ward to S.L.C., January 1, 1864, *Letters,* I, 93. Reprinted by permission.

29. San Francisco *Morning Call,* January 3, 1864.

30. Joseph T. Goodman, "Artemus Ward."

31. See letter from Carson City, January 10, 1864, *MTE,* 129-30.

6. Ebbing Tide

1. Austin *Reese River Reveille,* October 31, 1863.

2. *Enterprise,* March 31, 1863.

3. Letter from Argentoro, Virginia City, December 15, 1863, San Francisco *Morning Call,* December 18, 1863.

4. Letter from Argentoro, Virginia City, December 10, 1863, San Francisco *Morning Call,* December 15, 1863.

5. Letter from J. Ross Browne, Virginia City, Stockton *Daily Independent,* November 11, 1863.

6. Letter from An Occasional Correspondent, Carson City, February 4, 1864, San Francisco *Evening Bulletin,* February 8, 1864.

7. Unionville *Humboldt Register,* n.d., reprinted in San Rafael *Marin County Journal,* December 12, 1863.

8. Stockton *Daily Independent,* January 16, 1864.

9. Virginia City *Union,* February 7, 1864.

10. Letter from Argentoro, Virginia City, January 14, 1864, San Francisco *Morning Call,* January 19, 1864.

11. Washoe City *Old Pah-Utah,* January 9, 1864.

12. Visalia, California, *Visalia Delta,* February 18, 1864.

13. Sacramento *Daily Union,* January 21, 1864.

14. *Enterprise,* January 17, 1864.

15. See letter from Carson City, November 7, 1863, *MTE,* 87, 88.

16. See letter from Carson City, January 4, 1864, *MTE,* 122.

17. *MTE,* 130-31.

18. Marysville *Express,* n.d., reprinted in Gold Hill *Daily News,* January 26, 1864.

19. Grass Valley *National,* n.d., reprinted in Gold Hill *Daily News,* January 26, 1864.

20. Washoe City *Old Pah-Utah,* n.d., reprinted in Sacramento *Daily Union,* January 26, 1864.

21. San Francisco *Daily Alta California,* January 20, 1864.

22. *Enterprise,* n.d., reprinted in Gold Hill *Daily News,* January 5, 1864.

23. *Biography,* IV, 1377.

24. *Enterprise,* n.d., reprinted in Gold Hill *Daily News,* February 9, 1864.

25. See letter from Carson City, January 28, 1864, *MTE,* 147.

26. Virginia City *Union,* January 30, 1864.

27. *Enterprise,* n.d., reprinted in Marysville *Daily Appeal,* March 1, 1864.

28. *Enterprise,* March 1, 1864.

29. *Enterprise,* n.d., reprinted in Columbia *Tuolumne Courier,* March 5, 1864.

30. Allen Lesser, *Enchanting Rebel,* 117.

31. *Ibid.,* 110.

32. See letter from San Francisco, September 13, 1863, *MTE,* 78-79.

33. Sacramento *Daily Union,* December 7, 1863.

34. San Francisco *Daily Alta California,* August 25, 1863.

35. Gold Hill *Daily News,* November 19, 1863.

36. *Ibid.,* February 27, 1864.

37. *Enterprise,* n.d., reprinted in *The Golden Era,* March 11, 1864.

38. Stockton *Daily Independent,* March 14, 1864.

39. Unionville *Humboldt Register,* March 19, 1864.

40. Virginia City *Union,* March 10, 1864.

41. *Enterprise,* n.d., reprinted in Gold Hill *Daily News,* March 12, 1864.

42. Bernard Falk, *The Naked Lady,* 67.

43. *Biography,* I, 248.

44. Marysville *Daily Appeal,* April 8, 1864.

45. Dan De Quille, "Salad Days of Mark Twain," San Francisco *Examiner,* March 19, 1893.

46. Grass Valley *National,* n.d., reprinted in San Jose *Mercury,* May 5, 1864.

47. *Ibid.*

7. The Weekly Occidental

1. Reprinted in *The Golden Era,* March 27, 1864.

2. *Ibid.,* April 3, 1864.

3. Reprinted in San Francisco *Evening Bulletin,* March 18, 1864.

4. *Ibid.,* March 23, 1864.

5. Reprinted in Downieville *Mountain Messenger,* May 14, 1864.

6. Reprinted in Unionville *Humboldt Register,* April 9, 1864.

7. Marysville *Daily Appeal,* March 11, 1864.

8. Virginia City *Union,* March 6, 1864.

9. See Dan De Quille, "Reporting With Mark Twain," 173-74.

10. "Recollections and Reflections of Thomas Fitch," San Francisco *Sunday Call,* October 4, 1903.

11. *Ibid.*

12. Dan De Quille, "Reporting With Mark Twain," 173.

13. "Recollections and Reflections of Thomas Fitch."

8. The Army of the Lord

1. Gold Hill *Daily News,* April 23, 1864.

2. Virginia City *Union,* n.d., reprinted in San Andreas, California, *Register,* April 23, 1864.

3. Carson City *Independent,* n.d., reprinted in Napa, California, *Register,* May 14, 1864.

4. Letter from Argentoro, Virginia City, May 17, 1864, San Francisco *Morning Call,* May 20, 1864.

5. Letter from Virginia City, May 21, 1864, Nevada City *Nevada Daily Gazette,* May 24, 1864.

6. Virginia City *Old Piute,* n.d., reprinted in Quincy, California, *Union,* April 30, 1864.

7. Virginia City *Old Piute*, n.d., reprinted in Nevada City *Nevada Daily Gazette*, May 7, 1864.

8. *Enterprise*, n.d., reprinted in Unionville *Humboldt Register*, May 14, 1864.

9. *Enterprise*, n.d., reprinted in Nevada City *Nevada Daily Gazette*, April 28, 1864.

10. *Enterprise*, n.d., reprinted in *The Golden Era*, May 1, 1864.

11. *Enterprise*, n.d., reprinted in Jackson *Amador Weekly Ledger*, April 30, 1864.

12. *Enterprise*, May 11, 1864.

13. Gold Hill *Daily News*, n.d., reprinted in Marysville *Daily Appeal*, April 24, 1864.

14. Gold Hill *Daily News*, May 17, 1864.

15. *Enterprise*, May 20, 1864.

16. Letter from Argentoro, Virginia City, May 17, 1864, San Francisco *Morning Call*, May 20, 1864.

17. S.L.C. to mother and sister, May 16, 1864, *MTE*, 188-89.

18. *Enterprise*, n.d., reprinted in Nevada City *Nevada Daily Gazette*, May 31, 1864.

19. Virginia City *Old Piute*, May 17, 1864.

20. Advertisement, San Francisco *Daily Alta California*, June 13, 1864.

21. Nevada City *Nevada Daily Gazette*, May 31, 1864.

22. Redwood City, California, *San Mateo County Gazette*, May 27, 1864.

23. Austin *Reese River Reveille*, June 15, 1864.

24. *Ibid.*

9. Coffee and Pistols for Several

1. New York *The Independent*, Vol. XVI, No. 795 (February 25, 1864).

2. *Ibid.*

3. Advertisement, New York *The Round Table*, Vol. I, No. 9 (February 13, 1864).

4. Letter from Carson City, May 21, 1864, *MTE*, 200-201.

5. S.L.C. to Mrs. Orion Clemens, May 20, 1864, *MTE*, 190-91.

6. S.L.C. to Mrs. W. K. Cutler, May 23, 1864, *Letters*, I, 97-98. Reprinted by permission.

7. S.L.C. to Orion Clemens, May 25, 1864, *MTE*, 202.

8. S.L.C. to W. K. Cutler, May 28, 1864, William Wright Correspondence, Bancroft Library, University of California.

9. Virginia City *Union*, May 21, 1864.

10. *Enterprise*, May 24, 1864.

11. *Ibid.*

12. *Ibid.*

13. *Ibid.*

14. *Ibid.*

15. *Ibid.*

16. *Ibid.*

17. Gold Hill *Daily News*, May 24, 1864.

18. Carson City *Independent*, n.d., reprinted in Austin *Reese River Reveille*, June 6, 1864.

19. Mariposa, California, *Weekly Mariposa Gazette*, June 4, 1864.

20. San Francisco *Evening Bulletin*, May 27, 1864.

21. San Francisco *Morning Call*, May 28, 1864.

22. S.L.C. to Orion Clemens, May 25, 1864, *MTE*, 202.

23. S.L.C. to Orion Clemens, May 26, 1864, *MTE*, 203.

24. Gold Hill *Daily News*, May 30, 1864.

25. Virginia City *Old Piute*, n.d., reprinted in Unionville *Humboldt Register*, June 11, 1864.

Envoy

1. Cleveland, Ohio, *Daily Leader*, July 16, 1895.

2. S.L.C. to Robert Fulton, May 24, 1905, *Letters*, II, 773. Reprinted by permission.

BIBLIOGRAPHY

Unpublished Material

The Grant H. Smith Papers, Bancroft Library, University of California, Berkeley.

Lillard, Richard Gordon, "Studies in Washoe Journalism and Humor," Ph.D. Dissertation, State University of Iowa, 1943.

The Mark Twain Papers, University of California, Berkeley.

Ryan, Ella Ward, "Federal Relations With Nevada Territory," M.A. Thesis, University of California.

William Wright Correspondence, Bancroft Library, University of California, Berkeley.

Books and Articles

Absalom Grimes: Confederate Mail Runner. Edited by M. M. Quaife. Yale University Press, 1926.

Annual Report of the President and Secretary of the Gould and Curry Mining Company. San Francisco, 1863.

Barnes, George E. "Mark Twain," San Francisco *Morning Call,* April 17, 1887.

Benson, Ivan. *Mark Twain's Western Years.* Stanford, 1938.

Browne, J. Ross. "A Peep at Washoe," *Harpers New Monthly Magazine,* Vol. XXII, Nos. CXXVII-CXXIX (December, 1860 —February, 1861), 1-17, 145-62, 278-305.

Church, John A. *The Comstock Lode.* New York, 1879.

Clemens, Will M. *Mark Twain, The Story of His Life and Work.* San Francisco, 1892.

Colcord, R. K. "Reminiscences of Life in Territorial Nevada," *California Historical Society Quarterly,* Vol. VII, No. 2 (June, 1928), 112-19.

Congressional Record, Vol. 86, Part 1, Washington, D. C., 1940.

Daggett, Rollin M. "Brisk Days on the Comstock," San Francisco *Morning Call*, September 10, 1893.

———. "Daggett's Recollections," San Francisco *Examiner*, January 22, 1893.

De Quille, Dan. *A History of the Comstock Mines*. Virginia, Nevada, 1889.

———. "Artemus Ward in Nevada," *The Californian*, Vol. IV, No. 3 (August, 1893), 403-406.

———. "No Head Nor Tail," *The Golden Era*, December 6, 1863.

———. "Reporting With Mark Twain," *California Illustrated*, July, 1893, 170-78.

———. "Salad Days of Mark Twain," San Francisco *Examiner*, March 19, 1893.

Falk, Bernard. *The Naked Lady*. London, 1934.

Fatout, Paul. "Mark Twain's *Nom de Plume*," *American Literature*, Vol. XXXIV, No. 1 (March, 1962), 1-7.

Ferguson, Delancey. "Mark Twain's Comstock Duel: The Birth of a Legend," *American Literature*, Vol. 14, No. 1 (March, 1942), 66-70.

Gillis, William R. *Gold Rush Days With Mark Twain*. New York, 1930.

Goodman, Joseph T. "Artemus Ward in Nevada," San Francisco *Chronicle*, January 10, 1892.

———. "The 'Enterprise's' Poets," San Francisco *Examiner*, January 22, 1893.

Goodwin, C. C. *As I Remember Them*. Salt Lake City, 1913.

Graham, J. B. *Handset Reminiscences*. Salt Lake City, 1915.

Harte, Bret. "Artemus Ward," *The Golden Era*, December 27, 1863.

Hingston, Edward P. *The Genial Showman*. London, n.d.

Howells, William Dean. *My Mark Twain*. New York, 1910.

Kelly, J. Wells. *First Directory of Nevada Territory*. San Francisco, 1863.

———. *Second Directory of Nevada Territory*. Virginia, Nevada, 1863.

Lesser, Allen. *Enchanting Rebel*. New York, 1947.

Lillard, Richard G. "Contemporary Reaction to 'The Empire City Massacre,'" *American Literature*, Vol. 16, No. 3 (November, 1944), 198-203.

———. "Dan De Quille, Comstock Reporter and Humorist," *Pacific*

Historical Review, Vol. XIII, No. 3 (September, 1944), 251-59.

Long, E. Hudson. *Mark Twain Handbook*. New York, 1957.

Loomis, C. Grant. "The Tall Tales of Dan De Quille," *California Folklore Quarterly*, Vol. V, No. 1 (January, 1946), 26-71.

Lord, Eliot. *The Drama of Virginia City*. n.p., n.d.

Lyman, George D. *The Saga of the Comstock Lode*. New York, 1957.

Mack, Effie Mona. *Mark Twain in Nevada*. New York, 1947.

———. *Nevada: A History of the State from the Earliest Times Through the Civil War*. Glendale, California, 1935.

Mark Twain, Business Man. Edited by Samuel Charles Webster. Boston, 1946.

Mark Twain Himself, A Pictorial Biography Produced by Milton Meltzer. New York, 1960.

Marye, George Thomas, Jr. *From '49 to '83 in California and Nevada*. San Francisco, 1923.

McEwen, Arthur. "In the Heroic Days," San Francisco *Examiner*, January 22, 1893.

Mercantile Guide and Directory for Virginia City, Gold Hill, Silver City and American City. Compiled by Charles Collings. Virginia, Nevada, 1864-65.

Michelson, Miriam. *The Wonderlode of Silver and Gold*. Boston, 1934.

Miscegenation; The Theory of the Blending of Races, Applied to the White Man and the Negro. New York, 1863.

Paine, Albert.Bigelow. *Mark Twain: A Biography*. 4 Vols. New York, 1912.

Pellowe, William C. S. *Mark Twain, Pilgrim From Hannibal*. New York, 1945.

"Recollections and Reflections of Thomas Fitch," San Francisco *Sunday Call*, October 4, 1903.

Reminiscences of Senator William M. Stewart of Nevada. Edited by George Rothwell Brown. New York, 1908.

Rodecape, Lois Foster. "Tom Maguire, Napoleon of the Stage," *California Historical Society Quarterly*, Vol. XXI, No. 2 (June, 1942), 141-82.

Seitz, Don C. *Artemus Ward*. New York, 1919.

Smith, Grant H. *The History of the Comstock Lode, 1850-1920*. Nevada State Bureau of Mines and the Mackay School of Mines, Geology and Mining Series No. 37, 1943.

Stevens, Walter B. *Centennial History of Missouri.* 4 Vols. Chicago, 1921.

Study and Stimulants. Edited by A. Arthur Reade. Manchester, England, 1882.

Twain, Mark. "All About the Fashions," *The Golden Era,* September 27, 1863.

———. "Concerning Notaries," *The Golden Era,* February 28, 1864.

———. "The Facts Concerning the Recent Carnival of Crime in Connecticut," *Tom Sawyer Abroad.* New York, 1910, 302-25.

———. "First Interview With Artemus Ward," *Sketches New and Old.* New York, 1917, 334-38.

———. "For Sale or to Rent," New York *Sunday Mercury,* February 17, 1864.

———. "The Great Prize Fight," *The Golden Era,* October 11, 1863.

———. "How I Escaped Being Killed in a Duel," *Tom Hood's Comic Annual for 1873,* 90-91.

———. "How to Cure a Cold," *The Golden Era,* September 13, 1863.

———. *The Innocents Abroad.* New York, 1927.

———. "The Lick House Ball," *The Golden Era,* September 27, 1863.

———. *Life on the Mississippi.* New York, 1903.

———. *Mark Twain's Autobiography.* 2 Vols. Edited by Albert Bigelow Paine. New York, 1925.

———. *Mark Twain's Letters.* 2 Vols. Edited by Albert Bigelow Paine. New York, 1917.

———. *Mark Twain of the Enterprise.* Edited by Henry Nash Smith and Frederick Anderson. Berkeley, California, 1957.

———. "Memoranda," *The Galaxy,* Vol. IX, No. 6 (June, 1870), 858-60.

———. "The Private History of a Campaign That Failed," *The Century Magazine,* Vol. XXI, No. 2 (December, 1885), 193-204.

———. *Roughing It.* New York, 1913.

———. "Those Blasted Children," New York *Sunday Mercury,* February 21, 1864.

———. *A Tramp Abroad.* 2 Vols. New York, 1907.

———. "Washoe—Information Wanted," *The Golden Era,* May 22, 1864.

Ward, Artemus. *The Complete Works of Artemus Ward.* New York, 1898.

————. *To California and Back.* n.p., n.d.

The Washoe Stock Circular, Vol. 1, No. 3. Virginia, N. T., May 25, 1864.

Wilson, John Lyde. *The Code of Honor; or Rules for the Government of Principals and Seconds in Dueling.* Charleston, South Carolina, 1858.

INDEX